Using

MICROSOFT®

Works 4.5

que®

Using

MICROSOFT®

Works 4.5

que®

Debbie Walkowski

Using Microsoft Works 4.5

Library of Congress Catalog No.: 97-69801

ISBN: 0-7897-1492-2

99 98   6 5 4 3 2

Interpretation of the printing code: the rightmost double-digit number is the year of the book's printing; the rightmost single-digit number, the number of the book's printing. For example, a printing code of 97-1 shows that the first printing of the book occurred in 1997.

Screen reproductions in this book were created using Collage Plus from Inner Media, Inc., Hollis, NH.

Contents at a Glance

Table of Contents

About the Authors

Debbie Walkowski has worked in the computer industry since 1981 writing documentation, designing online user interfaces, and teaching computer courses. Her company, The Writing Works, specializes in writing computer self-help books and providing writing services to companies such as Microsoft Corporation, Digital Equipment Corporation, and AT&T Wireless Services. Debbie has a degree in scientific and technical communication and has authored and co-authored fourteen books on popular computer software, including WordPerfect, Microsoft Excel, Microsoft PowerPoint, Microsoft Office, Microsoft Works for DOS and Works for Windows, Microsoft Project, Lotus 1-2-3, and Quicken.

Acknowledgments

Writing a Que book is always a pleasure because the people I get to work with are the best. Thanks to Lisa Swayne, Acquisitions Editor, for being conscientious, responsive, and *always* on top of things; thanks to Melanie Palaisa and Henly Wolin, Product Directors, for their expert guidance on content, form, and tone for this Using series book (also to Henly for his input on Internet Explorer); and thanks to Tom Lamoureux, Production Editor, and Sherry Kinkoph, Technical Editor, for their excellent editing, comments, and suggestions for making this book the best it could be.

Introduction to Works 4.5

The basics

Learn about the four primary components of Works (word processor, spreadsheet, database, and communications) and the uses of each.

A jumpstart

See a sample screen from each of the four Works tools.

Works extras

Learn about four additional tools included in Works: Microsoft Draw, ClipArt, Word Art, and Note-It.

The advantages of integration

Discover how you can use all the Works tools together to create truly professional documents.

Welcome to Microsoft Works 4.0 for Windows. You have made an excellent investment in one of the easiest-to-use integrated software programs available today. If you're new to Works, this chapter will get you feeling comfortable with your new software program.

Microsoft Works 4.0 contains four software applications in one: a *word processor* with a drawing package, a *spreadsheet* with a charting package, a *database*, and a *communications* package. Each component is designed to help you create, present, illustrate, organize, sort, report on, and print information in the ways that are most important to you. Works also contains several "mini-applications" that let you add drawings, clip art, notes, and stylized text to documents. Works is often called an *integrated* software program because all of its applications are designed to work together.

Integrated software programs offer two distinct advantages over separate, or *stand-alone*, programs. First, they offer *consistency*, enabling you to use the same methods for performing basic tasks (For instance, you save a file in the same way in different applications). Second, integrated programs allow you to share data effortlessly among the applications. For example, you can easily add a spreadsheet, picture, or chart to a letter or report; copy or move information between documents; combine two documents into one, and so on. Were you to buy separate word processor, spreadsheet, database, and communications packages, it might be difficult, if not impossible, to accomplish these tasks.

A third advantage Works offers is that it is *truly* easy to use. It was designed for users who might be using a computer for the first time. This makes it the perfect package for home users, students, and small business owners. ■

The Word Processor

Most people get started with Works by using the word processor, which helps create documents that primarily contain text. You can use a word processor to create a letter, memo, newsletter, announcement, bulletin, article, and even a book. The greatest advantage to using a word processor is that if you make an error, you can erase and retype it; if you decide to rearrange paragraphs, you can move or copy them easily; if you want to add more information or remove something you've already typed, you can do that easily, too.

With Works you can create truly professional-looking documents. You can choose from a wide variety of typefaces and sizes and add features like bold, underline, or italic. You can set margins and tabs anywhere you like; adjust line spacing; align text right, left, or center; or alter the size of a page. Other sophisticated features in the word processor allow you to:

- Print in columns
- Insert footnotes in a document
- Add titles, page numbers, or other information at the top and bottom of each page
- Add tables or figures to a document
- Check and correct your spelling
- Replace a word with a synonym
- Search a document for a word or phrase and replace it with something different

A sample word processing document is shown in Figure 1.1. The logo was created by using a ClipArt illustration, described later in this chapter.

▶ Refer to Chapters 2-6 to learn how to work with the word processor.

The Spreadsheet

A spreadsheet is an electronic version of a paper worksheet used to do numeric calculations. The advantage of the electronic spreadsheet over a paper one is that it calculates numbers automatically, and when you change numbers, it recalculates automatically, too. Spreadsheets are generally used to calculate financial data, although they can also be used to calculate and analyze mathematical and scientific data as well. Spreadsheets are most commonly used for tasks such as budgets, balance sheets, income statements, and sales forecasts. An example is shown in Figure 1.2.

FIG. 1.1
A word processing document with a ClipArt logo.

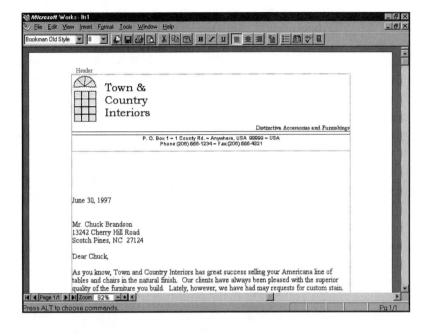

FIG. 1.2
A sample income statement prepared with the Works spreadsheet.

	A	B	C	D	E	F	G	H
1			Town and Country Interiors					
2			Income Statement					
3			1997					
4								
5		Q1	Q2	Q3	Q4	Total		
6	INCOME							
7	Retail Store	$19,839	$18,093	$21,993		$59,925		
8	Private Clients	$33,546	$32,198	$39,872		$105,616		
9	Mail Order	$8,901	$7,989	$8,912		$25,802		
10	Total Income	$62,286	$58,280	$70,777		$191,343		
11								
12	EXPENSES							
13	Cost of Goods	$20,297	$18,988	$23,978		$63,263		
14	Rent	$5,000	$5,000	$5,000		$15,000		
15	Labor	$7,310	$6,229	$7,900		$21,439		
16	Insurance	$1,500	$1,500	$1,500		$4,500		
17	Utilities	$850	$720	$899		$2,469		
18	Total Expenses	$34,957	$32,437	$39,277		$106,671		
19								
20	Net Income					$84,672		
21								
22								
23								
24								

A Works spreadsheet is arranged in rows and columns, just like a paper worksheet, and it contains numbers and formulas.

You can enhance a worksheet by adding bold, underline, or italic to selected data, or by changing the size and style of the characters you use. Before printing, add a title or file name that will appear at the top or bottom of each page and add page numbers that will appear at the bottom of each page.

Spreadsheet information can sometimes be difficult to interpret without the aid of a graph or chart, so the spreadsheet tool in Works includes a charting tool. You can choose from several chart styles, including variations of bar, line, and pie charts. Once you create a chart, you can incorporate it into the spreadsheet or add it to a word processing document. A sample chart appears in Figure 1.3.

▶ Refer to Chapters 7-10 to learn how to work with the spreadsheet.

FIG. 1.3
The chart is drawn directly from the data in the spreadsheet shown in Figure 1.2.

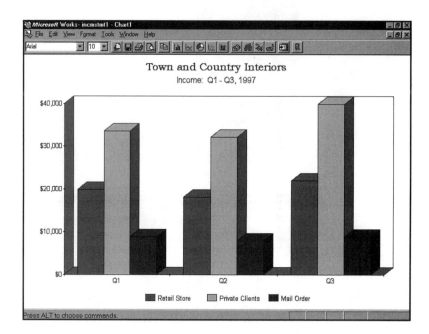

The Database

In simple terms, a database is nothing more than a collection of related information. You might think you have never used a database, but you have. The telephone book is an example of a database of names, addresses, and phone numbers. You can use the database in Works to create a database of client or supplier names, addresses, and phone numbers. Other examples of databases include a product list that contains item numbers, descriptions and prices, or an inventory list that contains items and quantities.

Figures 1.4 and 1.5 show examples of database information displayed in two different ways.

The first time you start Works, a welcome screen appears asking if you want to see an introduction to Works. To bypass the welcome screen the next time you start Works, click the Skip Welcome Screen option. (You can view the introduction any time by selecting it from the Works folder—see Figure 2.1—or from the Help menu inside of Works.)

The Works Task Launcher

After you close the welcome screen, you'll see the Works Task Launcher dialog box shown in Figure 2.2. The Task Launcher is like "Command Central" in Works. It is your starting point for any task you choose and it is the point to which you return when you want to choose a different task.

Ch
2

FIG. 2.2

The Works Task Launcher is your starting point for all Works tasks.

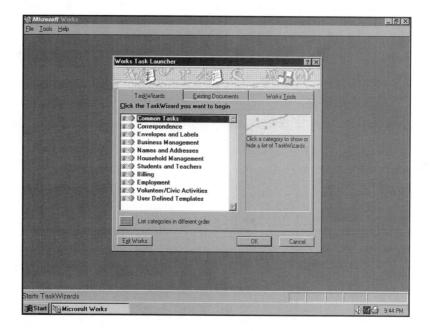

The Task Launcher dialog box contains three tabs: TaskWizards, Existing Documents, and Works Tools. Each tab you choose presents a different set of options, as you'll see pictured throughout this chapter. To have Works help you create a document with a TaskWizard, click the TaskWizards tab. To work on a document you have already created, click the Existing Documents tab. And to start a new word processor, spreadsheet, database, or communications document, click the Works Tools tab. (Each of these options is discussed in more detail later in this chapter.)

 To display the Task Launcher at any time, click the Task Launcher button on the toolbar, or choose the File, New command.

About Works Windows

As you've already seen, Works displays a window on the screen when you start the program. When you choose a task from the Task Launcher dialog box, (such as the word processor tool to type a letter) Works displays another window—a *document* window—inside of the Works window. The document window is where you actually do your work (see Figure 2.3).

The document window is separate from the overall Works window so that you can open multiple document windows at once. This allows you to work on more than one document (say a spreadsheet and a word processor document) at the same time. And because you can see both windows on the screen at once, you can switch easily from one document to the other. You'll learn more about working with more than one document window later in this chapter. For now, think of the Works window as a container for one or more document windows.

Works window, word
processor (document
window) title bars

Minimize, maximize/
restore, and close
buttons for Works window

FIG. 2.3

The Works window can
contain one or more
document windows.

Menu bar

Toolbar

Minimize, maximize/
restore, and close
buttons for document
window

Status bar, scroll bars,
control menu button for
Works window

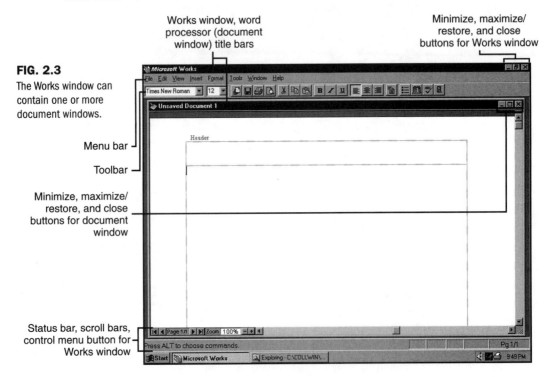

> **N O T E** If your screen doesn't show the Help window as illustrated in Figure 2.3, your Help display option is turned off. See "Getting Help," later in this chapter. ■

The document windows that Works displays are slightly different depending on the application you are using. For instance, a word processor window has a blank area for displaying text whereas a spreadsheet window contains a grid of rectangles for holding numbers. Some of the *elements* of the window, however, are the same regardless of the Works application you use.

FIG. 2.13

The Page Setup dialog box displays paper source, size, and orientation settings for the current document.

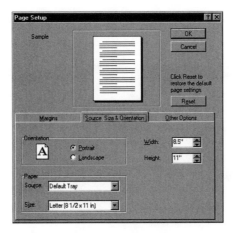

Depending on the type of printer you are using, you can choose the correct paper source (such as the default tray, auto sheet feeder, manual feed) from the Paper Source drop-down list. The Paper Size list offers a variety of standard paper and envelope sizes.

Paper orientation refers to the direction the document is printed on the paper. Most documents printed on standard 8-1/2 × 11-inch paper are printed in *portrait* orientation (the default setting). In other words, portrait orientation uses the 11-inch dimension as the *height* of the paper. For documents that are printed in *landscape* orientation, the image is rotated on the paper 90 degrees so that the 8-1/2-inch dimension is used as the height of the paper.

To change source, size, and orientation settings, follow these steps:

1. Choose File Page Setup. The Page Setup dialog box is displayed.
2. Choose the Source, Size, and Orientation tab. The dialog box shown in Figure 2.13 is displayed.
3. Choose any of the following options:
   - Choose a paper source from the Paper Source drop-down list.
   - Choose a paper size from the Paper Size drop-down list.
   - Choose a paper orientation by clicking either the Portrait or Landscape option button.
4. When all settings are correct, click OK. The Page Setup dialog box closes and you are returned to your document.

Setting Other Page Options

The third tab in the Page Setup dialog box is Other Options. The options on this tab vary depending on the type of document you're printing. If you're printing a word processor document, the tab looks like the one shown in Figure 2.14 and lets you specify the page number on the first page of the document, whether you want headers or footers to print on the first page, and where you want footnotes to be printed. For other types of documents, the Page Options dialog box lets you choose settings such as printing gridlines on a spreadsheet or page breaks between database records.

FIG. 2.14
The Other Options tab in the Page Setup dialog box displays miscellaneous page settings.

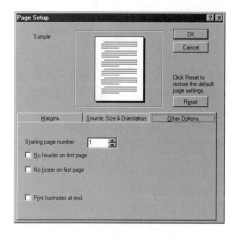

▶ **See** "Printing Special Features of a Word Processor Document," **p. 44**

▶ **See** "Creating a Header or Footer" **p. 82**, and "Creating a Footnote," **p. 99**

▶ **See** "Printing Special Features of a Spreadsheet," **p. 134**

Previewing a Document

One of the most important steps you can take before printing a document is to *preview* it. Previewing allows you to see on the screen how your document will look on the printed page. When you preview a document, Works displays a full-page view of the document, one page at a time. This is your chance to see that margins are the appropriate size, line spacing is appropriate, page separations are correct, header and footer text is positioned correctly, inserted objects appear in the proper locations, and so on. When included in a document, all of these elements appear on the preview screen.

 To preview a document, choose File, Print Preview or click the Print Preview toolbar button. The current document is displayed in a preview screen like the one shown in Figure 2.15.

Because you are viewing a full-page version of the document, the reduced size of the text displayed in the preview screen is difficult to read. On this screen, it is more important to check the document's layout than to proofread the content.

The first thing you notice is that the mouse pointer is shaped like a magnifying glass when you point anywhere on the page. If you want to view an area up close, you can click the left mouse button or the Zoom In command button. If you need to magnify the document further, click the left mouse button once more anywhere on the page, or click the Zoom In button again. To zoom back out, click the mouse button a third time, or click the Zoom Out button.

FIG. 2.15
Previewing a document shows you how the document will appear when printed.

Current page number —

Preview command buttons —

Full-page view of document —

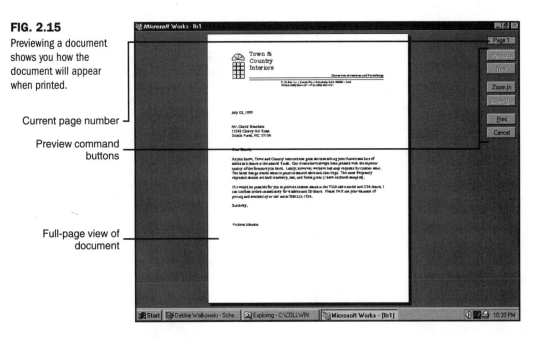

If your document is longer than one page, display the page you want to preview by clicking the Previous or Next button, or use the Page Up and Page Down keys on the keyboard.

If you notice something in the document you want to change, click Cancel to return to the document. If the document is ready to print, you can print directly from the preview screen by choosing the Print button. This button displays the Print dialog box shown in Figure 2.16. You learn how to use the Print dialog box in the next section.

Printing

When you're ready to print a document, choose File, Print, which displays the Print dialog box shown in Figure 2.16. You use the Print dialog box to specify the printer you're using, the particular pages you want to print, the number of copies you want to print, and the quality of printing you want to use. The printer that is currently selected is shown at the top of the dialog box. If the printer shown is not correct, select the correct printer from the Name drop-down list.

N O T E If you have access to more than one printer on your computer and you switch printers often, remember to click the Properties button in the Print dialog box. This is where you specify the paper size, orientation, and settings for printing graphics for the current printer. ■

Notice that a Preview command button is available in the Print dialog box. If you forget to preview a document before choosing File, Print, you can choose the Preview button in the Print dialog box.

FIG. 2.16

The Print dialog box for a word processor document.

Current printer selection ————

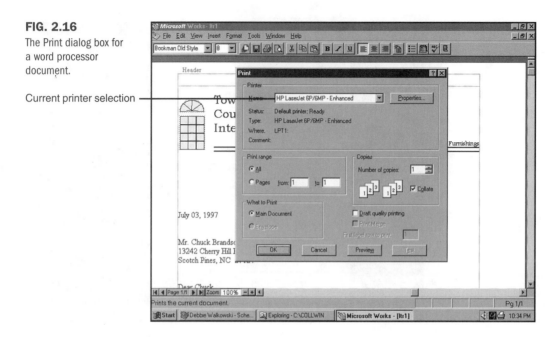

Table 2.2 describes the options in the Print dialog box.

Table 2.2 Options in the Print Dialog Box

Option	Description
Number of Copies	The default setting is 1; to print more than one copy of the current document, enter a different number.
Print Range: All	The default setting is to print all pages of the current document.
Print Range: Pages	To print selected pages, choose the Pages option button, then enter the first page to print in the From box and the last page to print in the To box.
Main Document	Prints the document itself rather than an envelope. This is the default setting.
Envelope	Choose this option to print envelopes.
Print merge	Allows you to merge a word processor document with a database document.
Draft quality printing	If your printer is capable of printing draft quality, choose this setting to print more quickly but at a lower print quality.

To print a document, follow these steps:

1. Open the document you want to print.

2. Choose File, Print. The Print dialog box shown in Figure 2.16 is displayed.

3. Choose the appropriate print settings, then choose OK.

Working with Multiple Document Windows

Earlier in this chapter you learned that Works displays a document window inside of a Works window. Works allows you to open multiple documents of any type at one time. Each is displayed in a separate document window and the windows can be various sizes. However, only one document at a time can be active, indicated by the highlighted title bar. The menu and toolbar automatically reflect the active window; that is, their commands are specific to the application you are using. When you create a new document, Works opens a new document window on top of the window you are currently using and the new window becomes the active window. In Figure 2.17, three document windows appear in the Works window.

FIG. 2.17
Three separate document windows are open at once.

Task Launcher button

Word processor window

Spreadsheet window

Database window

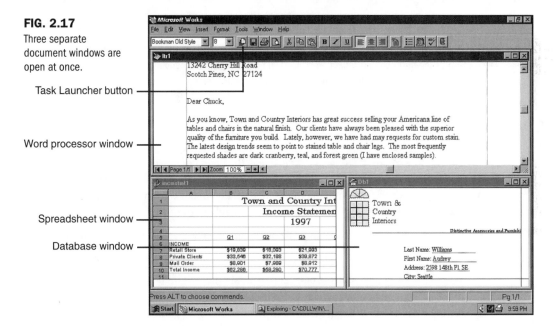

To create a new document of any type, follow these steps:

1. Click the Task Launcher button, or choose File, New.

2. Click the Works Tools tab, then click the button for the type of document you want to create. A new document window appears inside of the Works window.

To open an existing document in a new window, follow these steps:

1. Click the Task Launcher button, or choose File, New.

2. Click the Existing Documents tab, then double-click the file name. Your existing document appears inside of a new window.

There are two other quick ways to open an existing document. If you've recently worked on the document, it will appear at the bottom of the File menu. Just click the File menu, then click the file you want to open. The other way to open an existing document is to select File, Open; then in the Open dialog box, double-click the file you want to open.

Switching from One Window to Another

Switching from one document window to another is easy to do if the other window is visible. Just click anywhere in the new window to bring it to the front. If the window you want isn't visible (because the current window is maximized), follow these steps to switch to another window:

1. Choose Window from the menu bar.
2. At the bottom of the Window menu, find the document you want to open and click the name, or type the number that appears to the left of the name.

 If you like using keyboard shortcuts, another way to activate a hidden window is by pressing Ctrl+F6, which activates the next open document. Press Ctrl+F6 repeatedly until the document window you want is active, or press Shift+Ctrl+F6 to move backwards through open documents.

Arranging Open Windows

There are many ways to arrange open windows on the screen. You can choose to *cascade* all open windows (see Figure 2.18), a style that stacks the windows in a descending arrangement leaving the title bar of each window visible. Or you can *tile* all open windows (see Figure 2.19). This arrangement varies depending on the number of document windows that are open. To choose an arrangement select Window, Cascade or Window, Tile.

You can also arrange open windows by resizing and moving them to new locations on-screen:

- To resize a window, click and drag any of the window borders.
- To resize in two dimensions at once and maintain the height-to-width proportions of the window, click and drag any of the window corners.
- To move a window, click and drag the title bar to a new location, then release the mouse button.

Another way to arrange open windows on-screen is to minimize them. Minimizing a window shrinks it to the size of an icon but leaves the document open. In Figure 2.20, the database window is active and the word processing and spreadsheet windows are minimized.

To minimize a window, click the document window's minimize button. To make a minimized window active again, click the restore button. The window is restored to its previous size and position on-screen.

FIG. 2.18
All open document
windows are cascaded.

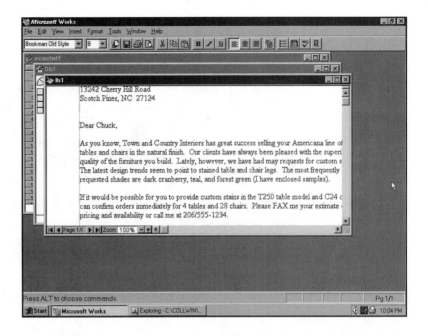

FIG. 2.19
All open document
windows are tiled.

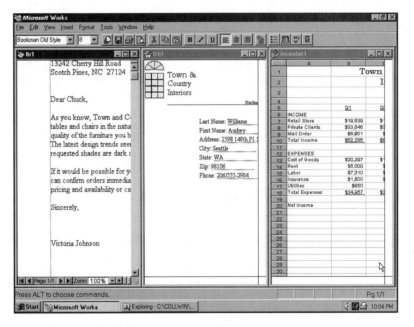

N O T E If you confuse the Works *program* window's minimize button with the *document* window's minimize button, you will shrink the Works window instead of just the document window. If you make this mistake, just click the Works icon to restore the Works window. (Refer to Figure 2.3 for examples of these and other window control buttons.) ■

FIG. 2.20
Minimized document windows appear as icons at the bottom of the Works window.

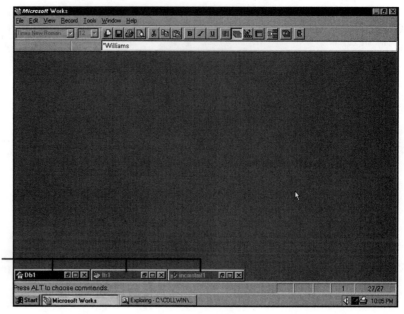

Icons indicate document windows that are minimized

Using Zoom

Works lets you change the magnification of a document on the screen using *Zoom*. You may often use Zoom to magnify a particular area of a document. Zoom also can reduce the displayed size of a document. The Zoom dialog box, displayed by choosing View, Zoom, contains five preset magnification/reduction levels. (You can also display the Zoom dialog box by clicking the Zoom button at the bottom of the window.)

To use the Zoom feature in Works, follow these steps.

1. From the View menu, choose the Zoom command. Works displays the Zoom dialog box shown in Figure 2.21.
2. Select a magnification level or enter a number from 25 to 1000 in the Custom text box.
3. Choose OK. Works displays the current document at the magnification level you choose.

When working with a word processor document, the Zoom dialog box also lets you choose one of the following options rather than a magnification percentage:

Page Width   Choose this option when you want to display your document from left to right margins, regardless of the window size. For example, if your document window size is reduced, the entire page width of the document is still visible.

Whole Page   Choose this option when you want your document to fit within the width of the document window. This is useful when using Landscape orientation so you don't have to scroll horizontally to see all the text.

Margin Width   Choose this option when you want to maximize the amount of available typing space within the window.

Using TaskWizards

A *TaskWizard* is a tool in Works that helps you create a specific type of document, such as a résumé, bibliography, newsletter, or invoice. TaskWizards are particularly useful for users who are new to Works, those who are not quite confident in their ability to create documents, or for users who are just in a hurry to get a task done. The wizard does all the planning, designing, and layout of a document. All you do is choose from suggested styles, then fill in the document's unique information.

When you use a TaskWizard, an on-screen "script" asks questions that you respond to interactively. Using the information you supply, the TaskWizard either completes a task or creates the framework of a document for you. In the Task Launcher dialog box, you'll find a variety of TaskWizards under each of the following categories:

Common Tasks
Correspondence
Envelopes and Labels
Business Management
Names and Addresses
Household Management
Students and Teachers
Billing
Employment
Volunteer/Civic Activities

Within each of these categories, TaskWizards help you create a variety of documents including newsletters, brochures, résumés, invoices, order forms, address books, and phone lists. To see a complete list of documents, display the TaskWizards tab in the Task Launcher dialog box. To expand or collapse a TaskWizard category, click the icon to the left of the category name. To see a description of the type of document, highlight the document name. The description appears on the right side of the dialog box.

To use a TaskWizard, follow these steps:

1. Click the Task Launcher toolbar button to display the Task Launcher dialog box.
2. Click the TaskWizards tab.
3. Click a category. To start a TaskWizard, double-click a document name in the list.
4. Click the Yes, Run the TaskWizard button.
5. Follow the step-by-step instructions on the screen for creating the document.

When you finish the TaskWizard steps, the document framework is created for you and you are ready to enter your unique text and save your file.

Using Templates

A *template* is a generic term for any type of model, pattern, or guide. In the context of Works, you use a template to create a Works document much the same way a clothing designer might use a pattern to make a garment or a woodworker might use a template to create four matching table legs. A template has two purposes: to provide consistent results each time you use it, and to save you the trouble of "reinventing the wheel" for each new project.

A fax cover sheet and a purchase order form are two good examples of business documents that could be created from templates. They require the same information each time you use them, and the format should be consistent for each document.

When you make a template, you create the *framework* of the document, including all repetitive text and formatting—essentially, you are creating a form. You can create the document "from scratch" or use a TaskWizard to help you build the document. Once the document is complete, you save the document as a template rather than as a standard document file. (Works recommends you store all templates in the Template folder under MSWorks.) When you want to use the template to create a working document, Works opens a *copy of* the template as a new document. You fill in the document with unique information and save it, and the original template remains unchanged.

To create a template, follow these steps:

1. Open the word processor, spreadsheet, or database tool and create the repetitive parts of the document exactly as you want the template to appear, or use a TaskWizard to create your document.
2. Choose File, Save As. The Save As dialog box is displayed.
3. In the Save In drop-down box, choose the Template folder.
4. Select the Template command button. The Save As Template dialog box is displayed.
5. Type in a name for the template document in the text box.
6. If you want the template to be the default document when you open the Works word processor, spreadsheet, or database, click the Use This Template check box.
7. Choose OK.

To create a new document using a template, open the Task Launcher dialog box (click the Task Launcher toolbar button from any Works application window). Scroll to the bottom of the TaskWizards list and double-click User Defined Templates, then double-click the template name. Works creates a new "blank" document using the template.

Getting Help

If you are new to Works, you will appreciate the fact that Help is always at your fingertips. When you have a question or you want simple step-by-step instructions, just press F1 or click the Help menu. The help commands on the Help menu are shown in Table 2.3.

Table 2.3 Help Menu Commands and Their Functions

Help Command	Description
Contents	Displays a table of contents listing all help topics, categorized by the four Works applications. Use for browsing just like you would in a book.
Index	Displays an extensive alphabetic list of topics, similar to an index in the back of a printed book.
Introduction to Works	Provides an introduction/overview of Works and its tools.
How to Use Help	Gives brief instructions on using Help.
Hide/Show Help	Hides or shows the help window on the screen when Help is running.
Office Compatible	Tells you the ways in which Works is compatible with Microsoft Office.
Launch Works Forum	If you are a subscriber of Microsoft Network, connects you directly to the Works Forum, a bulletin board.
About Microsoft Works	Microsoft Works 4.0 for Windows 95 copyright and version information.

Ch
2

Whenever you start Works and create a new document a Help window like the one shown in Figure 2.21 is displayed on the right side of your screen. (The Works document window automatically shrinks to make room for the Help window.) The Help window has two tabs. The Step-by-Step tab provides numbered instructions for accomplishing a particular task. The More Info tab gives you an overview of the topic or lists troubleshooting information.

FIG. 2.21

A typical help topic in Works.

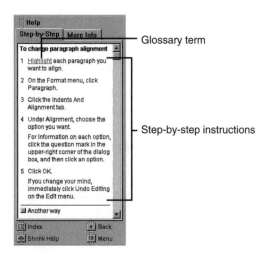

Glossary term

Step-by-step instructions

Because the Help window takes up a lot of room on your screen, you might consider turning it off when you don't need it, using one of these methods.

- To hide the Help screen, choose Help,Hide Help.

- To shrink the Help window to a Help bar on the right side of your screen (next to the vertical scroll bar), click the Shrink Help button (?) at the bottom of the Help window.

- To eliminate the Help window whenever you start up Works, choose Tools, Options, then click the View tab and remove the check mark from the Show Help at Startup option.

Help pages sometimes include *glossary terms* that appear in green underlined characters. Click a glossary term to display a definition in a pop-up window. To return to Help, click anywhere on the Help window or press any key on the keyboard.

At the bottom of the Help window are four buttons for navigating and controlling Help. These buttons are described in Table 2.4.

Table 2.4 Command Buttons Available in Help Windows

Command Button	Uses
Index	Click to see the Index or Contents to Help and choose a topic.
Back	Retrace your steps through the Help pages you have viewed.
Shrink Help	Shrinks the Help window to a vertical bar, displayed to the right of the document window. To bring the Help window back, click either button at the bottom of the vertical bar.
Menu	Displays a list of Help topics for the application that is currently active (such as the word processor).

N O T E   If you leave the Help window open on the screen when you exit Works, it will appear on the screen the next time you start Works. ■

Exiting Works 4.5

When you're finished using Works, choose File, Exit Works to close the program, click the Works window's close (X) button, or double-click the Works program icon. If you still have open document files that have not yet been saved, Works displays a dialog box for each file asking if you want to save the changes. Click Yes to save the most recent changes, click No to abandon the most recent changes, or click Cancel to return to Works. ●

Creating, Saving, and Printing a Word Processor Document

Now that you've learned the basics of using Works, you're ready to begin creating documents. Documents created with a word processor (those that contain primarily text) are by far the most common type of document most users create. ■

The word processor menus and toolbar

Menu commands and toolbar buttons in the word processor make it easy for you to create, edit, format, and print text documents.

How to enter text and correct minor errors

Entering text is one of the easiest things you'll do in a word processor document, and when you make an error, you can correct it quickly on the spot.

How to find your way around in a document

Word processor documents can become quite large. You'll learn how to move throughout the document to find a particular location where you might want to make changes.

How to print your document

Although the basics of printing any Works document were covered in Chapter 2, in this chapter you learn about some special considerations for printing word processor documents.

The Word Processor Window

Recall from Chapter 2, "Getting Started with Works," that each Works application displays a unique document window inside the Works program window. The window shown in Figure 3.1 is the basic word processing window that opens when you choose the Word Processor tool from the Task Launcher dialog box. In the figure, the window is maximized so that the Works window and the word processing window blend together. The title bar, (shared by both windows) shows the temporary file name, Unsaved Document 1.

FIG. 3.1

The word processor window has its own menu bar, toolbar, status bar, and scroll bars.

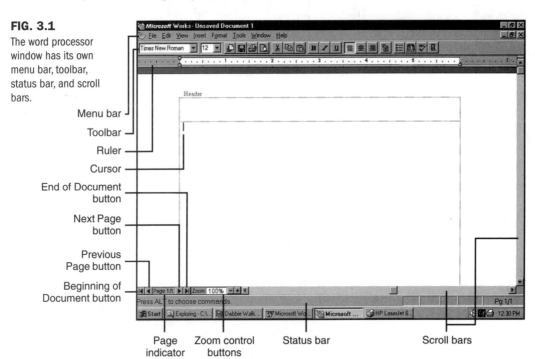

The menu bar and toolbar shown in Figure 3.1 contain commands and buttons that pertain to word processor tasks. The white area of the screen represents the page; the faint dotted lines outline the text area on the page and define the "header" area at the top of the page.

 TIP In Works, you can choose to display the toolbar or turn it off. If the toolbar isn't visible in the word processor window, choose View, Toolbar. (The toolbar is already visible in the window when a check mark appears to the left of the Toolbar option on the View menu.)

The blinking vertical bar is the *insertion point* or *cursor*; it is the point at which characters are inserted when you type.

Just below the word processor toolbar is the ruler. The white area of the ruler (between 0 and 6 inches) indicates the width of the page area in which you can type text. The pointers (they appear at the 0 and 6" positions in Figure 3.1) indicate where the right margin, right indent, and left margins are located. When appropriate, the ruler also indicates tab locations.

▶ **See** "Moving and Deleting Tabs," **p. 92**

 If you do not see the ruler on your screen, your ruler is turned off. To display the ruler, choose View, Ruler. (A check mark appears next to the Ruler command on the View menu when your ruler is displayed.)

Like all other document windows, the word processor window has both a vertical and a horizontal scroll bar so you can scroll a long document up and down or a wide document right to left.

The left end of the horizontal scroll bar indicates the page where the cursor is currently located and the total number of pages (as in page 5 of 10, noted as 5/10). Just to the left of the page indicator are the Beginning of Document and Previous Page buttons. To the right of the page indicator are the Next Page and End of Document buttons. Click these buttons to help you move through the document quickly.

Also along the horizontal scroll bar is a Zoom indicator, a Zoom button, and plus (+) and minus (-) buttons. The Zoom indicator shows the current zoom percentage (100%). When the zoom percentage is 100% you see the document at its actual size; if the document is displayed at 70%, you see it at 70% of its actual size. To zoom in closer on a document, click the plus (+) button; to zoom out, click the minus (-) button. Or, click the Zoom indicator and a pop-up menu appears from which you can choose a standard zoom percentage or enter a custom setting.

The status bar appears just below the horizontal scroll bar at the bottom of the window. Its function is to provide a variety of important information. At the far right end is a page indicator just like the one in the horizontal scroll bar. The left end of the status bar provides brief instructions (such as Press ALT to choose commands), or describes the current menu command that is highlighted. For instance, if you highlight the Print command on the File menu, the status bar reads: Prints the Current Document. When you're first learning to use Works, the messages in the status bar can be very useful in helping you remember command functions. When you press the Num Lock and Caps Lock keys on the keyboard, indicators also appear on the status bar to the left of the page indicator.

As you learned in Chapter 2, every Works application has a set of *menus* which contain *commands*. Table 3.1 describes the word processor menus and the commands they contain.

 To review how to select menus and commands, refer to Chapter 2, "Getting Started With Works."

Just as each Works application has a unique menu, each has a unique toolbar (refer to Figure 3.1). Each button on the toolbar represents a particular command. To activate the command, you just click its button. If the button you select requires more information before a command can be completed, Works displays either a drop-down menu or a dialog box. Table 3.2 shows a picture of each button and describes its use.

Table 3.1 The Word Processor Menus

Menu Name	This Menu Contains
File	All the commands necessary for creating, opening, saving, and printing files. The four most recently opened files are always listed at the bottom of the File menu, providing a quick way to open a file.
Edit	Commands for cutting, copying, and pasting text and for undoing the most recent change to a document.
View	Commands that determine how a document is displayed; for instance, View commands determine whether the document apppears in normal view or page layout view (see "Changing Your View of a Document," later in this chapter), with or without the ruler, the toolbar, hidden characters, and so on. Commands for displaying footnotes, headers, and footers also appear on this menu.
Insert	Commands for inserting any type of graphics object (such as a drawing, ClipArt, word art, chart, or spreadsheet) in a document. Use this menu also to insert page breaks, special characters, footnotes, EasyText, and so on.
Format	Commands that let you to choose a font and text style, specify a paragraph's format, set tabs, add a border to selected text, create columns of text, and format a picture.
Tools	Special tools for working with a word processor document. Here you have access to your address book, the spell checker, thesaurus, hyphenation, and word count features in Works. You also use this menu to customize the toolbar and other Works options.
Window	Commands that help you arrange all open documents on your screen and to select the active window.
Help	Commands for getting help in the form of an Index, Contents, and Introduction to Works.

Table 3.2 The Buttons on the Word Processor Toolbar

Button	Function
Bookman Old Style	Displays a drop-down list of all available fonts.
8	Displays a drop-down list of all available point sizes for the current font.
	Displays the Task Launcher dialog box.
	Saves the file using the current file name and settings. (If the document has not yet been saved, the Save As dialog box appears.)

Button	Function
	Prints the current document using the current print settings.
	Shows a preview of your document before printing.
	Removes the selected text and places it in the Clipboard.
	Copies the selected text and placed it in the Clipboard.
	Inserts (pastes) the contents of the Clipboard into the current document at the location of the cursor.
	Applies bold to selected text.
	Applies italic to selected text.
	Applies underline to selected text.
	Left-aligns selected text.
	Centers the selected text between the left and right margins.
	Right-aligns selected text.
	Applies an EasyFormat to the selected text.
	Places a bullet to the left of the selected paragraph.
	Lets you look up a reference in Bookshelf or Encarta if you have either of these programs installed on your computer.
	Begins spell checking the current document.
	Runs the Address Book TaskWizard.

Ch
3

Changing Your View of a Document

A *view* defines the way Works displays a document on-screen. In the word processor, Works offers two different views: Page Layout and Normal, both described below. Each view has its advantages and unique characteristics.

- *Page Layout view* To view inserted objects or drawings, headers, footers, footnotes, and columns on-screen, use Page Layout view. This view presents all aspects of your document on-screen as they will appear when printed. The top, bottom, right, and left page margins are presented accurately on-screen. Headers and footers appear at the top and bottom of every page, footnotes appear at the bottom of the appropriate pages, and if you use multiple columns in a document, they appear on-screen as well. An example of a document displayed in Page Layout View is shown in Figure 3.2.

FIG. 3.2

In Page Layout view, the document is displayed as it will look when printed.

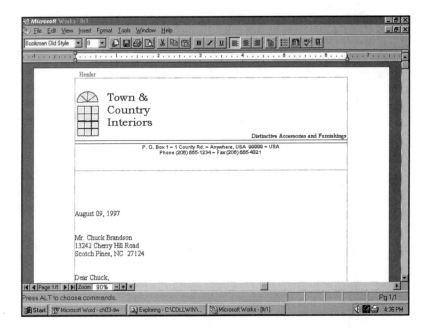

- *Normal view* Works uses this view by default; unless you choose another view, Works displays all documents in Normal view. Normal view reflects most aspects of your document as they will appear when printed. That is, Works displays accurate font and point sizes, text alignment, and paragraph formats. Missing from Normal view are margins, headers, footers, footnotes, inserted objects or drawings, and columns in their proper locations (see Figure 3.3).

The more document enhancements, features, and special effects you choose to display on-screen, the more computer resources Works requires. Page Layout view requires the most computer resources and may cause slow response on a computer lacking adequate memory. Normal view, on the other hand, requires fewer computer resources and is often the best view to use on a slow or low-memory computer. Typically you enter and edit a document in Normal view.

FIG. 3.3

In Normal view, headers, footers, and inserted ClipArt are not displayed.

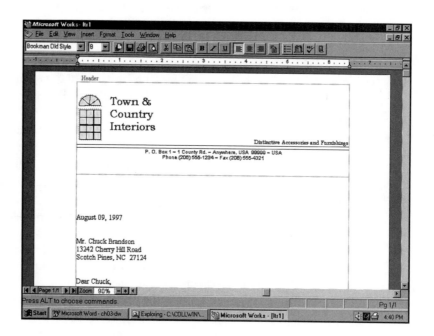

To change your view of a document, follow these steps:

1. Choose the <u>V</u>iew menu. A check mark appears to the left of the view you currently are using.

2. To select another view, choose <u>N</u>ormal or <u>P</u>age Layout. Works places a check mark next to the view you select and immediately switches your document to that view.

Entering Text

Entering text in a word processing document is one of the simplest things you can do—you just start typing. Characters appear on the screen to the left of the cursor, and the cursor moves to the right as you type. When you reach the end of the first line, continue typing. Works automatically *wraps* text to the next line so you don't have to press Enter at the end of each line. The only time you need to press Enter is when you want to return the cursor to the left margin to begin a new paragraph.

As you type a document on a word processor, the characters appear in the visible display area of the window. When you fill this area, the document scrolls upward to reveal a new blank page for you to type on. For example, if you typed three pages of text without stopping, the window would display the third page and the cursor would be located to the right of the last character you typed. The page indicator on the status line would say 3/3 (page 3 of 3).

Moving Around in a Document

There are many ways to move the cursor within a document. The method you choose often depends on personal preference, where the cursor is located in a document, and how far you want to move the cursor. The most common methods are described below:

- *Arrow keys* The up- and down-arrow keys on the keyboard move the cursor up or down one line at a time. The left- and right-arrow keys move the cursor right or left one character at a time. You can press and hold any of these keys to repeat the action.

- *Page Up and Page Down keys* These keys move the cursor one window back and one window forward respectively. Note that, in this context, a *page* is defined as one window's worth of information. The Page Up and Page Down keys also repeat when held down.

- *Navigation buttons* Located at the left end of the horizontal scroll bar, there are four navigation buttons (refer to Figure 3.1). To the left of the page indicator are the Beginning of Document and Previous Page buttons. To the right of the page indicator are the Next Page and End of Document buttons. Click any of these buttons to move quickly through a document.

- *Go To Command* When you want to go to a specific page in a document, the Edit, Go To command is a handy feature. When you choose this command, the Go To dialog box shown in Figure 3.4 is displayed. Type the page number you want in the Go To box, then click OK. Works moves the cursor to the beginning of the page you specify.

- *Scroll bars* The scroll box inside the vertical scroll bar indicates your approximate position in a document. For example, if a document is 10 pages long and the scroll box is located halfway down the vertical scroll bar, you are probably viewing page 5. Using the mouse, drag the scroll box to the approximate location in the document you want to view, then click anywhere within the working area to move the cursor. You can also move the document up or down one line at a time by clicking the scroll arrows at either end of the vertical scroll bar.

 TIP Scrolling alone does not move the cursor, it only shifts your view of the document. To move the cursor, you must click inside the window.

- *Keyboard shortcuts* Before most computer programs supported a mouse, a user would rely on the keyboard to navigate a document. These keyboard shortcuts, listed in Table 3.3, still work and are often quicker than the mouse or scroll bars.

Table 3.3   Keys for Moving the Cursor

Keys	Moves Cursor
Home	To the beginning of the current line
End	To the end of the current line
Ctrl+Home	To the beginning of the document

Keys	Moves Cursor
Ctrl+End	To the end of the document
Ctrl+right arrow	To the next word
Ctrl+left arrow	To the previous word
Ctrl+up arrow	To the previous paragraph
Ctrl+down arrow	To the next paragraph
Right arrow	One character to the right
Left arrow	One character to the left
Up arrow	One line up
Down arrow	One line down
PgUp	Up one window
PgDn	Down one window

 T I P To display the Go To dialog box quickly, press F5 or Ctrl+G.

FIG. 3.4
The Go To dialog box lets you move directly to a specific page in a document.

Correcting Minor Errors

When you're entering new text, it's easiest to correct minor errors as you type. These include typing mistakes, punctuation errors, or a minor change to a word or phrase.

To delete characters, you use either the Backspace or Delete keys. Backspace deletes characters to the left of the cursor; the Delete key deletes the character to the right of the cursor. Whichever key you choose, use the arrow keys to position the cursor, then press Backspace or Delete.

Both the Backspace and Delete keys repeat their functions when you hold them down, so you can delete a sequence of characters quickly—but be careful. On a fast computer, these keys can delete more characters than you might intend to remove.

Refer to the following sections for information on more extensive editing: "Deleting Large Areas of Text," Chapter 6; "Inserting Text and Typing Over Text," Chapter 6; "Automatically Replacing Text," Chapter 6.

▶ **See** "Adding Special Features to a Word Processor Document, **p. xxx** (CH 6)

Printing a Word Processor Document

Chapter 2, "Getting Started with Works," includes an extensive section on printing Works documents. In general, all Works documents, regardless of the type, are printed the same way. That is, you set margins, paper source, paper size, and print orientation using the File, Page Setup command (which displays the Page Setup dialog box). When all settings are correct, you preview the document, then print.

▶ **See** "Printing a Document," **p. 22**

The default margin settings (1 inch for top and bottom margins and 1.25 inches for left and right margins) are generally fine for most word processor documents. In some cases, however, you might want to change these settings to achieve some of the following results:

- In order to fit more (or less) text on a page
- To align text with graphic elements on the page (such as a company logo)
- To arrange a special type of document on the page, such as a thank you note or party invitation

Printing Special Features of a Word Processor Document

The settings on the Other Options tab in the Page Setup dialog box varies depending on the type of document you're printing.

For example, four common elements of word processor documents are page numbers, headers, footers, and footnotes. Use the Other Options tab in the Page Setup dialog box to specify how you want these elements to be printed. For instance, if you want the first page of the document to start with a page number other than 1, you can change the starting page number. If the first page of your document is a title page, you can eliminate the header and/or footer from the first page of the document.

When your document contains footnotes, they typically are printed on the page of the document where the footnote marker appears. If you prefer to print all footnotes at the end of the document, choose the Print Footnotes at End option. ●

CHAPTER 4

Changing a Document

In this chapter you learn about the most important feature of a word processor—the ability to change a document. Unlike a typewriter, a word processor allows you to make changes to a document. These changes can range from minor ones such as changing a word, to major ones such as moving paragraphs or entire pages. ■

Deleting and inserting text

In this chapter you learn how easy it is to make the most common changes to a document—removing text and inserting new text.

Moving and copying text

Probably the second most common changes you make in a document are moving or copying text; you'll learn just how easy this tasks is.

Undoing changes

Thank goodness most changes are not permanent! You learn how to undo changes, when necessary.

Finding and replacing text in a document

One of the best uses for the Replace function is to use one document for two different purposes, such as an identical letter to two different clients; just replace the first client's name in the second document.

Checking your document for accuracy

Be sure your documents are as professionally prepared as possible by using the spell checker and thesaurus.

Selecting Text to Change It

Whenever you want to make changes to text you must select it first so that Works knows what portion of text you want to change. When you select—or *highlight*—text, the background color behind the text changes (usually to black) so that the text appears highlighted (in white). See Figure 4.1. There are a variety of methods for selecting text using the mouse, the keyboard, or both. The method you choose depends on your own personal preference and the amount of text you are selecting.

When using the mouse, the method is called "click and drag." With this choice, you click the left mouse button and hold it down as you move the mouse pointer over the portion of text you want to select. This is the best method to use when you are selecting irregular areas of text (for example, part of a word, sentence, or paragraph). As you move the mouse, the text that you drag the pointer across is automatically highlighted (see Figure 4.1).

FIG. 4.1
The selected text is highlighted.

Selected text ——

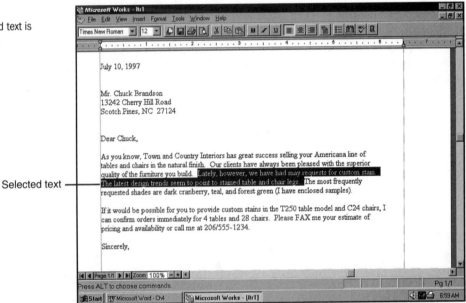

When you move the mouse vertically through lines of text, one line at a time is added to the selection. When you move the mouse horizontally across words on the same line, one word at a time is added to the selection. After the text you want to select is highlighted, release the mouse button.

N O T E Works selects entire words at a time because the Automatic Word Selection option is selected by default. (This setting appears on the Editing tab when you choose Tools, Options). If you prefer to have Works select a character at a time rather than an entire word, you can turn off the Automatic Word Selection option by clicking the check box for this option to remove the check mark. ■

Works incorporates some special "mouse clicks" that allow you to efficiently select certain portions of text. You determine how much text is selected by where you click or double-click the mouse, sometimes in combination with other keys.

These methods are summarized in Table 4.1. After making your selection, be sure to release the mouse button to avoid selecting any unwanted text.

Table 4.1 Selecting Text by Clicking the Mouse	
To Select	**Do This**
One word	Double-click anywhere on the word
One line	Click in the left margin next to the line
One paragraph	Double-click in the left margin next to the paragraph
One sentence	Press and hold the Ctrl key, then click anywhere in the sentence
The entire document	Press and hold the Ctrl key, then click anywhere in the left margin
From cursor	Press and hold the Shift key, then click where you want the selection to end to any other point

Sometimes you might prefer to select text using the keyboard (or Shift) method. Using this method is sometimes easier than using the mouse because you don't need to reach for the mouse and take your hands away from the keyboard.

You can also select text using a combination of the Shift key and the Page Up, Page Down, Home, End, and arrow keys. When you have highlighted all the text you want to select, release all keys on the keyboard.

The Shift key methods of selecting text are summarized in Table 4.2. If you select the wrong text, or decide you don't need to select text, cancel the selection by pressing any of the arrow keys or clicking anywhere in the document.

Table 4.2 Using the Shift Key To Select Text	
Selection	**Press and hold the Shift key, then...**
One character at a time	Press the right- or left-arrow key
One line	Press the up- or down-arrow key
From the cursor to the beginning of the current line	Press Home
From the cursor to the end of the current line	Press End
From the cursor to the previous paragraph	Press Ctrl+up arrow
From the cursor to the next paragraph	Press Ctrl+down arrow
From the cursor to the beginning of the document	Press Ctrl+Home key
From the cursor to the end of the document	Press Ctrl+End key

Ch

4

Deleting Large Areas of Text

In Chapter 3, "Creating, Saving, and Printing a Word Processor Document," you learn about two simple keys that help you change text: Backspace and Delete. These keys are useful for making minor changes such as correcting a word or phrase. But sometimes you need to make major changes like deleting several paragraphs, or changing existing text and inserting new text.

To delete large areas of text, use the Edit, Cut command. Using this command removes the selected text from the document as if you had removed a section of text with scissors. If the text you remove is in the middle of a paragraph, the text that follows the selection is automatically realigned with the surrounding text.

Although the text that you cut is removed from the document, it isn't permanently lost. It is stored on the Clipboard, a temporary storage area for text that you cut or copy. Think of the Clipboard as a convenient "safety net" for those times when you delete text by mistake. When this happens, you can reinsert the text, as you'll learn later in this chapter.

To select text to cut, use any of the selection methods you just learned. Be sure to select the lines and spaces surrounding the text that you want to cut. For instance, if you are cutting a paragraph, you need to select the blank line that precedes or follows the paragraph, otherwise you'll be left with two blank lines between the two remaining paragraphs. If you are selecting several sentences, be sure to select the space or spaces that follow the last sentence (see Figure 4.2).

To delete text from a document, follow these brief steps:

1. Select the text you want to delete, including the blank lines and spaces.
2. Choose Edit, Cut, or click the Cut toolbar button.

FIG. 4.2

The paragraph is selected to be cut. Notice that the blank line following the paragraph is selected as well.

Blank line is also selected

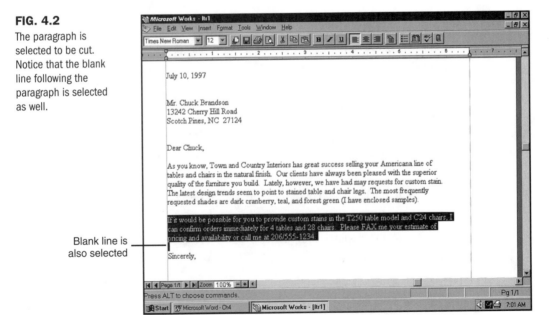

CAUTION

Don't use the Delete key on the keyboard in place of the Edit, Cut command. The Delete key deletes selected text from your document, but does *not* place it on the Clipboard. Using the Delete key permanently removes the selected text from the document and you cannot retrieve it.

Inserting Text and Typing Over Text

The word processor automatically operates in *insert mode*. This means that the characters to the right of the cursor are shifted to the right to make room for the new text you type. Insert mode is the "safest" mode in which to work because your original text isn't typed over.

The alternative to insert mode is *overtype* mode. In this mode, any text to the right of the cursor is automatically replaced by the new text you type. Overtyping is a method you might choose when you are certain you want to replace an existing phrase, sentence, or paragraph with new text. What's the advantage? Overtyping saves you the trouble of selecting and deleting existing text, then inserting new text; you simply do it all in one step. However, overtype mode is riskier because it automatically replaces existing text. If you forget that you are using overtype mode and begin typing in the middle of a sentence or paragraph, your original text is replaced by the new text you type.

Because insert mode is selected by default, you must select overtype mode if you want to use it. To do so, choose Tools, Options. In the Options dialog box, choose the Editing tab (see Figure 4.3), then choose the Overtype check box and click OK. Notice that the OVR indicator appears near the right end of the status line. This setting remains in effect until you change back to insert mode. To switch back to insert mode, turn off the Overtype option in the Options dialog box.

You can quickly turn overtype mode on by pressing the Insert key on your keyboard or the Zero key (0) on the 10-key pad. Again, the OVR indicator appears on the status line. The Insert and Zero (0) keys toggle on and off, so press it again to turn overtype mode off.

By default, Works uses the Typing Replaces Selection setting (see the Editing Tab in the Options dialog box, Figure 4.3). With this setting, all text that you select is automatically replaced by new text that you type. If you prefer not to have Works automatically replace selected text, click the Typing Replaces Selection option to remove the check mark from the box.

Moving and Copying Text

When you use a word processor to create and revise documents, moving and copying are editing changes you make frequently. With a few simple keystrokes, you can move or copy any selection of text, anywhere in a document. These features make it easy for you to completely rearrange a document without losing any of its original text.

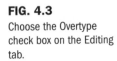

FIG. 4.3

Choose the Overtype check box on the Editing tab.

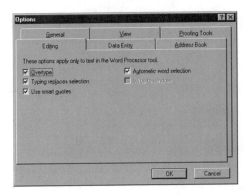

You can move and copy text using menu commands or using a special mouse technique called drag-and-drop. You learn both methods in the following sections.

Moving and Copying Using Menu Commands

When you move text, you use Edit, Cut to remove the text from its original location, then you use Edit, Paste to insert the text in its new location. While you're in the process of moving text, Works uses the Windows Clipboard as a temporary storage area for the selected text.

Follow these steps to move text:

1. Select the text you want to move, including the spaces and blank lines surrounding the text (see Figure 4.4).

2. Choose Edit, Cut; or click the Cut button on the toolbar. The selected text is removed from the document and placed on the Clipboard.

3. Move the cursor to the location where you want to move the text.

4. Choose Edit, Paste, or click the Paste button on the toolbar. Works inserts the selected text where the cursor is located (see Figure 4.5).

When you copy text, you use the Copy and Paste commands on the Edit menu. Again, Works uses the Clipboard to store a copy of the selected text until you choose a location to paste it. Here's how to copy a selection:

1. Select the text you want to copy, including the appropriate spaces and blank lines surrounding the text.

2. Choose Edit, Copy; or click the Copy button on the toolbar. The selected text is copied to the Clipboard.

3. Move the cursor to the location where you want to copy the text.

4. Choose Edit, Paste, or click the Paste toolbar button. Works inserts the selected text where the cursor is located. The original text you selected remains intact in its previous location.

FIG. 4.4

A sentence is highlighted for moving.

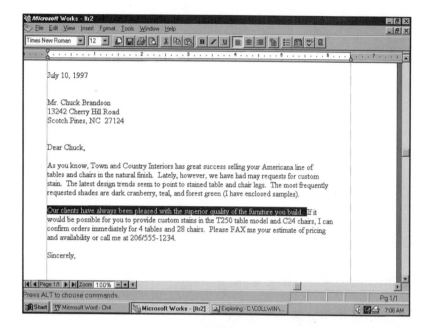

FIG. 4.5

The sentence in its new location.

The moved sentence ——

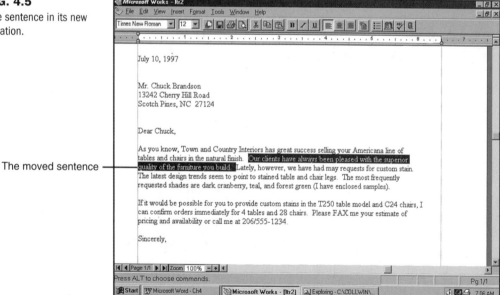

Ch

4

The keyboard shortcut for Edit, Cut is Ctrl+X; for Edit, Paste, Ctrl+V; for Edit, Copy, Ctrl+C.

CAUTION

When you move or copy text in a document, be sure to complete the operation before doing any other editing. That is, paste the selection somewhere in the document immediately after you cut or copy it, otherwise you might lose it. The Clipboard can hold only one selection at a time. If you cut a paragraph, then cut a sentence, the sentence replaces the paragraph on the Clipboard and you have no way to retrieve your paragraph.

 To select the Cut, Copy, or Paste commands quickly from within the document, right-click the mouse button to display the shortcut menu.

Moving and Copying Using Drag-and-Drop

If you prefer, you can use the mouse rather than menu commands to move and copy text. This is called the *drag-and-drop* method.

To use drag-and-drop to move text, follow these steps:

1. Select the text you want to move or copy. The word DRAG appears next to the mouse pointer.
2. Move the mouse pointer over the selected text, press and hold the left mouse button and the word MOVE appears next to the mouse pointer on-screen.
3. Drag the selection to its new location, then release the mouse button. Works moves the text to its new location.

To use drag-and-drop to copy text, follow these steps:

1. Select the text you want to move or copy. The word DRAG appears next to the mouse pointer.
2. Move the mouse pointer over the selected text, press and hold the Ctrl key and the left mouse button and the word COPY appears next to the mouse pointer on-screen.
3. Drag the selection to its new location, then release the mouse button and the Ctrl key. Works copies the text to its new location and leaves the original text intact.

Undoing Changes

Fortunately, Works provides a way for you to undo changes that you make by using Edit, Undo. This command reverses the most recent editing changes you make in a document. Editing changes include typing, replacing text, deleting, moving, and copying. Although Undo is useful in all these cases, you'll most appreciate Undo when you delete text by mistake.

The most important thing to remember about Undo is that you must use it *immediately* after the editing change you make. If you delete several paragraphs, then type a new word, using Undo will remove the new word you typed; it will not bring back your paragraphs.

Suppose you delete a paragraph by mistake, retrieve it using Undo, then decide you really do want to delete the paragraph. You could select and delete the paragraph again, or you could just choose Undo again.

N O T E   In the word processor, the Undo command also works to reverse formatting changes, including changes to the font, size, style (such as bold, underline, italic), color, alignment, and so on. You learn more about using these features in Chapter 5, "Creating Great-Looking Documents." ■

Finding and Replacing Text in a Document

One of the most useful features of a word processor is its ability to search for and replace characters in a document. Imagine typing a 50-page sales proposal, then discovering that you misspelled the client's company name throughout the document. Finding and correcting every occurrence of the company name would be a great deal of work.

With the find and replace features in Works, you can search an entire document or just a selected section of a document. You can search for a single character, a word, a phrase, or any string of characters, such as a part number like 120-NB98. You can even search for tabs and paragraph markers. You can choose whether to replace all occurrences of a word or phrase, or replace only selected occurrences.

Ch
4

N O T E   When you press the Tab key or press Enter to begin a new paragraph, Works inserts special "hidden" characters in your document: an arrow when you press Tab, a paragraph marker when you press Enter (for a new line). Generally you keep these characters hidden so they are not distracting. However, if necessary, you can display these characters by choosing View, All Characters. ■

To search for text without replacing it, you use the Edit, Find command. The Edit, Replace command lets you search for text and automatically replace it with something else.

Table 4.3 illustrates exactly how you can widen or narrow your search depending on whether you choose the Match Case or Find Whole Words Only options.

Table 4.3   How Works Searches for Characters Using Edit, Find and Edit, Replace

If You Search For:	Works Finds:
in	in, IN, In, printing, within, Indicate
In (Match case)	In, IN, Indicate
In (whole word)	in, IN, In

continues

Table 4.3 Continued

If You Search For:	Works Finds:
In (match case and whole word)	In
Tab (→)	tab characters in the document
Paragraph (¶)	paragraph markers in the document

N O T E If you begin searching in mid-document and search to the end, Works lets you choose whether to continue searching from the beginning of the document. ■

To find text in a document, follow these steps:

1. Move the cursor to the beginning of the document, or highlight the text you want to search.
2. Choose Edit, Find. The Find dialog box shown in Figure 4.6 is displayed.

FIG. 4.6

The Find dialog box.

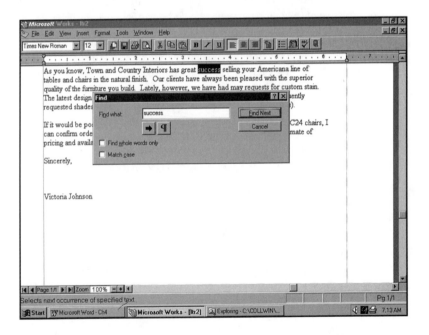

3. In the Find What text box, type the word, phrase, or character string to find.
4. Choose any of the following options:
    *   To match the whole word or the case of the text, check the Find Whole Words Only check box or the Match Case check box, or both.
    *   To search for tab or paragraph markers, click either of these buttons. (Works inserts a ^T for tab, a ^P for paragraph markers in the Find What text box.)

5. Choose the Find Next button or press Enter. Works finds the first occurrence of the text. Repeat step 5 to find additional occurrences. A message box appears when all occurrences have been found. Click OK.

6. After you finish searching, close the Find dialog box by choosing the Cancel button.

 TIP After returning to your document, pressing Ctrl+F redisplays the Find dialog box if you want to search again. This keyboard shortcut is useful when you have finished a search and closed the Find dialog box, then realized you wanted to continue searching.

NOTE If your document does not contain text that matches your criteria, Works displays a message saying it could not find a match. ■

The Edit, Replace command works just like Edit, Find, except that you also specify text or characters you want to use as a replacement for the text you find. You can choose to replace all occurrences of the characters you're looking for (using the Replace All button), or replace occurrences selectively.

To replace text throughout a document, follow these steps:

1. Move the cursor to the beginning of the document, or highlight the section of text you want to search and replace.

2. Choose Edit, Replace. The Replace dialog box shown in Figure 4.7 is displayed.

3. In the Find What text box, enter the word, phrase, or character string to find. To search for a tab character or paragraph marker, click the appropriate button.

4. In the Replace With text box, enter the replacement text. To replace with a tab character or paragraph marker, click the appropriate button.

5. To match the whole word or case of the text to search for, check the appropriate check box.

6. Choose the Find Next button. Works finds the first occurrence of the text and highlights it in the document.

7. If you want to replace all occurrences of the text, choose the Replace All button. If you want to replace only the current occurrence, choose the Replace button. If you want to skip this occurrence without replacing it and find the next, choose the Find Next button.

8. Repeat step 7 until you finish searching for and replacing text. A message appears after Works has searched the entire document. Click OK.

9. Close the Replace dialog box by choosing the Cancel button.

NOTE You are not required to enter anything in the Replace With text box; you can choose nothing as your replacement text. This is an easy way to delete a word or phrase that occurs repeatedly in a document. Say your document contains the name "Acme Corporation" 25 times. To avoid the monotony and redundancy of such a long name, you could search for "Corporation" and leave the replacement text blank—all references would be changed to simply "Acme." ■

Ch
4

FIG. 4.7

The Replace dialog box.

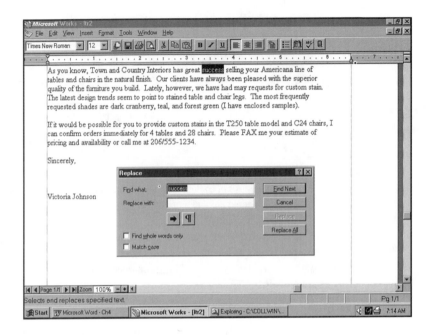

N O T E Unlike the Edit, Find command, Edit, Replace does not go back to the beginning of the document to continue searching if you started the command in mid-document. Works displays a message asking if you want to search from the beginning. To do so, click Yes, then continue searching. ■

Sometimes you might not be certain about the spelling of a word you're searching for. In these cases, you can use a *wild card*, represented by a question mark, to take the place of any single character. For instance, if you search for *t?p*, Works finds *tap*, *tip*, and *top*. If you enter *t???p*, Works finds all five-letter words that begin with *t* and end with *p*. Wild cards can be very useful for finding names like Ander*so*n or Ander*se*n when you're not sure of the spelling.

In addition to tabs and paragraph markers, you might want to search for other special or hidden characters. These are listed in Table 4.4. To search for one of these characters or document elements, type the code in the Find What text box of the Find or Replace dialog boxes.

Table 4.4 Wild Cards and Special Character Codes

To Find This Character	Type This Code
Any single character	?
Question mark	^?
End-of-line marker	^n
Page break	^d
White space (one space between words)	^w

To Find This Character	Type This Code
Optional hyphen	^_
Non-breaking space	^s

 T I P You can replace two spaces between words with one space between words by searching for ^w^w and replacing with ^w.

N O T E Some of these elements, such as optional hyphens and non-breaking spaces, are not familiar to you yet but you will learn about inserting them in a document in Chapter 6, "Adding Special Features to a Word Processor Document." ■

Using the Spelling, Thesaurus, and Word Count Commands

Works provides several tools for helping you check the accuracy of your documents. One is the Spelling checker. It checks all the words in your document against a dictionary file that contains hundreds of thousands of words. When the Spelling Checker finds a word that's not in the dictionary file, it highlights the word, but it isn't necessarily misspelled. It could:

■ be an unknown word (not in the dictionary)

■ have incorrect hyphenation

■ have irregular capitalization (such as wOrks)

■ be a word repeated consecutively (such as "and and")

The Spelling Checker gives you several commands for handling these ambiguous situations. Table 4.5 defines these commands and explains how they can help you spell check your document.

Table 4.5 Spell Checker Command Buttons

Button	Description
Ignore	If the highlighted word is spelled correctly, use this button to leave the word unchanged and continue checking the document.
Ignore All	If the highlighted word is spelled correctly and it occurs frequently in the document, use this button to leave all occurrences of the word unchanged.
Change	Choose this button if you want to replace the highlighted word with the word shown in the Change To box.
Change All	Choose this button if you want to replace all occurrences of the word throughout the document with the word shown in the Change To box.

continues

Table 4.5 Continued	
Button	**Description**
Add	If you want to add a word to the dictionary, choose this button. For instance, if the name of your company is Smithson Tool Works, the dictionary will always question *Smithson* as a misspelled word unless you add it to the dictionary file.
Suggest	When the Always Suggest check box is not selected, choose this button to see a list of suggested replacement words.
Cancel	Close the Spelling Checker without checking the remainder of the document.
Help	Display the help topic that describes the Spelling Checker dialog box.

To use the spell checker, follow these steps:

1. Move the cursor to the beginning of the document, or highlight the portion of the document you want to check.

2. Choose Tools, Spelling or click the Spelling Checker button on the toolbar. The Spelling dialog box shown in Figure 4.8 is displayed. The first unrecognized word is highlighted in the document.

FIG. 4.8

The Spelling dialog box displays the unrecognized word and suggested replacement words.

Selected word in the document

Word not in dictionary

Suggested replacement spelling

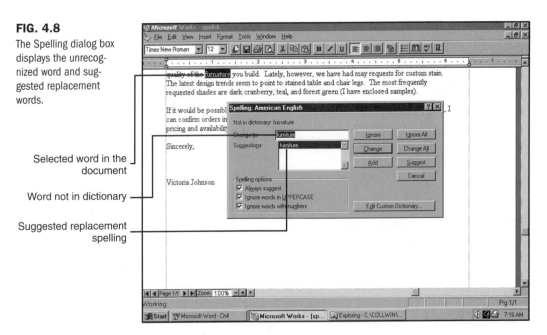

3. If the word is spelled correctly, choose the Ignore, Ignore All, or Add button (see Table 4.5 for more information about these commands).

4. If the word is spelled incorrectly, select a replacement word from the Suggestions list or use the word shown in the Change To box. (If the Always Suggest check box is not checked, click the Suggest button to display a list of suggested words.) If no words are suggested, type the correct spelling in the Change To box, then choose the Change or Change All button (see Table 4.5).

5. (Optional) In the Spelling Options area check the following options:

- Always suggest   Check this option if you want the Spelling Checker to automatically suggest word spellings. Click to remove the check mark to turn off this feature.
- Ignore words in UPPERCASE   Check this option when the document contains abbreviations and acronyms, or addresses that the Spelling Checker does not recognize and therefore highlights as "misspelled."
- Ignore words with numbers   Use this feature in documents that contain model numbers, addresses, or telephone numbers that the Spelling Checker does not recognize and therefore highlights as "misspelled."

6. After you choose a command button, Works highlights the next unrecognized word in the document. Repeat step 3 until Works displays a message saying it has reached the end of the document.

7. Choose OK to dismiss the message and return to your document.

N O T E   If you start the Spelling Checker anywhere other than at the beginning of a document, Works checks spelling from the location of the cursor to the end of the document. Works then displays a message signaling the end of the document and asks if you want to continue checking from the beginning of the document. Choose OK to continue or Cancel to close the Spelling Checker. ■

Ch
4

A *thesaurus* is a book that lists synonyms and related words. A thesaurus helps you find just the right word to use in a particular context; it also helps you improve the style and readability of a document by eliminating overuse of the same word. Works includes an online thesaurus that works in much the same way as the Spelling Checker. You position the cursor anywhere on the word you want to check, then choose Tools, Thesaurus. Works displays the Thesaurus dialog box shown in Figure 4.9.

To use the thesaurus, follow these steps:

1. In the document, move the cursor in or near the word you want to look up. The word is highlighted in the lookup box.

2. Choose Tools, Thesaurus. The Thesaurus dialog box shown in Figure 4.10 is displayed.

3. The Meanings box suggests possible meanings for the word. Highlight the word that most closely resembles the meaning of the selected word in its context.

4. In the Replace With Synonym list, highlight the word you want to use as the replacement.

FIG. 4.9

The Thesaurus lists the word you looked up, its meaning, and possible synonyms.

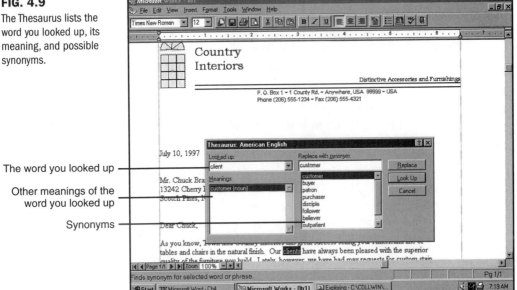

The word you looked up

Other meanings of the word you looked up

Synonyms

5. If none are appropriate and you want to look up a different word, highlight the word, click the Look Up button, then repeat Step 4.

6. Choose the Replace button to change the selected word in the document to the highlighted synonym. Works returns to your document and changes the highlighted word.

Works provides another tool that you might find useful in specific situations. Sometimes you need to know the number of words in a document. For instance, if you are writing a 500-word essay or submitting a 1000-word article for publication, Works can tell you how close you are to your limit.

To count the number of words in an entire document, choose the Tools, Word Count command. Works displays a message indicating the total number of words in the document (see Figure 4.11). Note that if your document contains footnotes, header text, and footer text, these are included in the word count. You also can count the number of words in a selection of text by first selecting the text before you choose the Word Count command. Note that Works counts the exact number of words and does not estimate word length. Click OK to close the word count box.

FIG. 4.10

The Word Count dialog box tells how many words are in the current document.

CHAPTER 5

Creating Great-Looking Documents

A document is much easier—and more enjoyable—to read when it contains a variety of fonts for headings and body text, uses indentation and alignment effectively, provides ample spacing between paragraphs and headings, and includes color, bold, and italic used effectively. These features are all referred to as *formatting*. ■

Change text attributes in a document

Font, size, color, style, and position are all features of text that you learn to change to make a document more attractive and interesting to read.

Change paragraph attributes in a document

Indentation settings, alignment styles, line spacing, paragraph breaks, and borders are features you can set on a paragraph-by-paragraph basis to make a document easier to read and to comprehend.

Using Easy Formats to Automate Changes

Easy Formats is a formatting tool designed to make your life easier. It lets you apply one of more than two dozen formatting styles to a selected paragraph. These easy-to-use formats take the guesswork and experimentation out of creating formats from scratch for common paragraph styles used in many documents. Easy Formats are especially helpful to beginning users who don't feel comfortable experimenting with formatting, and for users who are in a hurry and need to get a polished document out quickly.

A common paragraph format is the simple *indented paragraph* in which the first line is indented one-half inch and the remaining lines are left-aligned. Another format used frequently for numbered or bulletted lists is called a *hanging indent*, in which the first line of a paragraph is left-aligned and the remaining lines are indented one-half inch. A third type of commonly used format is one that indents a paragraph one-half inch on both the right and left sides. This type of format is used to distinguish certain types of text such as quotations, notes, tips, or warnings.

To use an Easy Format, choose the Format, Easy Formats command, which displays the Easy Formats dialog box (see Figure 5.1).

FIG. 5.1

The Easy Formats dialog box lists more than two dozen predefined paragraph formats.

The Easy Format you choose is illustrated here

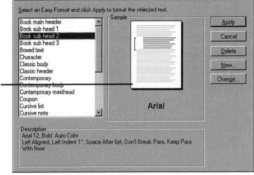

In the dialog box, the list on the left includes all Easy Formats. The Description area lists in detail the format features of the current Easy Format. As you scroll down the list, watch how the example in the Sample area changes to reflect the different settings.

To use an Easy Format, follow these steps:

1. Place the cursor anywhere within the paragraph you want to format.

2. Choose Format, Easy Formats. The Easy Formats dialog box shown in Figure 5.1 is displayed.

3. Click an Easy Format. The Sample area displays how the format will look.

4. Click Apply. The paragraph you selected is automatically reformatted using the Easy Format characteristics.

You can change any of the characteristics using the steps covered in the remainder of this chapter. See the last section of this chapter, "Creating Your Own Easy Formats," to learn how to add your own formats to the existing list, and how to change existing formats.

Changing the Attributes of Existing Text

To specify text attributes for existing text, use the Format, Font and Style command, which displays the Format Font and Style dialog box shown in Figure 5.2. You can also display this dialog box via the shortcut menu by pressing the right mouse button anywhere in the document, then choosing the Font and Style command.

FIG. 5.2

The Format Font and Style dialog box lets you choose font, size, color, style and position for selected text.

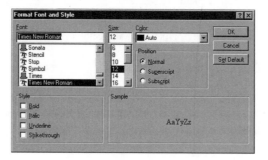

In the Font and Style dialog box you see settings for the font, size, color, style, and position of text. The following list describes these attributes:

- *Font* A font refers to a specific style or design for a set of characters that Works displays on-screen and prints on paper. Each font has a particular shape (or other characteristics) that distinguish it from other fonts. For example, this sentence appears in the Dom Casual font.

N O T E In addition to the fonts Works provides, additional fonts are sometimes added by other programs when you install them. When this occurs, the fonts are included in the Font list in the dialog box. Some printers can print only a limited number of fonts. Whether or not you can print all of the screen fonts available through Works is entirely dependent on the capabilities of your printer. ■

- *Size* Font sizes are measured in *points.* (A point is equal to $\frac{1}{72}$ of an inch.) The most common point sizes for body text in a typical document are 10 or 12. Other elements in a document, such as titles or headings, often appear in larger sizes, such as 14, 16, 18, or 24 points.
- *Color* If you have a color monitor, you can display selected text in a variety of colors. If you have a color printer, you also can print the colors that you display in your document.
- *Style* Text style refers to bold, italic, underline, or strikethrough. Bold, italic, and underline are common styles used to emphasize text. Strikethrough prints a line through the text, indicating that the text is marked for deletion, but the text still is readable.

Ch
5

■ *Position*   Position refers to the horizontal placement of text on the line. Superscript raises a selected character slightly above the normal line level and is often is used in documents that contain mathematical notations such as 8.25×7^3. In contrast, Subscript drops a selected character slightly below the normal line level, as in H_2O, the symbol for water.

As you make font, size, color, style, and position choices, keep an eye on the Sample area of the dialog box. It displays sample text that conforms to the choices you make so you can see exactly how text will look in your document.

To apply a text attribute to existing text using menu commands, follow these steps:

1. Select the text you want to format.
2. Choose Format, Font and Style, or right-click and choose the Font and Style command from the shortcut menu. The Format Font and Style dialog box appears on-screen (refer to Figure 5.2).
3. From the Font, Size, and Color lists, select one option.
4. From the Position section, select one option.
5. From the Style section, select any styles you want to apply to the selected text.
6. When the text shown in the Sample section appears as you want it, choose OK. Works automatically reformats the selected text.

The word processor toolbar includes several buttons that let you apply text attributes to selected text. Figure 5.3 illustrates the buttons for Font and Size, as well as Bold, Italic, and Underline. The Font and Size buttons contain drop-down lists from which you select a font and point size. The bold, italic, and underline buttons toggle on and off, so if you want to remove an attribute, select the affected text, then just click the appropriate button again.

FIG. 5.3

Choose a text attribute
from the word processor
toolbar.

Font Name   Font Size   Bold   Italic   Underline
button   button

You can apply some text attributes using the keyboard shortcuts listed in Table 5.1. To use a keyboard shortcut, select the text you want to format, then press the key sequence shown in Table 5.1. Note that all the shortcuts listed except Ctrl+Space Bar (for plain text) toggle on and off.

Table 5.1   Keyboard Shortcuts for Character Style

Character Style	Key Combinations
Bold	Ctrl+B
Underline	Ctrl+U
Italic	Ctrl+I

Character Style	Key Combination
Superscript	Ctrl+Plus Sign (+)
Subscript	Ctrl+Equal Sign (=)
Plain text (remove all text attibutes)	Ctrl+space bar

N O T E There is no toolbar button or keyboard shortcut for changing the color of text; you still must use the Format Font and Style dialog box. ■

Choosing Text Attributes for New Text

You can preset text attributes for new text just as easily as you can apply them to existing text.

1. Place the cursor where you want the new text attribute to begin.
2. Choose Format, Font and Style, or right-click and choose Font and Style from the shortcut menu.
3. Select the text attributes you want to use, then click OK.
4. Begin typing.

All new text you type conforms to the text attribute you specify until you perform one of the following actions:

■ Change one or more text attributes.

■ Move the cursor to an area of the document where different text attributes have already been applied.

Copying Text Attributes

Works gives you the ability to copy text attributes, which offers three advantages. First, copying saves you the trouble of remembering (or checking each time) the attributes you assign to text. Second, this method is fast because it copies all attributes at one time. And third, copying eliminates the likelihood of errors; you cannot possibly get the text attributes wrong when you copy them.

To copy text attributes from one selection to another, follow these steps:

1. Select the text whose text attributes you want to copy. (You don't need to select all the text, such as an entire paragraph. Just select any portion that uses all the attributes you want to copy.)
2. Choose Edit, Copy, or right-click and choose the Copy command from the shortcut menu.
3. Select *all* the text to which you want to copy the character style.

Ch
5

4. Choose Edit, Paste Special or right-click and choose the Paste Special command from the shortcut menu. Works displays the Paste Special dialog box shown in Figure 5.4.

5. Choose Character Style, then click OK. Works applies the style or format to selected text.

FIG. 5.4

The Paste Special dialog box.

You also can copy a text attribute to a blank line where you intend to type new text. Follow the preceding steps, but instead of selecting text in step 3, move the cursor to where you want the copied text attribute to take effect. Complete steps 4 and 5, then begin typing. Everything you type conforms to the copied text attribute until you change the text attribute or move the cursor to text that uses a different style.

Removing Text Attributes from Text

As you begin experimenting with text attributes, you might change your mind many times. Attributes you *add to* text (such as bold, italic, underline, strikethrough, subscript, and super-script) toggle on and off, whether you select the setting using the Format Font and Style dialog box, the toolbar, or a keyboard shortcut. To remove any of these text attributes, select the affected text, then select the appropriate dialog box option, the toolbar button, or the keyboard shortcut to remove the attribute.

Unlike attributes that are added to text, attributes such as font, size, and color *change the characteristics* of text. Technically, you can't remove these attributes from text, but you can change them. Select the affected text, then choose Format, Font and Style, or choose the Font and Style command from the shortcut menu to change any or all of the current attributes.

 When text contains several "toggle" attributes (such as bold, italic, underline, strikethrough, superscript, subscript), you can remove all attributes quickly by selecting the text then pressing Ctrl+Space Bar. This keyboard shortcut changes all selected text back to plain text and saves you the trouble of removing each attribute individually.

Indenting Paragraphs

Just as certain text attributes can make a document easier to read, changing the indentation of paragraphs can add structure to a document that makes it easier to follow. You can indent a paragraph on the left side, the right side, both sides, or you can indent just the first line of a paragraph.

The ruler in the word processor window indicates how a paragraph's indentation is set. In Figure 5.5, two *indent markers* appear at the zero point. The bottom marker, the *left indent marker*, marks the overall indentation of the paragraph from the left margin. The top marker, the *first line indent marker*, marks the indentation of only the first line of the current paragraph. At the 6-inch point, *the right-indent marker* indicates the point at which text is indented from the right margin. These are the default settings Works uses for any new paragraph you type: left indent is at 0, first line indent is at 0, and right indent is at 6.

FIG. 5.5

Left indent, right indent and first line indent markers appear on the ruler.

First line indent marker

Left indent marker

Right indent marker

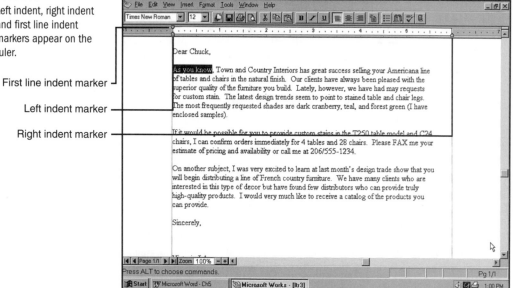

 TIP If you're ruler isn't displayed, choose View, Ruler.

The settings shown on the ruler always reflect *the paragraph where the cursor is currently located.* As you move the cursor through the paragraphs of a document, you'll see the indent markers on the ruler change to reflect the settings of paragraphs that are indented differently. In Figure 5.6, notice that the same paragraph is indented ½" on the left, ½" on the right, and the first line indent marker is at 1".

The quickest and easiest way to change a paragraph's indentation is to drag the indent markers along the ruler. Suppose you wanted to change the paragraph shown in Figure 5.6 to a left indent of 0", a first line indent of ½", and a right indent of 6". Use these steps:

1. Place the cursor anywhere within the paragraph.

2. Drag the left indent marker to the 0" mark on the ruler. (Notice the first line indent marker moves along with the left indent marker.)

TIP If the First-Time Help dialog box is displayed, you can choose to see a demo on one of the listed topics or click the Don't Display This Message In The Future box and choose OK.

3. Drag the right indent marker to the 6" marker on the ruler.

FIG. 5.6

Indent markers now appear in different positions on the ruler to reflect the format of the current paragraph.

Left indent ——

First line indent ——

Right indent ——

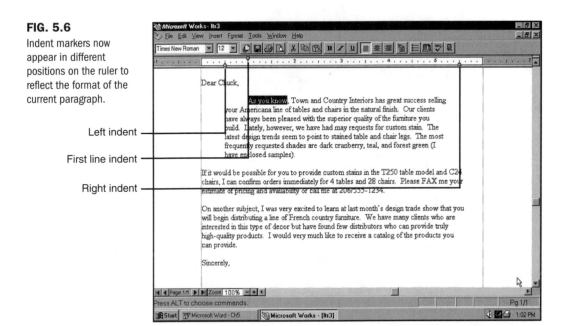

It's just that simple; the paragraph reformats as you drag the markers. But why did the first line indent marker move along with the left indent marker in step 2? Because Works automatically *maintains* the first line indent marker's relative position to the left indent marker. In other words, if the left indent and the first line indent are ½" apart, Works maintains that spacing; if they are 2" apart, Works maintains that spacing. To move the left indent marker independently of the first line indent marker, hold down the Shift key as you drag the left indent marker.

N O T E   When you want to apply the same indentation to several contiguous paragraphs, select them all at once, then change the indent settings on the ruler bar. ■

You can also set paragraph indentation by choosing the Format Paragraph command, then clicking the Indents and Alignment tab (see Figure 5.7) in the Format Paragraph dialog box. This method allows you to specify exact measurements to one-tenth of an inch or smaller. Use these steps:

1. Select the paragraph or paragraphs you want to indent.

2. Choose Format, Paragraph, or right-click and choose Paragraph from the shortcut menu. The Format Paragraph dialog box appears on-screen.

3. Click the Indents and Alignment tab.

4. In the Left, Right, and First Line boxes, click the up or down arrows to specify indentation to one-tenth of an inch. If you want to use even smaller increments, you can type a number (such as 1.35) in the boxes. The Sample area of the dialog box reflects the new settings you specify.

5. When the settings are correct, click OK.

FIG. 5.7

Use the Indents and Alignments Tab in the Format Paragraph dialog box to set paragraph indentation.

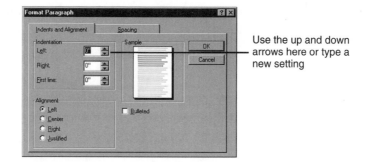

Use the up and down arrows here or type a new setting

Aligning Paragraphs

Another attribute you can set for a paragraph is *alignment*, which refers to the way the left and right edges of a paragraph line up. For instance, this paragraph is left-aligned because the characters begin at the left margin and the characters at the right margin are "ragged." Left-aligned text is commonly used in business documents because it is considered easy to read and not too stiff or formal.

In Works, you can left-align, right-align, center, or justify paragraphs. In a right-aligned paragraph, characters at the right margin are aligned vertically and characters at the left margin are ragged. Right alignment is a style often used in brochures, flyers, or other advertising literature You'll often see it used for a caption that appears to the left of a figure, chart, or table.

A centered paragraph has ragged left and right edges, and each line is centered at the midpoint on the line. In a justified paragraph, a more formal style, characters at both the right and left margins are aligned vertically by adjusting the space between letters on each line. An example of each of these alignment styles is shown in Figure 5.8.

You have three choices for setting paragraph alignment; using menu commands, keyboard shortcuts, or the toolbar. The quickest and easiest way is to use the toolbar. Just place the cursor anywhere in the paragraph you want to align (or select several paragraphs at once), then click the Left Align, Center Align, or Right Align button on the toolbar. The paragraph is immediately realigned. (Note that the toolbar doesn't include a Justified Align button.)

To set alignment of a paragraph using menu commands, use the Format Paragraph dialog box shown earlier in Figure 5.7. Follow these steps:

1. Select the paragraph or paragraphs to align.
2. Choose Format, Paragraph, or right-click and choose the Paragraph command from the shortcut menu to display the Format Paragraph dialog box (see Figure 5.7). (If the Indents and Alignment tab is not selected, choose it now.)
3. From the Alignment section, select Left, Center, Right, or Justified.
4. Choose OK. Works realigns the current paragraph(s).

Ch
5

FIG. 5.8
This example shows four types of text alignment styles.

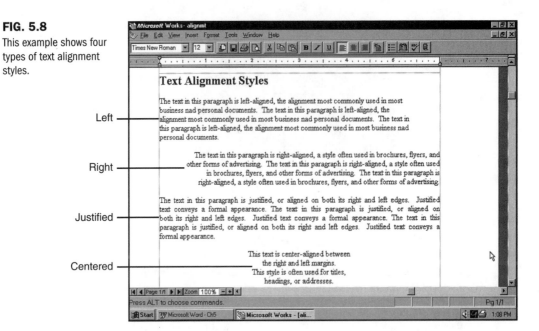

If you prefer to use the keyboard, you can set paragraph alignment using a keyboard shortcut. Move the cursor anywhere in the paragraph you want to align, then press one of the following key sequences:

Key Sequence	Function
Ctrl+L	Left-aligns the current paragraph
Ctrl+E	Centers the current paragraph
Ctrl+Shift+R	Right-aligns the current paragraph
Ctrl+J	Justifies the current paragraph

Setting Line Spacing and Paragraph Breaks

Line spacing and paragraph breaks also affect the appearance and readability of a document. *Line spacing* refers to the amount of space between lines of text. A *paragraph break* is the line at which the paragraph divides when it falls across a page break. You adjust both of these settings using the Spacing tab in the Format Paragraph dialog box, shown in Figure 5.9.

Most business documents are single-spaced; the amount of space between lines is adequate to make the document readable. When you are creating a draft version of a document for readers to review, however, it's helpful to add extra space between lines allows readers to write comments and notes more easily.

On the Spacing tab in the Format Paragraph dialog box, the Line Spacing setting is represented in numbers of lines. The default setting is *Auto*, which means the line space is equal to the height of the largest character in the current font and size. (If you change the font and size of the current text, Works automatically adjusts the line spacing.) You can enter any whole positive number for Line Spacing (2, 5, 10, and so on) or any number fraction (1.3, 3.2, 5.8, and so on). To return to the default setting, choose Auto.

FIG. 5.9

Using the Spacing tab in the Format Paragraph dialog box, you can control spacing of lines, spacing before and after paragraphs, and the location of paragraph breaks.

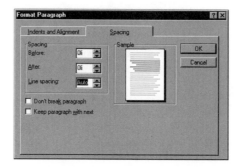

N O T E If you prefer to set line spacing using a different unit of measurement, you can type a designator following the number you enter, such as 3 cm for 3 centimeters. You can enter *in* or " (for inches), *cm* (for centimeters), *mm* (for millimeters), *pi* (for picas—a unit of measure used in the publishing industry), or *pt* (for points).

You can set a paragraph to single, double, or one-and-one-half spaced lines quickly by placing the cursor anywhere in the paragraph, then pressing one of the following key sequences:

Key Sequence	Function
Ctrl+1	Single spaces the current paragraph
Ctrl+2	Double spaces the current paragraph
Ctrl+5	Sets the spacing of the current paragraph to one-and-one-half

Sometimes you might want to specify the number of lines that precede and follow a paragraph. This setting is especially helpful for chapter names, titles, headings, opening paragraphs, or any other document elements that you want set off with extra space. You use the Before and After settings on the Spacing tab in the Format Paragraph dialog box to define this space (see Figure 5.9). Like the Line Spacing setting, the Before and After settings are measured in number of lines. For example, if you want one blank line before a heading and two blank lines after it, enter 1 and 2 respectively in these boxes.

The two check boxes below the Spacing options let you specify how paragraphs break in a document. When you choose not to break a particular paragraph (Don't Break Paragraph), Works moves the entire paragraph to the next page if it falls across a page break in the document. You would use this setting, for example, to keep all three lines of a three-line address together if the address fell at the bottom of a page.

You can also choose to keep two consecutive paragraphs together using the Keep Paragraph With Next option. You might use this option when the last paragraph on a page, for example, ends in a colon and introduces a bulleted list that follows. The Keep Paragraph With Next option would keep the paragraph together with its bulleted list.

On the Spacing tab in the Format Paragraph dialog box, the settings you choose are reflected in the Sample section.

Use the following steps to set line spacing and paragraph breaks:

1. Place the cursor in the paragraph you want to format.

2. Choose Format Paragraph, or right-click and choose Paragraph from the shortcut menu. The Format Paragraph dialog box is displayed. If the Spacing tab is not selected, choose it now.

3. In the Spacing section, set the amount of space in the Line Spacing, Before, and After boxes.

4. To prevent the current paragraph from splitting at a page break, select the Don't Break Paragraph check box.

5. To keep the current paragraph together with the paragraph that follows it, select the Keep Paragraph With Next check box.

6. Choose OK. Works adjusts line spacing and page breaks according to the choices you make.

Bordering a Paragraph

Sometimes you'll create documents with special types of text that you want to be very visible. One way to make a paragraph stand out is to place a border around it. You can create a paragraph border using a single line, double line, bold line, or a color.

The term *border* is something of a misnomer because it implies that a line completely surrounds a paragraph. This type of border is called an *outline* border. You also can create *partial* borders that fall on the top, bottom, left, or right sides of a paragraph. Or you can use any combination of the four partial borders. For example, you may want to use a bottom border to "underline" an entire line, or you might use right and left borders to set off notes and cautions. You could use a right or left border in a draft document to mark all paragraphs in which a change has been made. This type of border is called a *change bar* or *revision mark*. Figure 5.10 illustrates some sample border styles.

N O T E You can add a border to a single-line paragraph, a multiple-line paragraph, several contiguous paragraphs, or an entire page, but you cannot border individual words within a line of text. ■

You use the Borders and Shading dialog box shown in Figure 5.11 to define a line style, color, and border. Use the following steps to add a border to text:

1. Place the cursor in the paragraph where you want a border. To border contiguous paragraphs, select a portion of text in each paragraph.

FIG. 5.10

Use borders creatively to add style, draw attention, or mark revised text.

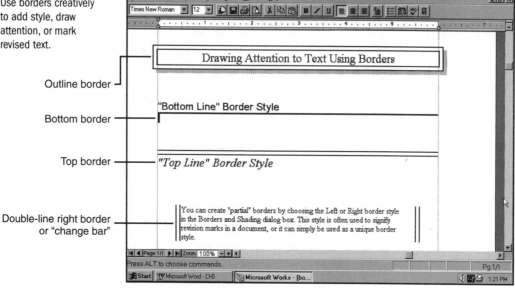

Outline border

Bottom border

Top border

Double-line right border or "change bar"

FIG. 5.11

Use the Borders tab in the Borders and Shading dialog box to select a border, line style, and color.

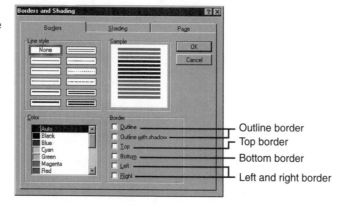

Outline border
Top border
Bottom border
Left and right border

Ch
5

2. Choose F**o**rmat, **B**orders and Shading, or right-click and choose Borders and Shading from the shortcut menu. The Borders and Shading dialog box is displayed. (If the Bor**d**ers tab is not selected, click it now.)

3. Select a style from the L**i**ne Style box.

4. Select a color from the **C**olor list.

5. Select a border style from the Bor**d**er box. The Sample area of the dialog box reflects the choices you make.

6. Choose OK. Works adds the specified border to the current paragraph.

To remove a border, use the preceding steps but choose None in the L**i**ne Style box.

Bordering a Page

You can also add a border to an entire page. To use this option, you use the Borders and Shading dialog box again, this time choosing the Page tab, shown in Figure 5.12.

FIG. 5.12

Use the Page tab in the Borders and Shading dialog box to choose a page border, line style, and color.

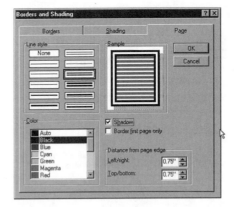

The Page tab is very similar to the Borders tab shown in the previous figure, but here you can choose to add a border to every page of a document or just the first page. In the Distance From Page Edge box, you can specify exactly where you want the border to fall on the page. (If you don't alter the settings in this box, Works automatically adds a page border at the page margins.)

To create a page border, follow these steps:

1. Place the cursor anywhere on the page you want to border.

2. Choose Format, Borders and Shading, or right-click and choose Borders and Shading from the shortcut menu. The Borders and Shading dialog box is displayed. (If the Page tab is not selected, click it now.)

3. Select a style from the Line Style box.

4. Select a color from the Color list.

5. Choose Shadow or Border First Page Only if you want either of these options.

6. To change the position and size of the border, enter the appropriate settings in the Left/Right and Top/Bottom boxes. The Sample area of the dialog box illustrates the settings you choose.

7. Choose OK. Works adds a border to the current page.

In Figure 5.13, the first page of a procedures manual is bordered using a heavy double line and a shadow. The page is shown at 45 percent so all of it is visible.

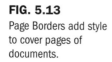

FIG. 5.13
Page Borders add style
to cover pages of
documents.

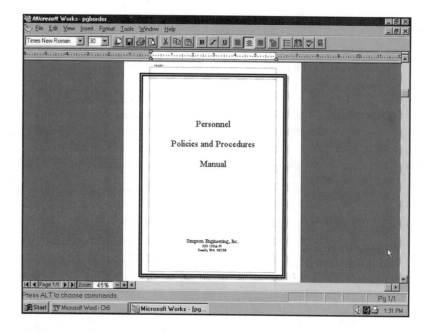

Copying Paragraph Attributes

Earlier in this chapter you learned that you can save time and ensure consistency by copying text attributes. You can do the same by copying a paragraph style. Paragraphs often contain many attributes (font, point size, space before, space after, line spacing, and so on) that you would have to check carefully before duplicating in another paragraph. The ability to copy a paragraph style saves you the trouble of checking all these attributes and then applying them to another paragraph; the paragraph to which you copy automatically takes on all the attributes you copy.

Follow these steps to copy a paragraph style:

1. Select a portion of the paragraph that you want to copy the paragraph style.
2. Choose Edit, Copy, or choose the Copy command from the shortcut menu.
3. Select the paragraph to which you want to copy the paragraph style.
4. Choose Edit, Paste Special, or choose Paste Special from the shortcut menu. The Paste special dialog box opens.
5. Select the Paragraph Format option then choose OK. Works applies the copied paragraph style to the selected text.

Ch
5

Inserting Page Breaks in a Document

Works keeps track of the number of lines you type in a document relative to the page size and margin settings you are using. Through a process called *pagination*, Works calculates where page breaks should occur and inserts a page break marker (a chevron character, shown in Figure 5.14) at the proper location in the left margin. These page breaks are called *automatic* page breaks. When you add or delete paragraphs in a document, Works automatically repaginates the document and adjusts automatic page breaks as necessary.

FIG. 5.14

A chevron character marks automatic page breaks in the left margin.

Automatic page break marker

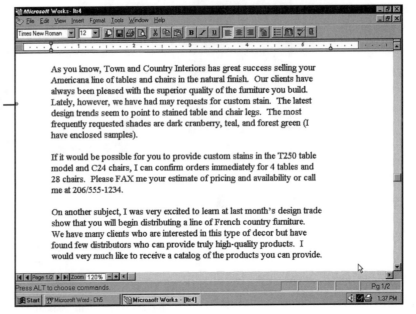

It's possible that Works might insert a page break where you don't want one. For instance, suppose Works inserts a page break following a section heading and the first paragraph in the section bumps to the next page. In this case, you can insert a page break just before the section heading so the heading and the first paragraph appear on the same page.

Page breaks that you insert are called *manual* page breaks. They are indicated on the screen by a dashed line that runs horizontally across the document in addition to the chevron character placed in the left margin (see Figure 5.15). Manual page breaks are sometimes called *hard* page breaks because Works will not adjust them when it repaginates a document. Only you can move or delete hard page breaks. If your document contains manual page breaks, be sure to preview every page before printing the final document to ensure the breaks are still positioned correctly.

Follow these steps to insert a manual page break:

1. Place the cursor at the leftmost character on the line that you want to appear on the new page.

FIG. 5.15
A dashed line across the document indicates a manual page break.

Manual page break marker

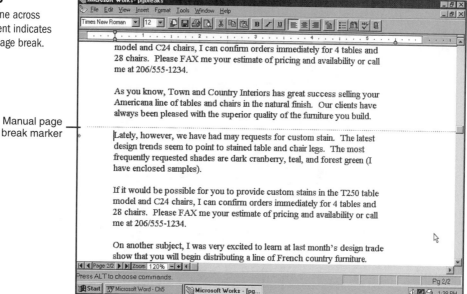

2. Choose <u>I</u>nsert, Page <u>B</u>reak; or press Ctrl+Enter. Works inserts a manual page break marker (a dashed line) in the document above the line with the cursor.

To remove a manual page break, move the cursor to the beginning of the dashed line, then press the Del key. When you delete a manual page break, Works automatically readjusts all automatic page breaks.

Creating Your Own Easy Formats

The first thing you learn in this chapter is how to use Easy Formats because they are already prepared for you and are quick and easy to use. Now that you know how to change the variety of text and paragraph attributes using the Format Font and Style and Format Paragraph dialog boxes, you're prepared to create your own Easy Formats and save them with the ones Works provides.

The easiest way to create a new Easy Format is to begin with an existing one, modify it the way you want it, then save it under a new name. Use these steps:

1. Place the cursor anywhere in the paragraph you want to reformat.
2. Choose F<u>o</u>rmat, <u>E</u>asy Formats, or choose the Easy Formats command from the shortcut menu. Works displays the Easy Formats dialog box.
3. Select the Easy Format that most closely resembles the new one you want to create.
4. Click <u>C</u>hange. Works displays the Change Easy Formats dialog box shown in Figure 5.16.

Ch
5

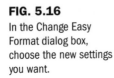

FIG. 5.16

In the Change Easy Format dialog box, choose the new settings you want.

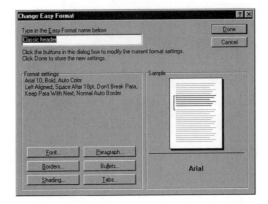

5. Type a name for the new Easy Format.

6. Click the Font, Borders, Shading, or Paragraph buttons to change any of these settings. The appropriate dialog box is displayed. Change the settings as you choose, then click OK.

7. When you have made all changes, double-check that you have typed a new name for the new Easy Format, then click Done. The new Easy Format is added to the existing list in the Easy Format dialog box.

N O T E If you forget to enter a new name for your Easy Format, the existing Works Easy Format you chose in step 3 will be changed. It's not a good idea to change the Easy Formats provided with Works unless you're sure you'll never use them. The only way to restore a deleted or changed Easy Format is to reinstall Works. ■

Note that in step 5, the Bullets and Tabs buttons were not mentioned. You learn about using these settings in Chapter 6, "Adding Special Features to a Word Processor Document."

If none of the existing Easy Formats resemble the one you want to create, choose the New button rather than the Change button in the Easy Formats dialog box, then follow the remaining steps outlined above.

If you create a new Easy Format, then decide you don't want to keep it, delete it from the list by highlighting it in the Easy Formats dialog box, then choosing the Delete key. ●

Adding Special Features to a Word Processor Document

The word processor in Works offers many ways to enhance a document with many special features that make a document look like it was professionally typeset. All of these features are designed to make your documents more attractive, more readable, and easier to understand. ■

Easy Text

Easy Text is a timesaving feature that lets you store words, phrases, clauses, or paragraphs and insert them automatically in a document.

Headers and footers

This is any type of text (such as a title, page number, file name, company name, date) that appears at the top (header) or the bottom (footer) of every page.

Numbered or bulleted lists

These are common elements in many types of documents, and in this chapter you learn how easy it is to create them.

Tables

Tables are often used to help condense information and make it more readable.

Footnotes

In Works, you can include footnotes at the bottom of each page or at the end of a document.

Columns of text

Format your text in two, three, or more columns just like text in a magazine or newspaper

Objects inserted from outside sources

Learn how to insert drawings, Clip Art, Word Art, and notes using tools included with Works.

Using Easy Text

Easy Text is a great feature for automatically inserting text (phrases or paragraphs) that you use over and over again. The object is to save you the time and trouble of continually retyping duplicate text. Examples of text you might want to save as Easy Text include a signature block, copyright information, standard clauses, disclaimers, warnings, notes, cautions, company information, addresses, and so on.

To create and save Easy Text paragraphs or phrases, use these steps:

1. Choose Insert, Easy Text, New Easy Text. The New Easy Text dialog box shown in Figure 6.1 is displayed.

2. In the first text box, type a name for the Easy Text (a name by which you can easily identify the text, such as Product Disclaimer).

3. In the Easy Text Contents box, type the complete text.

4. If you want to format the text using a Works Easy Format, click the Format button, choose a format, then click Apply.

5. In the New Easy Text dialog box, click Done. Works returns to your document. The name you specified for your Easy Text now appears on the Insert, Easy Text submenu.

FIG. 6.1

Use the New Easy Text dialog box to create new Easy Text entries.

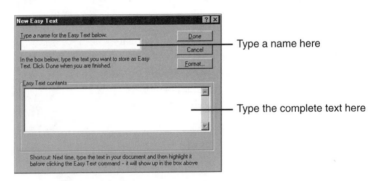

Type a name here

Type the complete text here

To insert an Easy Text entry in your document, follow these steps.

1. Place the cursor in your document where you want to insert Easy Text.

2. Choose Insert, Easy Text.

3. On the Easy Text submenu, highlight the name of the Easy Text entry you want to insert. Works automatically inserts the text in your document.

You can remove an Easy Text entry from a document at any time the same way you delete any other text from a document: select it and press the Delete key, choose Edit, Cut, or click the Cut button. If the entry is one you'll never use again and you want to delete it altogether, use these steps:

1. Choose Insert, Easy Text, More Easy Texts. The Easy Text dialog box is displayed.

2. Highlight the Easy Text entry you want to delete.

3. Click the <u>D</u>elete button. Works removes the Easy Text from the <u>I</u>nsert, Easy Te<u>x</u>t submenu and it is no longer available.

Using Headers and Footers in a Document

When your document is complete and you're ready to print, the final touch to add might be a title, page number, or other information that prints at the top or bottom of each page. Repetitive text that appears at the top of each page is called a *header*. Text that appears at the bottom of each page is called a *footer*. Headers and footers can include any type of information, such as the current date, current time, the document name, or instructions like *Company Confidential*. You can even include objects (such as Clip Art, a drawing, or Word Art) in a header or footer, and you can apply formatting, font, style characteristics, borders, and shading, just like you do to regular text in a document.

You can view headers and footers in the document window in either Page Layout view or Normal view. The most accurate view for examining headers and footers is Page Layout view, your default page view. Here, the header appears at the top of every page and the footer appears at the bottom of every page. These areas are bordered by a faint dotted outline and labeled *Header* or *Footer*. In Page Layout view, all special formatting and inserted objects are visible. An example of a header in Page Layout view is shown in Figure 6.2.

FIG. 6.2
In Page Layout view, headers and footers are visible at the top and bottom of every page in a document.

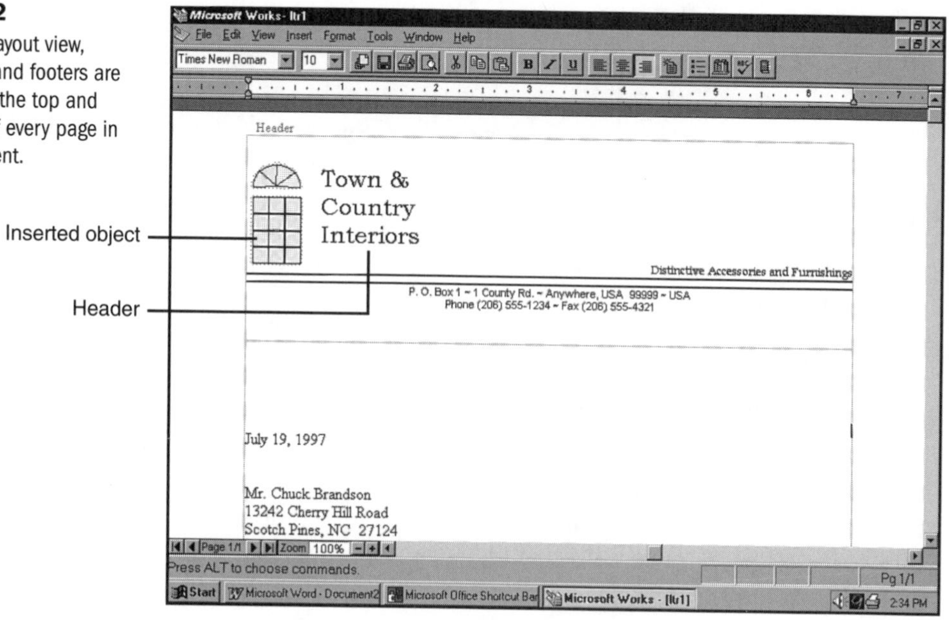

Inserted object

Header

Ch
6

When using Normal view, the text for headers and footers is visible only at the top of the first page of the document next to the H and F markers in the left page margin. In this view, you see all special formatting that is applied to the text, but if the header or footer contains an inserted object, it is not visible in Normal view. An example of header text in Normal view is shown in Figure 6.3. A footer marker appears but there is no footer text. Notice that the inserted Clip Art picture is *not* visible in Normal view. (You learn more about inserting objects such as Clip Art, Word Art, notes, and so on, later in this chapter. For more information about using these features, refer also to Chapter 14, "Using the Works Tools Together.")

FIG. 6.3

In Normal view, header and footer text appears next to the H and F markers in the left margin but inserted Clip Art is not visible.

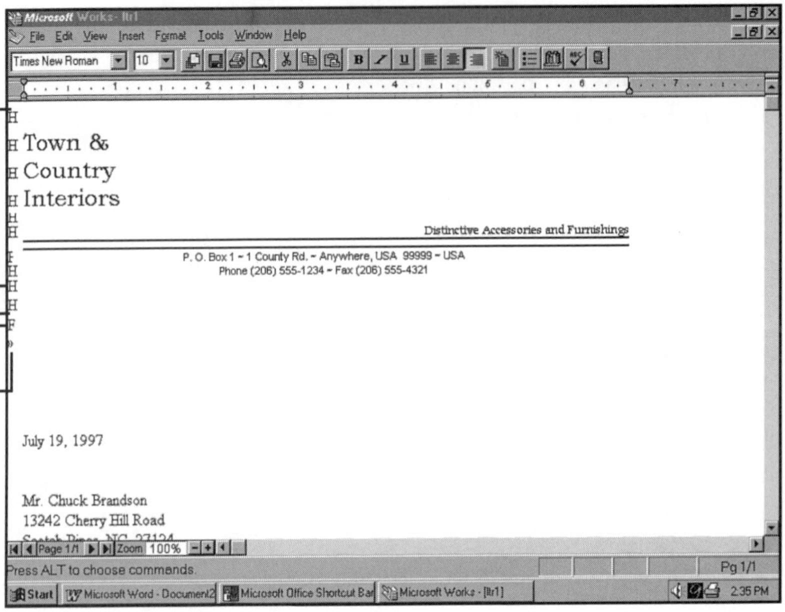

Header —

Header marker —

Footer marker —

Beginning of document marker

Creating a Header or Footer

In Works, you can create a header or footer in Normal view or Page Layout view. Regardless of the view you use, you can edit, format, and enhance the text just like you can modify any other text in a document. You can choose a different font, point size, or text color, and you can apply bold, underline, or italic. You can even add a border or shading to a header or footer.

To create a header or footer in Normal view, follow these steps:

1. Choose View, Normal.
2. If the H and F markers are not visible, choose View, Header or View, Footer. Works moves to the top of the document. (If a first-time Help dialog box is displayed, you can choose an option to view, or choose the Don't Display This Message In The Future box and choose OK.)
3. Place the cursor next to the H or F that appears in the left margin.
4. Type the text for the header or footer, pressing Enter when you want to begin a new line.
5. Format the text as you want it.

6. If you want, use the Insert menu to include Clip Art, a drawing, or Word Art in your header or footer.

7. When the header or footer is complete, click next to the Beginning of Document marker at the top of the first page to begin entering text, or click anywhere in the text area of the document to continue editing.

Refer to "Inserting Objects in a Document," later in this chapter. Refer also to Chapter 14, "Using the Works Tools Together."

If you're inserting an object of some kind in the header or footer, you might prefer to use Page Layout view so the object is visible exactly where you insert it. To create a header or footer in Page Layout view, use these steps:

1. Choose View, Page Layout.

2. If the header or footer is not visible, scroll to the top or bottom of any page.

N O T E   In Page Layout view, you can create or change a header or footer on *any* page, not just on the first page. ▪

3. Click inside the Header or Footer area.

4. Type the text for the header or footer, pressing Enter when you want to begin a new line.

5. Format the text as you want it.

6. If you choose, use the Insert menu to include Clip Art, a drawing, or Word Art in your header or footer.

7. When the header or footer is complete, click anywhere inside the text area of the document.

Inserting Special Information in Headers and Footers

Page numbers, the current date (or date of printing), the current time (or time of printing) and the document name are items that are commonly included in headers and footers. You can have Works insert these for you automatically by choosing the appropriate command from the Insert menu (see Figure 6.4).

When you choose Insert, Page Number or Insert, Document Name, Works automatically in-serts a **page** or a **filename** placeholder wherever the cursor is located. When you print the document, Works inserts the correct page number on every page and the document name in the location of these place holders. An example of these place holders is shown in Figure 6.5.

When you choose Insert, Date and Time, Works displays the dialog box shown in Figure 6.6. This dialog box displays a variety of date and time formats, including numeric or text formats, date and time separately, or date and time together. To insert a date or time, select a format, then click Insert. Works inserts the current date or time in the header or footer at the location of the placeholder.

Ch
6

FIG. 6.4

The Insert menu contains commands for inserting the date, file name, and page numbers in a document.

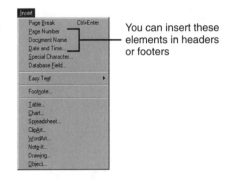

You can insert these elements in headers or footers

FIG. 6.5

Works inserts place-holders in a header or footer for page numbers and the document name.

Placeholders

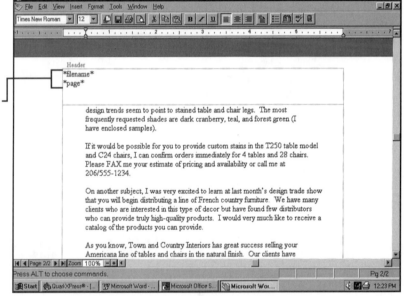

Works lets you specify if you want the date and time to be updated when the document is printed. If you do, click the Automatically Update When Printed check box in the Insert Date and Time dialog box. When you leave this box blank, Works prints the date and time that was current when you inserted these elements in the document.

Removing a Header or Footer

After you've created a header or footer, you might decide you don't want it anymore. To delete a header or footer (in either Normal view or Page Layout view), select all the text, then press Delete. In Normal view, the H and F markers remain on the screen. In Page Layout view, the Header and Footer areas remain visible on the screen but are empty.

FIG. 6.6
The Insert Date and Time dialog box offers many date and time formats.

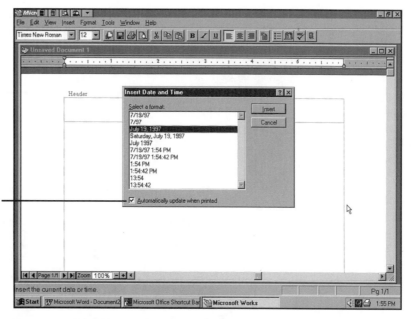

Click here if you want Works to update the current date and time when you print

Setting Header and Footer Margins

Figure 6.7 illustrates how Works measures page, header, and footer margins. The header margin is the space from the top of the paper to the bottom edge of the header area. The footer margin is the space from the bottom edge of the paper to the top edge of the footer area. It is within these spaces that you type header and footer text. Note that the header margin fits inside of the top page margin and the footer margin fits inside of the bottom page margin. Therefore, the header and footer margins must always be smaller than or equal to the top and bottom margins respectively. If they are larger, the header and footer will not print correctly.

The default top and bottom page margin settings are 1 inch. Within that space is a default header margin of .5 inch and a default footer margin of .75 inch. Because a one-line header always fits within a .5-inch margin and a one-line footer at a font of 10 or 12 points always fits within a .75-inch margin, you never need to adjust margins for a one-line header or footer. Depending on the font size you use, you might need to adjust header and footer margins for multi-line headers and footers.

In Chapter 3, "Creating, Saving, and Printing a Word Processor Document," you learn how to adjust top, bottom, left, and right margins using the Page Setup dialog box (see Figure 6.8). You use the same dialog box to adjust header and footer margins. Follow these steps:

1. Choose File, Page Setup.
2. Choose the Margins tab. The dialog box shown in Figure 6.8 is displayed.

Ch
6

3. In the He<u>a</u>der Margin and <u>F</u>ooter Margin boxes, type the setting you want to use in inches. Type a decimal for fractions of an inch (such as 1.25 for 1 ¼ inches). Remember to keep header and footer margins smaller than or equal to top and bottom margins.

4. After all margin settings are correct, choose OK.

FIG. 6.7
Headers and footers must fit within top and bottom margins.

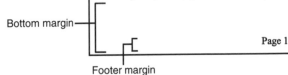

Chapter 2: Regular Pay
Payroll Manual

Top margin

Regular Pay

Header margin

Regular pay constitutes regular straight time earnings for non-exempt employees and salary for exempt employees. This chapter explains the procedures for handling all types of regular pay including performance bonuses, special bonuses, pay for overtime, vacation payments, and payments for sick time. All types of regular pay are subject to 401K deductions. Compensations that are not subject to 401K deductions are covered in Chapter 4, Compensations Other Than Regular Pay.

Regular Straight Time Earnings and Salaries

A non-exempt employee earns regular straight time earnings for regular house (up to 40 hours) worked in a pay period. An employee's hourly rate of pay determines the amount paid in a pay period. (See the Payments for Overtime section in this chapter for hours worked in excess of 40 peer pay period.0 An exempt employee's annual earnings is defined as salary. Salary is divided into 52 equal amounts and paid to the employee each pay period regardless of the number of hours worked.

Performance Bonuses

Performance bonuses are paid to exempt employees based on outstanding performance. (Non-exempt employees are not eligible for bonuses.) Managers determine which employees are to receive bonuses. Bonuses are paid twice yearly in January and July.

The employee's manager submits the appropriate paperwork to Personnel, who process the request. The paperwork is transmitted electronically into the Payroll system. In special cases, (such as late paperwork, or an employee who is leaving during the review months of January and July) bonus information must be entered into the Payroll System manually.

Performance bonuses are considered part of regular pay and therefore are subject to 401K deductions. When you enter an employee's review bonus into the Payroll System, the computer automatically calculates payroll taxes and other deductions

Bottom margin

Page 1

Footer margin

FIG. 6.8
Use the Margins tab in
the Page Setup dialog
box to adjust header
and footer margins.

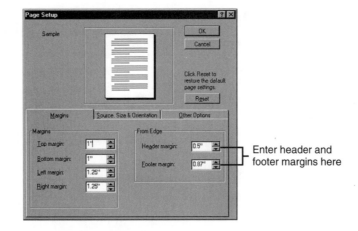

Enter header and
footer margins here

Creating a Bulleted List

Text documents often contain lists—lists of items, lists of numbers, lists of names. Marking the items with bullets makes them stand out from surrounding text. This format is so often used that Works provides a Bullets button on the toolbar.

There are two ways to create a bulleted list. Use this method when you've already typed your list of items.

1. Select all the items.
2. Click the Bullets button. Works automatically applies bullets to each new line.

If you decide later to remove the bullets, select all the items in the list, then click the Bullets button again. Works automatically removes the bullets.

You can also create a bulleted list for new items you type:

1. Click the Bullets button on the toolbar (see Figure 6.9).
2. Type the list of items, pressing Enter after each item. Works automatically inserts the bullet at the beginning of the line as you type.
3. After you type the last item, press Enter again. Works inserts a bullet at the beginning of the next line.
4. Click the Bullets button again to turn off the Bullets format and remove the bullet from the current line.

After typing a bulleted list, look at the indent markers on the ruler (see Figure 6.9). The left indent marker is positioned at ¼ inch; the first line indent marker is positioned at 0. This is known as a *hanging* indent because the first line *hangs* to the left of the rest of the paragraph. The position of the left indent marker is what causes multi-line entries to wrap at the ¼-inch point instead of wrapping at the left margin (zero).

Ch

6

FIG. 6.9

Bulleted lists use a hanging indent format; the left indent marker is at ¼ inch; the first line indent marker is at 0.

First line indent marker

Left indent marker

Bullets button

Bullet

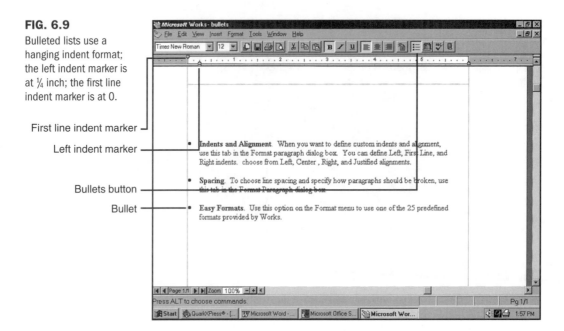

Choosing a Bullet Style

Although the bullet style shown in Figure 6.9 is probably the most commonly-used style, it is not the only style available in Works. You can choose from two dozen creative bullet styles by using the dialog box shown in Figure 6.10.

FIG. 6.10

The Format Bullets dialog box offers a variety of bullet styles and sizes.

To change a bullet style, use these steps:

1. Choose Format, Bullets to display the Format Bullets dialog box shown in Figure 6.10.
2. Click a bullet style.
3. In the Bullet Size box, click the up or down arrow key, or type a new size. Check the Sample area of the dialog box to see an example.
4. To turn off the hanging indent option, click the Hanging Indent check box to remove the check. (Turning this option off makes successive lines in the paragraph wrap at the left margin instead of indented from the bullet.)
5. Click OK.

Creating a Numbered List

A numbered list is similar to a bulleted list in that it uses a hanging indent format (see Figure 6.11). The Works toolbar, however, does not include a Numbers button, so you must type the numbers after you set up the hanging indent format.

FIG. 6.11

A numbered list uses a hanging indent format.

First line indent marker

Left indent marker

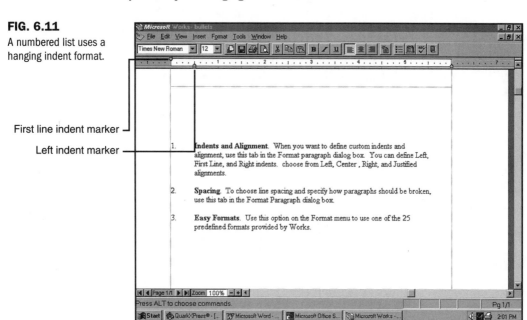

Use these steps to create a numbered list.

1. Type the items you want in the list, pressing Enter after each entry.

2. Select all items in the list.

3. Press and hold the Shift key, then drag the left indent marker on the ruler to the ½ inch point, or choose Format, Easy Formats, then choose the Hanging Indent format from the submenu.

4. Move the cursor back to the first item in the list.

5. Type **1.**, then press Tab.

6. Move the cursor to the next item in the list.

7. Type **2.**, then press Tab.

8. Repeat this process for all items in the list.

 You can quickly and easily indent lines using keyboard shortcuts. Press Ctrl+M to move the indentation of the current paragraph to the right in ½- inch increments. Press Ctrl+Shift+M to move the indentation of the current paragraph back to the left in ½- inch increments.

Creating Lists Using Tabs

An alternative to using indent markers is to create a simple one- or multi-column list using *tabs*. A tab marks a particular point on the ruler. When you press the Tab key, the cursor moves immediately to that location. Tabs let you align data or text in columns.

What's the difference between using tabs or indent markers to create multi-column lists? The difference is that a left indent marker marks the point at which *all* lines in a paragraph will be wrapped; a tab does not. If the left indent marker is placed at ½ an inch, all lines of the paragraph will wrap at ½ inch. In contrast, if you press Tab to indent text at ½ inch and keep typing past the end of the line, the following lines will wrap back at the left margin, not at the ½-inch tab.

The ruler includes default tab settings at ½ inch intervals, although they are not displayed on the ruler. (If you press the tab key repeatedly across a line, you'll see the cursor jump at ½" intervals.) Often these default tabs are sufficient for creating a multi-column list. If you choose, however, you can set custom tabs at any location. Custom tabs are always displayed on the ruler.

Works offers four types of custom tabs: left, center, right, and decimal. The names refer to the alignment of text or data in a column. For instance, when you type data at a left tab, all data in the column is left-aligned at the tab location; when you type decimal numbers at a decimal tab, the decimal points in the column are aligned. Notice that both columns of data in the list shown in Figure 6.12 are left-aligned.

FIG. 6.12

This two-column list uses a left-aligned tab for the Sales column.

Left-align tabs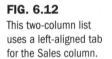

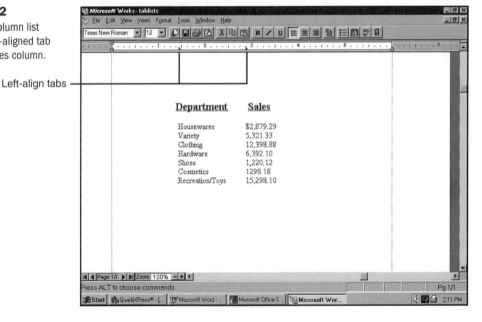

Left-alignment works well for the first column of text in Figure 6.12. It does not work well, however, for the second column, which includes numbers, because numbers are not generally left-aligned. In Figure 6.13, the list is redone using a decimal tab for the Sales figures.

FIG. 6.13

The decimal tab changes the alignment of numbers (compare to Figure 6.12).

Decimal tab

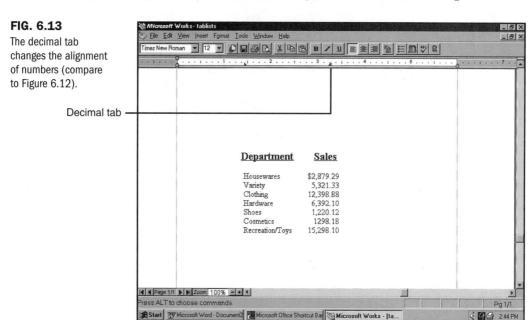

In Figures 6.12 and 6.13 you can see the tab marks for each type of tab (left and decimal) on the ruler. In these figures you see an L-shaped marker, used for a left tab, and the upside-down T-shape with a decimal point next to it for a decimal tab. The two types of tabs not shown in these figures include a right tab, which is the mirror-image of the L-shaped tab, and the center tab, represented by an upside-down T-shape (without the decimal point).

To set tabs on the ruler for multiple columns in a list, follow these steps:

1. Move the cursor to the line where you want to begin a multiple column list.
2. To set left tabs, click the proper location on the ruler. Works inserts left tab markers on the ruler.
3. Begin entering your text, pressing Tab when you want to move to the next column.

To set tabs for multiple columns using the Tabs dialog box, use these steps:

1. Move the cursor to the line where you want to begin a multiple-column list.
2. Choose Format, Tabs to open the Format Tabs dialog box (see Figure 6.14).
3. In the Tab Stop Position box, enter a number in inches indicating the location of the tab on the ruler.
4. In the Alignment box, select Left, Center, Right, or Decimal.
5. Choose the Set button. If you make a mistake, choose the Clear button or Clear All button.

Ch

6

FIG. 6.14
Use the Format Tabs dialog box to set precise tab positions and choose tab alignment styles.

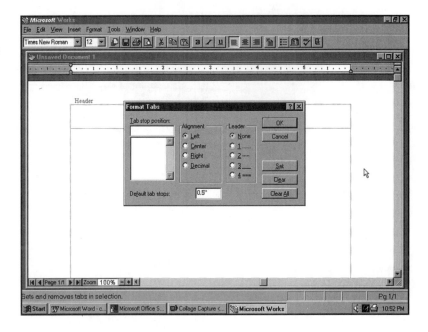

6. To set an additional tab or tabs, repeat steps 3-5.
7. When all tabs are set, correctly, click OK.

 TIP   To change the default tab interval, enter a setting in the Default Tab Stops box in the Format Tabs dialog box.

N O T E   Because inches often convert to unfamiliar decimal numbers (such as 1.625 for 1 ⅝ inches), you may have difficulty positioning a tab correctly when you type a setting in the Position text box in the Format Tabs dialog box. You might make several guesses before getting the tab in exactly the position you want. To save time and avoid experimenting with different settings, double-click the ruler where you want to set the tab. The Format Tabs dialog box opens and the tab you set is highlighted so that you can change its alignment, if necessary. ■

The tabs you set apply on the line where the cursor is located or to all lines of text that are currently selected. Begin typing the data for your list, pressing Tab to move to the next column. Press Enter to add a new line. Like character style and paragraph formats, tabs remain in effect until you change or remove them.

Moving and Deleting Tabs

When you begin to enter all the data for a list, you might find you need to move tabs that are not positioned correctly. Or you might decide to add or delete a column of data, requiring you to add or delete a tab. Works makes moving and deleting tabs easy.

Before you move or delete a tab, you must select the lines that the ruler tabs affect. If you don't select any lines, the changes you make affect only the line containing the cursor; the remainder of the list continues to use the original tab settings. If you select only a portion of the list, the changes you make apply only to the lines you select.

To move a tab, drag it to a new location on the ruler, then release the mouse button. The tab automatically assumes its new position on the ruler. To delete a tab, drag the tab off the ruler (up or down) then release the mouse button. Works automatically realigns the data in the list based on the new tab settings. If you move or delete a tab by mistake, you can restore it by choosing Edit, Undo or by pressing Ctrl+Z.

N O T E   If you want to delete a column, delete the data before you delete the tab. If you delete the tab first, the data will remain in the list and throw off the alignment of all remaining columns. In that case, finding the correct entries to delete then would be difficult. You can avoid this problem by deleting the data first then deleting the tab. ■

You also can use the Format Tabs dialog box to move or delete tabs. To move a tab:

1. Select all lines of text for which you want to change tab settings.
2. Choose Format, Tabs to display the Format Tabs dialog box.
3. Highlight the tab in the Tab Stop Position list.
4. Move the cursor into the Tab Stop Position box and type a new setting for the tab.
5. Choose the Set button to save the new setting.
6. Choose OK to return to your document.

To delete a tab, follow these steps:

1. Highlight the tab in the Tab Stop Position list.
2. Click the Clear button. Works removes the tab from the Tab Stop Position list.
3. Repeat these steps to delete additional tabs.
4. Click OK to return to your document.

Using Tab Leaders

A *leader* is a dotted line (or other character) that fills the space between columns in a tab list. Leaders help your eye track a row of data from one column to another. Figure 6.15 shows the same department sales figures shown in Figures 6.12 and 6.13, but the columns have been moved farther apart. Without the dot leader, it would be difficult for your eye to follow the row across to find the correct dollar figure in the second column. The dot leader makes it easy to see which dollar figures apply to each department.

To add a leader to a tab, select a style from the Leader options in the Format Tabs dialog box after you set the tab. Works automatically fills the space preceding the tab with the leader character you select (see Figure 6.15 for tab leader characters).

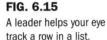

FIG. 6.15

A leader helps your eye track a row in a list.

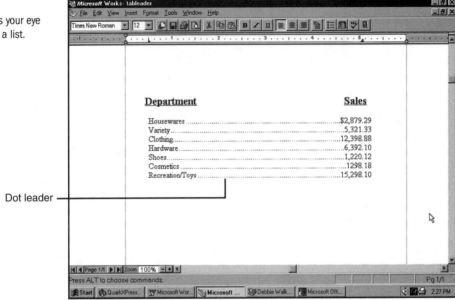

Dot leader

Department	Sales
Housewares	$2,879.29
Variety	5,321.33
Clothing	12,398.88
Hardware	6,392.10
Shoes	1,220.12
Cosmetics	1298.18
Recreation/Toys	15,298.10

N O T E You must select the entire list before you move or change tab options. If you don't, only a portion of the list will be reformatted. ■

Inserting a Table

A table is nothing more than rows and columns of text or data. Ideally, data displayed in a table is easier to understand than if it were presented as text.

Works has a built-in table generator that enables you to create multi-column tables instantly. The best feature of the table generator is that it includes dozens of preformatted table styles from which to choose. You don't have to make any decisions about colors, styles, sizes, fonts, and so on. Just choose the style that is appropriate for the data in your table. For instance, some table formats emphasize rows of data while others emphasize columns.

You use the Insert Table dialog box shown in Figure 6.16 to specify the number of rows and columns and choose a table style. When you highlight a format name, a sample of the table style is shown in the Example area.

To insert a table in a document, use these steps:

1. Move the cursor to the location where you want the table in your document.

2. Choose Insert, Table. The Insert Table dialog box shown in Figure 6.16 is displayed.

3. Enter a number in the Number Of Rows box.

4. Enter a number in the Number Of Columns box.

FIG. 6.16

The Insert Table dialog box lists a variety of formatting styles.

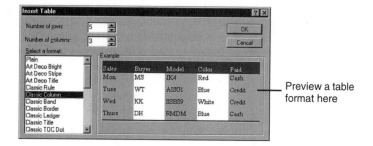

Preview a table format here

5. From the Select a Format list, choose a table format. (As you scroll through the list, the Example area illustrates each table style.)

6. Click OK. Works inserts the formatted framework for the table into your word processor document.

Figure 6.17 shows a five-column table created using the Insert Table command. The table format shown in Figure 6.17 is Plain; the font is Times New Roman 12, column headings are underlined, and rows and columns are not bordered or lined. This is the simplest format Works provides for tables and is appropriate when you want a very simple, unadorned table.

FIG. 6.17

A table displayed in the Plain format.

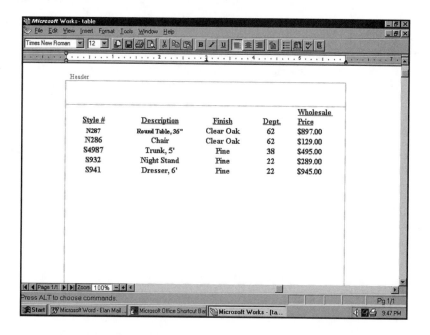

In Figure 6.18, you see the same table presented in the Classic Column format. This is a good example of a format that emphasizes rows rather than columns of data. It presents the column headings on a blue background, and the rows of data on alternating white and gray backgrounds. This color format makes it easier for your eye to follow each item across the table.

FIG. 6.18

The same table displayed in the Classic Column format.

Entering and Editing Table Data

With the table inserted in your document, you're ready to begin entering your data. When you select the table, the row and column dividers are visible, as shown in Figure 6.19. Notice that the standard word processor toolbar has been replaced by the spreadsheet toolbar. This is because the table feature in the word processor actually places a spreadsheet into your document. You operate in the table the same way you do within a spreadsheet document. That is, you type text or numbers in each *cell* (the intersection of a row and column).

Table 6.1 summarizes some of the most common text entry and editing techniques for spreadsheets.

Table 6.1 Text Entry and Editing Techniques for Spreadsheets

To:	Do This:
Move to the next cell in the current row	Press Tab
Select a cell	Click it
Select a row	Click the row marker at the far left of the row
Select a column	Click the column marker at the top of the column
Select the entire table	Click the square in the upper left corner of the table

To:	Do This:
Edit an entry	Highlight the cell; use the Backspace key to delete characters; type new characters
Change a font, alignment, number format, border, or shading	Highlight the cells you want to change, then right-click and choose Format from the shortcut menu. In the Format dialog box, click the tab for the change you want to make
Adjust column width	Point to the column divider until the Adjust pointer appears, then drag the column divider to a new width
Adjust row height	Point to the row divider until the Adjust pointer appears, then drag the row divider to a new height

FIG. 6.19
A table, when selected, is actually a spread-sheet within a word processor document.

Spreadsheet toolbar —

Cell —

Row —

Column —

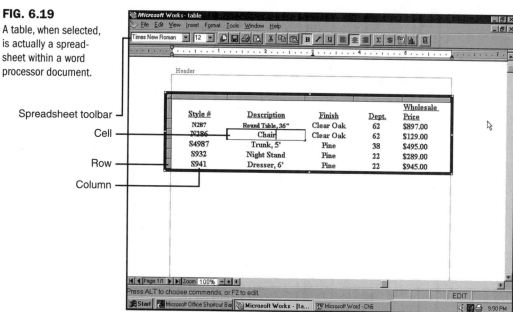

When you are finished entering data and editing data in a table, click anywhere in the document to move outside of the table. When you do, the word processor toolbar returns to the screen.

Using an Existing Spreadsheet for a Table

Another way to include a table in a document is by using an existing spreadsheet, created using the spreadsheet application in Works. You can incorporate spreadsheets into a document using one of two methods. The first method, called *embedding,* gives you full access to the Works spreadsheet functions from inside the word processor window if you want to make changes to the spreadsheet. The other method, called *linking,* ensures that any changes you

Ch

6

make to the spreadsheet in the spreadsheet application are automatically reflected in the table in your word processor document. To use either of these methods, refer to Chapter 14, "Using the Works Tools Together," which discusses linking and embedding.

Using Footnotes in a Document

Footnotes often are used in reports, proposals, and other business documents to cite the source of information or to provide additional information, comments, or remarks about a topic in the body text. A footnote marker appears in the body of the document where you place the marker, and the footnote text prints at the bottom of the page or at the end of the document (you specify which style you want). Footnotes (even the ones that appear at the bottom of the page) are counted as part of the body of the page, so they are not affected by top, bottom, header, or footer margins. You can use numbered footnote markers, or you can specify another character to mark the location of a footnote.

When using Normal view, Works displays a footnote pane at the bottom of the document window (see Figure 6.20). Works inserts the matching footnote marker and places the cursor next to the marker in the footnote pane. In this pane, you can enter, edit, and format the footnote text just like any other text in the document. After you complete the footnote, you move the cursor back into the body of the document and continue working. You can close the footnote pane by choosing the Footnotes command on the View menu. This command toggles the footnote pane on and off; choose the command another time to view footnotes again.

FIG. 6.20

In Normal view, you enter, edit, and format footnote text in the footnote pane.

Footnote marker

Footnote marker and text

Footnote pane

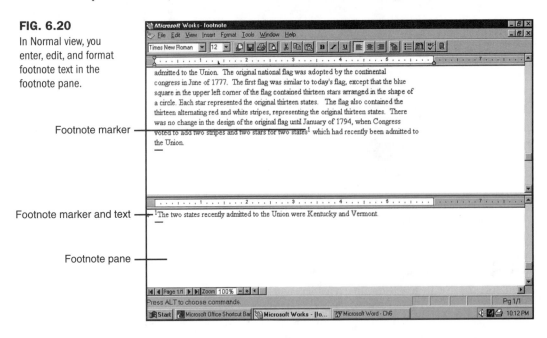

When using Page Layout view, Works inserts a footnote marker in your document where the cursor is located and a matching footnote marker at the bottom of the page. This is where you enter, edit, and format the footnote text (see Figure 6.21).

FIG. 6.21

In Page Layout view, enter, edit, and format footnote text at the bottom of the current page.

Footnote marker ———

Footnote marker and text ———

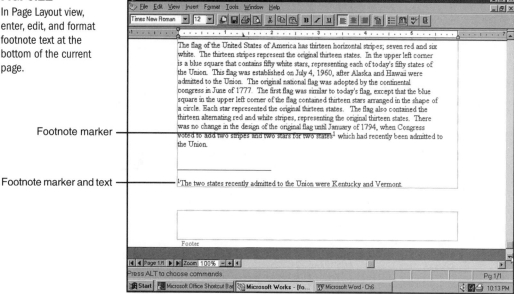

Creating a Footnote

To insert a footnote in a document, use the Footnote dialog box shown in Figure 6.22. In this dialog box you select Numbered or Special Mark for the footnote marker. A special mark is a character other than a number, such as an asterisk.

FIG. 6.22

Use the Footnote dialog box to choose a footnote marker.

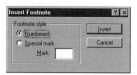

Follow these steps to create a footnote:

1. Move the cursor to the location in the document where you want to insert the footnote marker.

2. Choose Insert, Footnote. The Footnote dialog box shown in Figure 6.22 opens.

3. Select Numbered or Special Mark. If you select Special Mark, type the character in the Mark box.

4. Select Insert. If you're using Page Layout view, the cursor moves to the bottom of the page. If you're using Normal view, the cursor moves into a footnote pane at the bottom of the document window.

5. Type your footnote text and format it if you want.

6. To move the cursor back into the body of the document from Page Layout View, just click in the document text area of the screen. In Normal view, choose View, Footnotes to close the footnote pane and return to the document text area.

Moving or Copying a Footnote

Sometimes you might want to move a footnote in a document from one location to another, or you might want to copy a footnote to another page. You can move and copy footnotes in Works just like you move or copy any other text in a document. The important thing to remember is to select and move or copy the footnote *marker* in the body of the text rather than the footnote text itself. After you select the marker and move it, Works removes the footnote marker and footnote text from the original location; Works places the footnote marker and the footnote text in the location where you paste it. If the order of footnotes changes, Works automatically re-numbers footnotes appropriately.

To move a footnote, do this:

1. Select the footnote marker in the body of the document.

2. Click the Cut button on the toolbar or choose Edit, Cut.

3. Place the cursor where you want to move the footnote marker, then click the Paste button or choose Edit, Paste.

If you prefer to use the drag-and-drop method, you can drag the selected paragraph marker to a new location.

To copy a footnote, use these steps:

1. Select the footnote marker in the body of the document.

2. Click the Copy button on the toolbar or choose Edit, Copy.

3. Place the cursor where you want to copy the footnote marker, then click the Paste button or choose Edit, Paste. The original footnote remains in its original location and is copied to the new location. Works automatically renumbers the copied footnote.

Deleting a Footnote

You must delete a footnote by selecting the footnote *marker* in the body of the document, then deleting the marker. (Use Edit, Cut, use the Cut toolbar button, or press Delete. You can also Backspace over a footnote to delete it.) Works removes the text and marker from the list of footnotes and, in the case of numbered footnotes, automatically renumbers all remaining foot-notes. Note that you can't delete a footnote by selecting and cutting the *footnote text* from the bottom of the page or the footnote pane. If you try to delete the footnote, Works beeps and won't let you delete the text.

Printing Footnotes at the End of a Document

Works automatically assumes you want to print footnotes at the bottom of the appropriate page in a document. For some documents, however, you might decide to print all footnotes at the end of a document. To choose this option, you use the File, Page Setup command to display the Page Setup dialog box shown in Figure 6.23.

FIG. 6.23
Use the Other Options tab in the Page Setup dialog box to designate where you want footnotes to print.

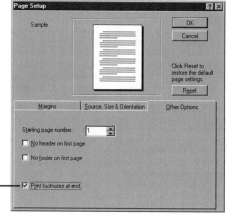

Footnotes printing option

Follow these steps to print footnotes at the end of a document:

1. Before printing your document, choose File, Page Setup. Works displays the Page Setup dialog box.
2. Choose the Other Options tab to open the dialog box shown in Figure 6.23.
3. Select the Print Footnotes at End check box.
4. Choose OK.
5. Print your document as you usually do.

To restore footnotes to their respective pages, clear the Print Footnotes at End check box before printing again.

Using a Bookmark

The same way you insert a bookmark in a printed book to mark the last page you read, you can insert an electronic *bookmark* in a document to mark a location where you want to return later. An electronic bookmark lets you return instantly to the location you mark. Without it, you could search for a location, but if you don't remember a particular word or phrase to search for, you might spend a long time looking for your place.

Ch
6

In Works, you assign a name to your bookmark using the Bookmark Name dialog box shown in Figure 6.24. To find the bookmark in the document, you use the Go To dialog box, which lists the name of the bookmark.

FIG. 6.24

Define a bookmark name in the Bookmark Name dialog box.

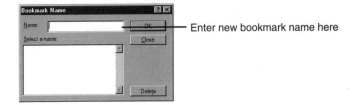

Enter new bookmark name here

Creating and Returning to a Bookmark

To create a bookmark, follow these steps:

1. Move the cursor to the location in the document where you want to place a bookmark.
2. Choose Edit, Bookmark. Works displays the Bookmark Name dialog box.
3. In the Name text box, enter the name for the bookmark.
4. Choose OK.

Works invisibly marks the location in the document; you don't see the bookmark on the screen. To return to a bookmark, choose Edit, Go To or press F5. In the Go To dialog box that opens, double-click the bookmark name in the Select a Bookmark list box, or highlight the bookmark name and choose OK. Works immediately moves the cursor in the document to the location of the bookmark.

Removing a Bookmark

When you no longer want to use an existing bookmark, you can delete it by following these steps:

1. Choose Edit, Bookmark. The Bookmark name dialog box opens.
2. In the Names list, highlight the bookmark you want to delete.
3. Choose the Delete button. Works deletes the bookmark.
4. Choose OK.

Creating Columns of Text

Certain types of documents lend themselves well to multiple columns of text. Newspapers and magazines use this style almost exclusively; you can use the same style to create newsletters, articles, brochures, or other types of documents.

When you format a document for multiple columns, you determine the number of columns and the amount of space between columns. The columns apply to the entire document except headers and footers. (You cannot use multiple columns on selected pages of a document.) Based on the number of columns you specify, the page size, and the margin settings, Works automatically calculates a uniform width for all columns. You also can add a vertical line between columns. An example of a multi-column document is shown in the Preview screen in Figure 6.25.

FIG. 6.25
Print Preview shows how a three-column document looks.

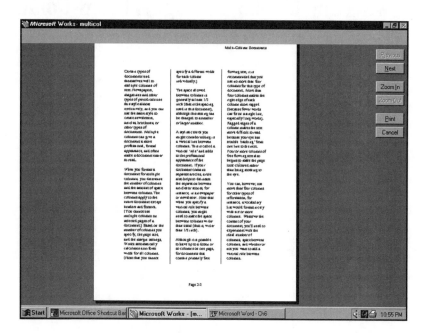

Choosing Column Specifications

To specify columns in a document, follow these steps:

1. Choose Format, Columns to display the Format Columns dialog box shown in Figure 6.26.
2. In the Number of Columns box, enter the number of columns to use.
3. In the Space Between box, enter a measurement in inches.
4. To print a vertical line between columns, select the Line Between Columns check box. Notice the example shown in the Sample area of the dialog box.

Ch
6

FIG. 6.26
Use the Format Columns dialog box to set the number of columns, space between columns, and vertical line between columns.

5. Click OK.

6. If you're using Normal view, Works displays a message suggesting that you switch to Page Layout view to view the document. Choose Yes. Works displays the columns on your screen.

Viewing and Moving through a Multi-Column Document

When using Normal view, Works displays your document as one narrow column on the left side of the screen; you can't tell where one column ends and another begins. It's best to use Page Layout view, which displays all columns side by side on your screen. Notice that the right and left indent markers on the ruler now are much closer together than normal—the markers define the width of a single column (see Figure 6.27). If you specify a vertical line between columns, you don't see it in Page Layout view, but the line is visible when you preview and print the document.

 TIP   To preview a document, click the Preview toolbar button or choose File, Print Preview.

FIG. 6.27
A three-column document shown in Page Layout view.

Left indent marker

Column width

Right indent marker

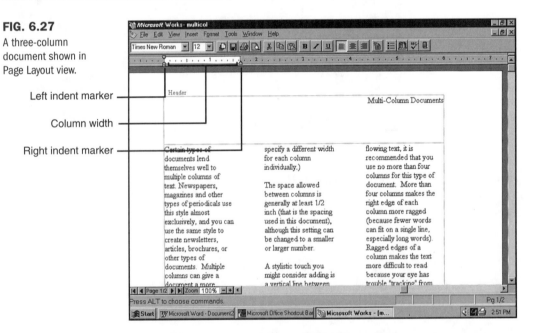

The text now follows a serpentine pattern on your page; that is, text flows from the bottom of one column to the top of the next. If you were to press and hold the right arrow key, you would find that the cursor moves from the bottom of the first column to the top of the second column, and so on. To position the cursor using the mouse, just click anywhere on the page. Use the scroll bars, the page navigation buttons, and the Page Up and Page Down keys as you normally would. For more information about working with Page Layout view, refer to Chapter 2, "Getting Started with Works."

Creating a Title Across Multiple Columns

If a multi-column format affects the entire document, how can you enter a title or a headline that runs across the top of all columns, as shown in Figure 6.28? You can do it by using Word Art, a tool built into Works that lets you add creative and artistic text to documents.

FIG. 6.28

A headline or title can span all three columns.

Inserted Word Art title ——

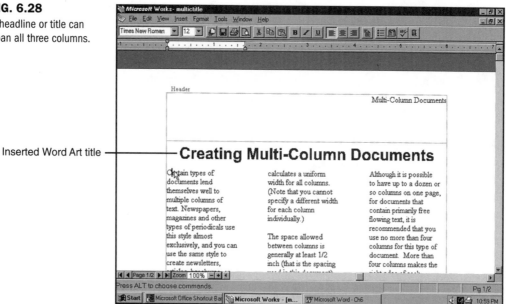

This section is not intended to provide a detailed discussion of Word Art and how to position it in your document. The instructions below briefly describe how to add a Word Art title across columns like the one shown in Figure 6.28.

To create a Word Art title for a multi-column document, use these steps:

1. Place the cursor at the top of the page where you want to insert a headline or title.

2. Choose Insert, Word Art.

3. In the Word Art pop-up window, type the headline or title text. Use the Word Art toolbar to change the font and size of the entry.

4. Click the Close button on the Word Art window. A Word Art object is placed in your word processor document.

5. Press Esc to restore the word processor toolbar.

6. With the Word Art object still selected, choose Format, Text Wrap.

Ch
6

7. In the Text Wrap dialog box, choose Absolute, then click OK.

8. With the Word Art object still selected, click the gray handle on the right side of the object and drag it to the right margin of the document. If necessary, drag the bottom gray handle to change the height of the Word Art object. The title is now displayed across all columns.

To learn the details of using Word Art, refer to Chapter 14, "Using The Works Tools Together." To learn more about positioning objects in a document, refer to the section "Inserting Objects in a Document," later in this chapter.

Changing or Removing Columns

Multiple columns are as easy to change or remove from a document as they are to define. Choose Format, Columns, then enter a number (enter 1 to take away all multiple columns) in the Number of Columns box and choose OK. Works reformats the document according to the number of columns you specify.

Inserting Objects in a Document

One of the most dramatic ways to make a document more visually appealing is to include graphic elements and illustrations. As you learned in Chapter 1, "Introducing Works 4.5," you have a variety of tools that enable you to insert such items.

- Using Clip Art, you can include a prepared drawing to add humor, draw attention, or illustrate a point.

- With Microsoft Draw, you can create your own drawings that are custom-designed to achieve the same purpose.

- Word Art's unique capability to bend and shape text offers a creative way to dress up and stylize titles, banners, headlines, or logos.

- Note-It enables you to insert eye-catching icons into a document that reveal a hidden note when you click the icon.

All four of these mini-applications insert *objects* into your document. The method for inserting an object varies from application to application, as you'll learn in Chapter 14, "Using the Works Tools Together."

▶ **See** "Using Draw," **p. 264**
▶ **See** "Using Clip Art," **p. 273**
▶ **See** "Using Word Art," **p. 275**
▶ **See** "Using Note-It," **p. 282**

Selecting, Sizing, and Moving Objects

Because all objects have height and width, the surrounding text in a document is "disrupted" when you insert an object. But before you decide how to format the surrounding text, you might want to move or resize the object to position it correctly.

To select an object, click anywhere on the object. The object's *frame*—the rectangular shape that surrounds the object—becomes visible. All objects have a rectangular shape when you select them. At the corners and midpoints around the frame are *handles*, used for resizing the object (see Figure 6.29).

FIG. 6.29

An object's frame and handles appear when you select the object.

Handle

Resize arrow

Object frame

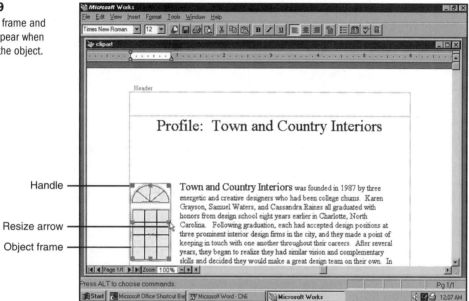

You can resize an object in several ways. When you place the mouse pointer on any of the handles, the pointer changes to a resize arrow. Click and drag a side, top, or bottom handle to resize in one dimension only. For instance, drag the top or bottom handle to make the object longer or shorter. Release the mouse button when the object is the size you want. To resize an object while maintaining its height-to-width ratio, click and drag any of the corner handles. The object resizes in two dimensions at the same time.

An alternative to resizing with the mouse is to specify exact dimensions for an object. To do so, use these steps:

1. Choose Format, Picture, which displays the Format Picture dialog box shown in Figure 6.30. Click the Size tab. The Original Size section at the bottom of the dialog box shows the original width and height of the object.

2. In the Width and Height boxes, type the dimensions you want for the object, or if you prefer to scale the object using a percentage of the original size, enter percentages in the Width and Height boxes in the Scaling section.

3. Choose OK to return to the document window.

To move an object, use these steps:

FIG. 6.30
Use the Size tab in the Format Picture dialog box to specify an object's exact dimensions and scale.

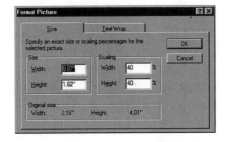

1. Point anywhere on the object. The I-beam mouse pointer changes to an arrow labeled DRAG.

2. Click the object and hold down the left mouse button; the DRAG label changes to MOVE.

3. Drag the object in any direction until it is positioned where you want it. Release the mouse button. Note that the surrounding text is still not formatted.

Formatting Text Surrounding Inserted Objects

Because most objects occupy more space than a single line of text in a document, you must make choices about how you want to format the surrounding text. Works offers two options for formatting the text that borders an inserted object: *in-line* or *absolute*. These options are illustrated in Figure 6.31, where the Format Picture dialog box is shown with the Text Wrap tab selected.

The Inline wrap option positions an object on the same line as the text that immediately precedes and follows the object. The height of the object determines the height of that line because Works treats the object as if it were a character on the line. The Absolute wrap option surrounds all sides of the object with text. See Figure 6.32.

The settings in the Picture Position area are available only when you select the Absolute wrap option. Initially, the Horizontal box shows where the object is positioned relative to the left edge of the paper; the Vertical box shows where the object is positioned relative to the top edge of the paper. The Page # box shows the page number where the object is located. In Figure 6.30, for example, the object is 3.23" from the left edge of the paper and 3.55" from the top of the paper.

If you prefer, you can use the Horizontal and Vertical boxes to position an object for you. Each box is a drop-down list that contains the choices Left, Center, and Right. If you want your object to appear in the exact center of the page, for instance, you can select the Center setting in both the Horizontal and Vertical boxes. If you want the object to appear in the lower left corner of the page, select the Left setting in the Horizontal box and the Bottom setting in the Vertical box. To change the page on which the object appears, enter a new page number in the Page # box.

FIG. 6.31

Use the Text Wrap tab in the Format Picture dialog box to specify how text is formatted around a picture.

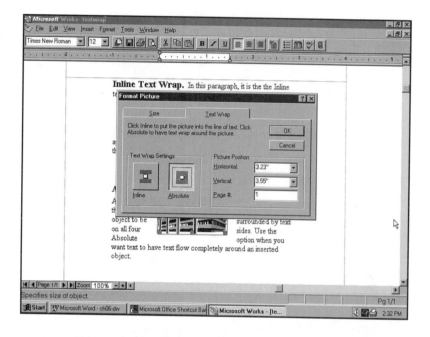

FIG. 6.32

Choose between Inline and Absolute Text Wrap to achieve the right effect for your document.

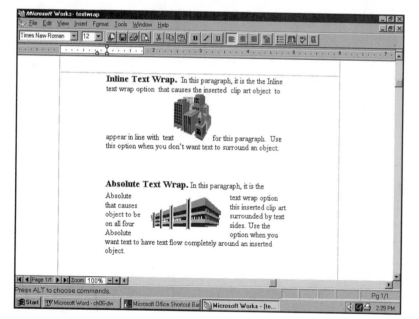

Ch

6

Creating and Printing a Spreadsheet

A spreadsheet is a life-saver for those who routinely perform numeric calculations manually. Essentially, a spreadsheet is an electronic version of a worksheet; calculations—and, more importantly, recalculations—are performed automatically when you insert a formula in the spreadsheet. This eliminates the need to recalculate figures when changes occur in the worksheet. ■

Spreadsheet window

Learn about the elements of the window that are different from the word processor window, and the menu commands and toolbar buttons that are unique to the spreadsheet.

Getting around in the spreadsheet

Learn several methods for moving around in the spreadsheet (since a spreadsheet can become quite large), and learn different methods for entering data and how to change it.

Printing a spreadsheet

There are a number of tasks leading up to printing such as selecting the area you want to print, setting margins, page and print options, and previewing your spreadsheet.

Becoming Familiar with the Spreadsheet Window

A typical spreadsheet window is shown in Figure 7.1. The general layout of the screen should look familiar to you, but in this section we'll take a look at how the spreadsheet window differs from the word processor.

FIG. 7.1

A typical spreadsheet window looks similar to a word processor window except for the grid in the working area.

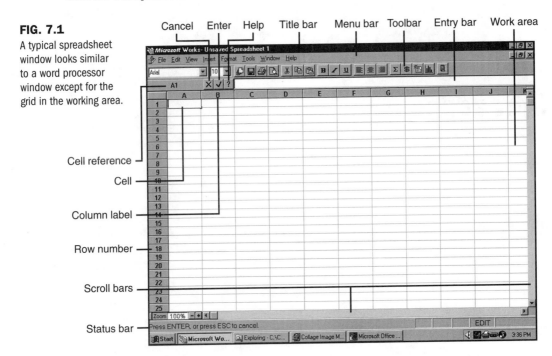

The spreadsheet window contains a grid of rows and columns. At the bottom of the spreadsheet is a horizontal scroll bar; on the right, a vertical scroll bar. Row numbers appear along the left, and column labels appear along the top. The title bar, menu bar, and toolbar appear above the grid. Various elements of the spreadsheet window are described below.

- *Work area* You can generally see seven or eight columns and up to 20 rows of the spreadsheet on the screen at a time. The entire spreadsheet is 256 columns by 16,384 rows. Columns are labeled A through Z, then AA, AB, AC...AZ; BA, BB, BC...BZ; CA, CB, CC...CZ; and so on until the last column, IV. Row numbers run consecutively from 1 to 16,384.

- *Cell* A cell is the part of the grid in which you enter data; it is the intersection of a row and column. Each cell is identified by its *address*, that is, its column letter and row number, such as E14 or N348. The *active* cell—the one where the cursor is located—is outlined in a heavy border to make it easy to spot on the screen. When you select a *cell range*, that is, two or more adjacent cells, the active cell is white and the remaining cells are black.

■ *Mouse pointer*   The mouse pointer is a large, bold cross unless you point to the toolbar or scroll bars, in which case the pointer changes to an arrow. When you point to the entry bar the mouse pointer changes to an I-beam so you can enter text or numbers.

■ *Title bar*   When you create a new file, the title bar displays the title `Microsoft Works - Unsaved Spreadsheet 1`. After you name a file, the file appears in the title bar.

■ *Menu bar*   The menu bar contains the same menu names as the word processor menu bar, but the commands on some of the menus are unique to spreadsheets, Two examples are the Insert, Row and Insert Column commands, which would be meaningless in the word processor.

■ *Toolbar*   The Toolbar contains buttons for commands that you'll use frequently. The toolbar is described in detail later in this chapter in the section "Using the Spreadsheet Menus and the Toolbar."

■ *Scroll bars*   The scroll bars allow you to adjust your view of the spreadsheet so you can see whatever area of the spreadsheet you're working on.

■ *Cell reference*   Works displays the address of the active cell, such as C3, or a cell range, such as C3:D5.

■ *Cancel button, Enter button, Help button, and Entry bar*   The entry in the active cell also appears in the entry bar. When a cell contains a formula, the formula is shown in the entry bar; the *result* appears in the cell. You use the entry bar to enter and edit data. Click the Cancel button to cancel an entry; click the Enter button to accept an entry. To get help creating a formula or entering data, click the Help button.

■ *Status bar*   In the status bar you'll see brief instructions (such as `Press Enter or press ESC to cancel`) or a description of the current menu command that is highlighted. The boxes at the right end of the status bar display `Num Lock`, `Extend Selection`, `Edit`, or `Point`, when these modes are active.

Using the Spreadsheet Menus and the Toolbar

The menu names in the spreadsheet are identical to many of those used in other Works tools. The commands on each menu, however, perform unique functions in the spreadsheet program. Table 7.1 briefly summarizes the commands on the spreadsheet menus.

Table 7.1 The Spreadsheet Menus	
Menu Name	**Description**
File	This menu contains commands for opening, saving, printing, and creating new files. The four most-recently opened files are listed at the bottom of the menu.

continues

Ch

7

Table 7.1 Continued

Menu Name	Description
Edit	This menu contains commands for cutting, copying, pasting, finding, and changing data, as well as undoing changes. Look here also for commands for selecting rows or columns and for filling cells with data.
View	These commands determine how your spreadsheet is displayed; for example, with gridlines or showing formulas rather than data, with or without the toolbar, ruler, status bar, and so on. Create headers and footers using this menu, and switch between Chart and Spreadsheet views. Use the Zoom command to reduce or enlarge the spreadsheet.
Insert	On this menu you find commands for inserting page breaks, rows and columns, functions, and range names in a spreadsheet.
Format	This menu holds the commands for font and style, number formats, borders, alignment, patterns, row height, and column width. Use AutoFormat to apply specially designed formats to spreadsheets. Set the print area when printing only a selected portion of a spreadsheet.
Tools	This menu contains special tools for working with a spreadsheet, such as spelling, sorting, recalculating, and working with charts. The Dial This Number command automatically dials a phone number for you if the number is in a cell of the spreadsheet.
Window	Using the commands on this menu, you can arrange all open documents on-screen, split the screen, or select a different open document as the active window.
Help	Use this menu when you need help working with the spreadsheet, or to see an overview of the spreadsheet tool.

The spreadsheet contains buttons on the toolbar that are unique to the spreadsheet tool. Table 7.2 describes the function of each of the spreadsheet toolbar buttons. Note that some buttons might require you to select data prior to clicking the button.

 TIP If you don't see the toolbar on your screen, it's hidden. To display it, choose View, Toolbar.

Table 7.2 The Buttons on the Spreadsheet Toolbar

Button	Function
Arial ▼	Displays a drop-down list of all available fonts.
10 ▼	Displays a drop-down list of all available point sizes for the current font.

Button	Function
	Displays the Works Task Launcher dialog box.
	Saves the file using the current file name and settings. If a spreadsheet has not yet been saved, the Save As dialog box appears.
	Prints the current spreadsheet using the current print settings.
	Previews your spreadsheet before printing.
	Removes (cuts) the selected text to the Clipboard.
	Copies the selected text to the Clipboard.
	Inserts (pastes) the contents of the Clipboard into the spreadsheet at the location of the cursor.
B	Applies bold to the contents of the selected cell.
I	Applies italic to the contents of the selected cell.
<u>u</u>	Applies underline to the contents of the selected cell.
	Left-aligns the selected cell entry.
	Centers the selected cell entry.
	Right-aligns the selected entry.
Σ	Automatically sums the nearest row of numbers or column of numbers.
$	Automatically formats the data in selected cells using the dollar symbol ($) and two decimal places.
	Displays the Easy Calc Wizard in which you create a formula.
	Click this button to create a new chart using selected data in the current spreadsheet.
	Displays the Address Book TaskWizard.

Ch
7

Moving Around the Spreadsheet

You can move around in the spreadsheet work area using the mouse, the arrow keys, or the keyboard shortcuts listed in Table 7.3.

Table 7.3 Keyboard Shortcuts for Moving Around in a Spreadsheet	
Press	**To move**
Arrow keys	Up, down, right, or left one cell at a time
Tab	One cell to the right
Shift+Tab	One cell to the left
Home	To column A in the current row
Ctrl+Home	To cell A1
End	To the last column containing data in the current row
Ctrl+End	To the last column and row containing data
Page Up	Up one screen
Ctrl+Page Up	Left one screen
Page Down	Down one screen
Ctrl+Page Down	Right one screen

N O T E When you use the scroll bars, you only shift your *view* of the spreadsheet; you must click in a cell to change the location of the active cell. ■

Using Go To

When you want to move to a specific cell in a spreadsheet, often the fastest way to do so is by choosing Edit, Go To, which displays the Go To dialog box shown in Figure 7.2.

 T I P You can also press Ctrl+G or F5 to display the Go To dialog box.

FIG. 7.2
Use the Go To dialog box to quickly move to a specific location in a spreadsheet.

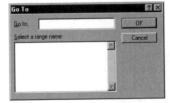

In the <u>G</u>o To text box, type the address of the cell you want to highlight, then choose OK or press Enter. You can type the address of a single cell or a cell range. Works closes the Go To dialog box and immediately highlights the cell or range you specify.

Selecting Cells

To enter data in a spreadsheet you must first select a cell by clicking it. You can also select a *range of cells*, any rectangular area of cells. A cell range can be any size or shape. You select cell ranges when you want to change something about all of the cells, or perhaps move or copy the entire range somewhere else in the spreadsheet. Cell ranges are identified by the address in the upper-left corner and the lower-right corner of the range, and separated by a colon. For instance, the range C3:F18 includes all cells in columns C, D, E, and F in rows 3 through 18. The cell range A6:D8 is shown in Figure 7.3.

FIG. 7.3

The cell range in this figure is A6:D8—the highlighted cells.

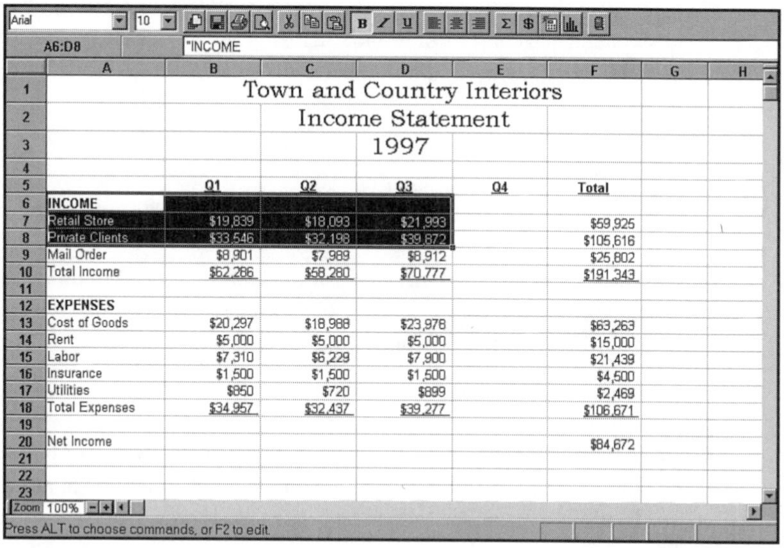

You can select a cell range in several ways:

- *Drag the mouse over a range of cells* Point to the first cell, then drag the mouse pointer to the last cell you want to include in the range and release the mouse button.

- *Click a column label or row number* Clicking a column label or row number automatically selects the entire column as a range or the entire row as a range. You can select several columns or rows at a time by dragging the mouse over more than one column label or more than one row number before you release the mouse button.

- *Use menu commands* The Edit menu contains commands for selecting a row or selecting a column. When you choose one of these commands, the row or column where the active cell is located is automatically selected. To select the entire spreadsheet, choose Edit, Select All.

- ■ *Use the shift key with the arrow keys or mouse* When you hold the Shift key, then use an arrow key or the mouse to select a new active cell, Works highlights all cells in the range from the previously active cell to the new active cell.

- ■ *Use the "extend" key, F8* Press F8, then press any of the arrow keys to extend the selection from the active cell to the final cell you want to select. (The EXT indicator appears on the status bar when you use F8 this way.) Press Ctrl+F8 to select the entire row of the active cell. Press Shift+F8 to select the entire column of the active cell. When you press Ctrl+Shift+F8, Works selects the entire spreadsheet.

Entering Text

You can enter three types of data in a spreadsheet: *text, numbers*, and *formulas*. The majority of most spreadsheets consists of numbers; text is used to label and describe the numbers. Formulas perform calculations on the numbers.

To enter text, use these steps:

1. Select a cell.

2. Type the entry. When you begin typing, a cursor appears in the entry bar. The characters you type appear in the entry bar as well as in the cell.

3. When you're finished, press Enter or click the Enter button on the reference bar. Or, you can confirm an entry and move to another cell in a single step by pressing an arrow key, the Tab key, or by clicking in a new cell.

Text entries are automatically left-aligned in cells using the *general* alignment format. If the text you type is too long to fit in a cell, it carries over into the cell to the right if that cell is empty. If the adjacent cell contains data, the cell in which you are typing only displays the amount of text that fits in the cell. You can still see the complete text entry in the entry bar when the cell is active. To display the entire text entry in the cell, however, you must increase the column width.

▶ **See** "Adjusting Column Width," **p. 124**

Any entry that begins with or includes a letter of the alphabet is considered a text entry. Sometimes you might want a numeric entry (such as a phone number or street address) to be interpreted as text. To do this, you precede the entry with a quotation mark ("). This ensures that Works interprets the entry as text rather than a number.

N O T E The exception to the "alphabetic rule" is that Works treats the names of months as numeric entries and formats them as dates. If you type "October" or "oct," Works displays "October" in the cell, interprets it as a number, and assigns the Date format to the entry. This is done so that calculations can be made on the date, if necessary. (If you want Works to interpret a date as text, precede it with a quotation mark.) ■

When an entry contains both alphabetic characters and numbers (such as a part number like PT413-N) Works automatically interprets the entry as text. Entries that include punctuation marks (, . : ; !) or other keyboard symbols (~ @ # $ % ^ & * ( ) _ [ ] { }) along with alphabetic characters are also interpreted as text.

Exceptions to alpha/numeric entries are those that begin with the following symbols:

- The addition symbol (+)
- The subtraction symbol (–)
- The equal symbol (=)
- The @ symbol

These symbols are used in formulas and functions and are therefore not allowed as the first character of an alpha/numeric entry. (If you type + – = or @ followed by text, Works displays an error message.) To type a text entry such as 2@.79, precede the entry with a quotation mark so that Works interprets the entry as text. Table 7.4 shows sample text entries and the reasons why Works interprets them as text.

Table 7.4   Entries Works Interprets as Text

Example Entry	Reason Works Interprets This Entry as Text
9802 9820 1198 1098	Spaces are interpreted as alphabetic characters
#2987	# is interpreted as an alphabetic character
3_10_97	Underscore characters in a date are interpreted as alphabetic characters
425/555-9871	Slash and hyphen are interpreted as alphabetic characters
"98035	The quotation mark designates this as a text entry
'98035	The apostrophe designates this as a text entry
539-BN-123	Alpha/numeric entries are interpreted as text
14412 124th Ave.	Alpha/numeric entries are interpreted as text

Entering Numbers

A *number* is any entry upon which a calculation can be performed. All entries that contain numbers and no alphabetic characters are automatically interpreted as numbers.

When a number includes commas used as thousands separators (5,280), a percent sign (48%), a period used as a decimal point (43.981), or a dollar symbol ($6.98), it is also automatically interpreted as a number. Works displays percent symbols, decimal points, and dollar signs, but commas are not displayed unless you assign the Comma format to a cell.

Ch
7

TIP To quickly insert the current date in m/d/yy format, press Ctrl+;. To insert the time in h:mm AM/PM format, press Ctrl+: (the Ctrl button plus a colon).

To enter a negative number, precede the number with a minus symbol (-); it isn't necessary to type an addition (+) symbol for a positive number. If you precede a number with an equal symbol (=) or an @ symbol, Works drops the symbol and enters a positive number.

Works automatically right-aligns numbers in a cell using the *general* alignment format. If the entry you type is too long to fit in a cell, Works either displays ##### in the cell or displays the number using scientific notation. Table 7.5 shows sample numeric entries and the reasons why Works interprets them this way.

Table 7.5   Entries Works Interprets as Numbers

Sample Entry	Reason Works Interprets This Entry as a Number
123.87	Decimal point is valid in a numeric entry
$44.98	Dollar sign and decimal point are valid in numeric entries
-298	Minus symbol signifies a negative number and is valid in a numeric entry
149%	Percent symbol is valid in a numeric entry
############	Long numbers in other formats are displayed as #########
5.89E+13	Numbers displayed in exponential format (scientific notation) are valid numeric entries

Filling Cells

Works offers a way for you to *fill* cells quickly with identical entries (such as a column filled with the entry *6.25%*), or numbers that occur in a series (such as *1, 2, 3, 4, 5*). A *series* is a set of numbers or dates that are automatically increased or decreased by a specific amount. It's faster to fill cells with entries of this type rather than typing individual entries. You can fill cells to the right of the current cell or below the current cell. For instance, if your income statement spreadsheet shows the same amount each month in the rent category, you can enter the amount for the first month, and then fill the cells for the remaining months with the same dollar amount. Figure 7.4 shows an example of cells that were filled to the right of the active cell.

To fill a range of cells to the right of the current cell or below the current cell, follow these steps:

1. Type an entry in the first cell in the range you want to fill.

2. Highlight the active cell and all cells to the right or below it that you want to fill (see Figure 7.4).

FIG. 7.4

Use the Edit, Fill Right command to fill a series of cells to the right of the active cell.

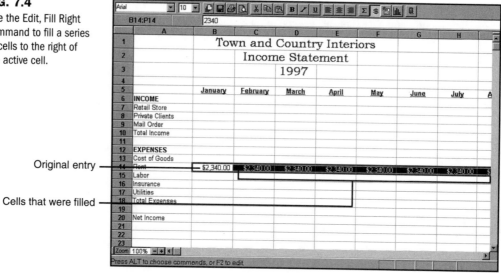

Original entry

Cells that were filled

3. Choose <u>E</u>dit, Fill Ri<u>g</u>ht or <u>E</u>dit, Fill Do<u>w</u>n. Works fills the range of cells you select with the entry in the first cell.

 TIP To quickly fill a range of cells that spans multiple columns or rows, select the range of cells, type the entry in the active cell, then press Ctrl+Enter.

When you want to fill a range of cells with a series of numbers, choose <u>E</u>dit, F<u>i</u>ll Series, which displays the Fill Series dialog box (see Figure 7.5).

FIG. 7.5

Fill Series offers many different options for filling cells.

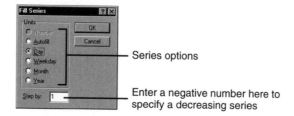

Series options

Enter a negative number here to specify a decreasing series

Use these steps to fill a range with a series:

1. Select the range of cells to fill.

2. In the active cell, type the first number in the series.

3. Choose <u>E</u>dit, F<u>i</u>ll Series, which displays the dialog box shown in Figure 7.5.

4. Choose the <u>N</u>umber option.

5. The <u>S</u>tep By box contains the number 1. To increment by a number other than 1, type a different number in the <u>S</u>tep By box.

6. Click OK.

Ch

7

Notice in Figure 7.5 that the Fill Series dialog box also contains options for Autofill, Day, Weekday, Month, and Year. This allows you to fill a range of cells with a series of days, weekdays, months, or years. For example, if you type Monday in the active cell and choose Autofill, Works enters Tuesday, Wednesday, Thursday, and so on for the range of cells you select. If you enter 7/21 (a Monday) and want Works to fill a series with dates for 4 more Mondays, you would choose the Day option and enter 7 in the Step By box. In this case, Works automatically fills in 7/28, 8/4, 8/11, 8/18 in the cell range you select. Or you might want to choose Weekday to fill a series of cells with weekday dates, automatically skipping weekends.

TIP To enter a series of dates, you must enter the first date in one of the following formats: 11/22/94; 11/22; 11/94; 22 November, 97; November, 1997; 22 November; November; or 1997.

Using Autofill

Autofill is a shortcut feature of Works that lets you fill cells without having to provide information in a dialog box. It works by highlighting a cell or range of cells, then dragging the mouse to fill a larger selected range of cells. Figure 7.6 shows an example of cells that were filled using Autofill.

FIG. 7.6
The Autofill feature filled these cells with data based on the original entries in row 3.

Original cells
Filled cells

Text entry
Numeric entry

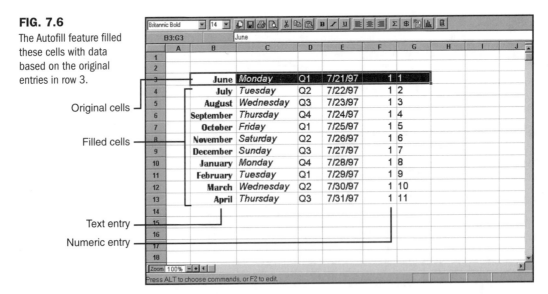

In the figure, the original entries were typed in row 3; rows 4 through 13 were filled downward using Autofill. Note the following explanation of how and why Works filled the cells as it did:

- B3 contains June, a valid date entry, formatted in the Britannic Bold font. Works filled B4:B13 with subsequent months in the same font.

- C3 contains Monday, a text entry, formatted in italic. Works filled C4:C13 with subsequent days formatted in italic.

- D3 contains Q3, a text entry. Because Works recognizes Q3 as a date (that is, Quarter 3), it filled D4:D13 with subsequent quarters (Q4, Q1, Q2, and so on).

- E3 contains 7/21/97, a valid numeric date format. Works filled E4:E13 with subsequent dates.

- F3 contains 1, a numeric entry. Works fills F4:F13 with the identical entry (just as if the Edit, Fill Down command had been used).

- G3 contains 1, entered as a *text* entry by preceding it with a quotation mark. Works fills G4:G13 with a series of numbers.

To use Autofill, follow these steps:

1. Select the cell or cells from which you want to fill a range.

2. Move the mouse pointer over the tiny square in the lower right corner of the selection until the pointer changes to cross and the word FILL appears (see Figure 7.7).

3. Drag the corner until all the cells you want to fill are highlighted.

4. Release the mouse button. Works automatically fills the cells based on the type of data the original cells contain.

FIG. 7.7
Autofill will fill these cells automatically.

Original entries

Selected cells to fill

Autofill mouse pointer

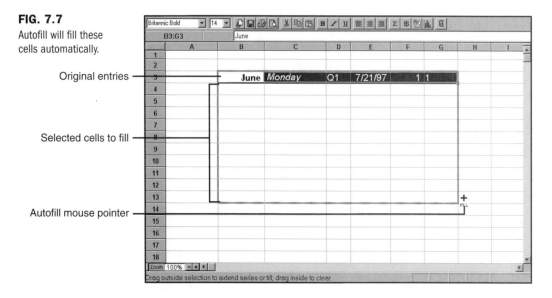

Ch
7

You can also use Autofill to fill cells with a series that increments at an interval greater than one unit (just as with the Edit, Fill Series command). You indicate the incremental value by typing the first few entries in the series. For instance, to fill cells with a series that increments by 5, type 5, 10, 15, in the first three cells, then use Autofill to fill the remainder of the series. Works "reads" the incremental value you have established by the first 3 entries and fills the range accordingly.

Adjusting Column Width

Works automatically sets the width of all columns in a new spreadsheet to 10 spaces. If 10 spaces is too wide, or too narrow, for the typical type of data you'll enter in the column, you can decrease or increase the width. For example, if your column contains the 2-letter code for states, such as CA or NY, you could narrow the width of that column. On the other hand, if the column includes phone numbers, including area code, 10 spaces is not adequate to display the entire entry and you might want to widen the column.

Works provides several methods for adjusting the width of columns. The quickest way is by dragging the column label border as described below:

1. Point to the border to the right of the column label until the mouse pointer changes to a left/right arrow labeled ADJUST (see Figure 7.8).

2. Hold down the mouse button and drag the column border right or left to adjust the column width.

3. Release the mouse button when the column is the size you want.

FIG. 7.8

It's easy to adjust column width by dragging the column border.

Mouse pointer —

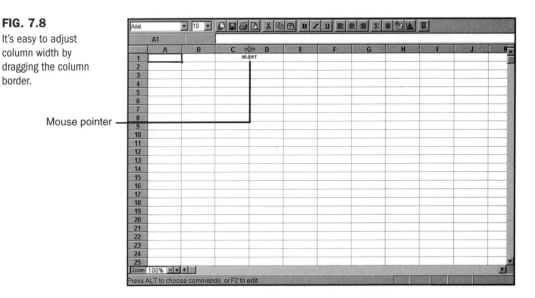

To size a column more precisely, you use the Format, Column Width command, which displays the Column Width dialog box shown in Figure 7.9. In the dialog box, you can specify an exact column width or you can have Works determine the best width based on the content of the cell.

To adjust column width using the Column Width dialog box, follow these steps:

1. Select any cell in the column you want to adjust. To adjust a column to the widest entry in the column, select the entire column. To adjust multiple columns at once, select multiple columns.

FIG. 7.9
The Column Width dialog box lets you specify column width or have Works determine the best fit.

2. Choose Format, Column Width. The Column Width dialog box in Figure 7.9 is displayed.

 T I P To display the Column Width dialog box quickly, right-click the mouse on the column label to display the shortcut menu, then choose Column Width.

3. In the Column Width text box, enter a number or select the Best Fit button to have Works determine an accurate column width. To set the column to 10, click the Standard button.

4. Choose OK. Works automatically adjusts the column width. (When you choose Best Fit, Works sizes the column to fit the entry in the active cell. If the entire column is selected, Works sets the column width to accommodate the widest entry in the column.)

 T I P To quickly adjust the column width for the widest entry in the entire column, double-click the column label. Works adjusts the column to accommodate the widest entry.

N O T E Works does not automatically readjust the column width if you change data in a column *after* sizing the column. To adjust the column for the new entry you type, you must double-click the column label or select the Best Fit option again in the Column Width dialog box. ■

Changing Cell Entries

Once you've created a spreadsheet file and entered data, you will inevitably want to change the data. You can change an entry in a cell by typing an entirely new entry or by changing a few characters in an existing entry.

To edit an entry, double-click the cell, or select the cell, then press F2. (Both methods display the Cancel and Enter buttons in the entry bar.) The cursor is displayed at the right end of the entry in the cell. Now use the arrow keys to move the cursor where you want to edit (see Figure 7.10). Another way to edit an entry is to select a cell, then click in the entry bar where you want to make the change. This method lets you position the cursor right away without using the arrow keys.

An alternative to editing or retyping an entry in a cell is to delete or clear a cell's contents. Here are three methods:

■ Select Edit, Cut; the Cut button on the toolbar; or Ctrl+X

Ch
7

FIG. 7.10
Position the cursor where you need to edit the entry.

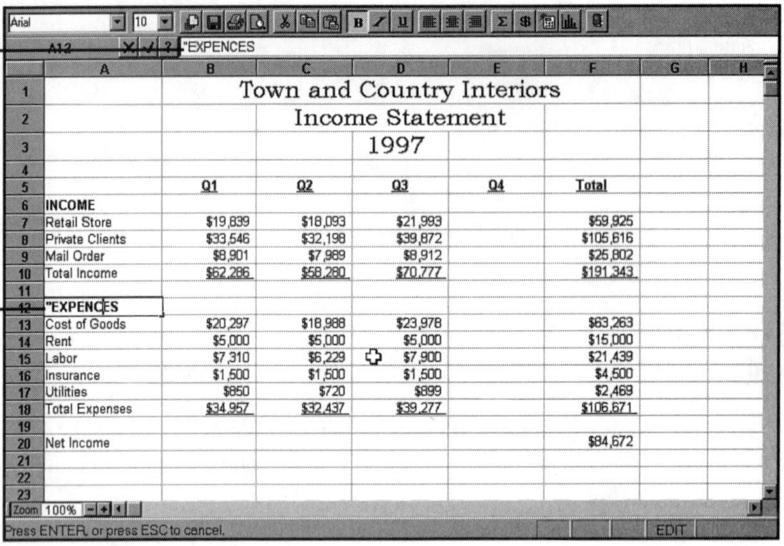

Position cursor here or here and edit the entry

- Use the Delete key on the keyboard
- Select Edit, Clear

What's the difference between the three methods? The Cut command places the entry on the Clipboard so you can paste it somewhere else if you like; Delete and Edit, Clear do not. When you use Delete or Edit, Clear, the only way to retrieve the entry is with Edit, Undo. Also, the Cut command removes any formatting from the cell as well. So if the cell is specially formatted, say in the Bodoni 16, bold, italic font and the entry was centered, all of this formatting is removed along with the entry if you use the Cut command. If you want to retain the formatting in the cell, use Delete or Edit, Clear.

Copying and Moving Cell Entries

The Edit, Copy command lets you copy identical data to a separate range of cells. Copying saves you the trouble of retyping identical entries in a spreadsheet and eliminates the possibility of errors while retyping. You can copy data from one or several cells in the *source* range to a *destination* range. Remember that when you copy data, the data remains unchanged in its source range and is duplicated in the destination range.

You can copy cell entries using menu commands (Copy and Paste on the Edit menu), the Copy and Paste toolbar buttons, or you can use the drag-and-drop method with the mouse. In any case, you select the source range, then place the cursor in the first cell in the destination ranges as shown in Figure 7.11.

To copy data, follow these steps:

1. Select the range of cells you want to copy.

FIG. 7.11

Entries in the source range will be copied to the cells in the destination range.

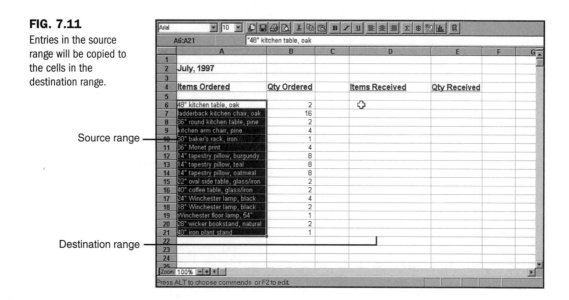

2. Choose <u>E</u>dit, <u>C</u>opy, or click the Copy button on the toolbar.

3. Click the first cell in the destination range.

4. Choose <u>E</u>dit, <u>P</u>aste, or click the Paste button on the toolbar. The selection is copied to the destination range of cells.

The drag-and-drop method of copying is illustrated in Figure 7.12. The outline of the cells is visible on the screen as you drag them. This makes it easier to see whether you're copying over existing data.

FIG. 7.12

When you use drag-and-drop to copy, you see the outline of cells as you drag the selection to a new location.

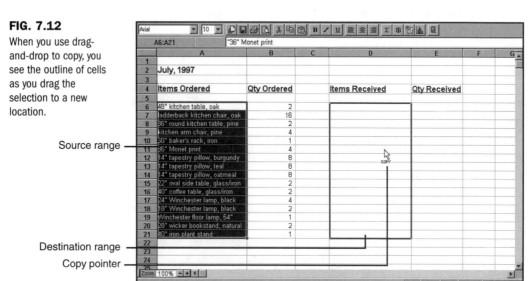

Ch

7

To copy data using the drag-and-drop method, use these steps:

1. Select the data to copy.

2. Move the mouse pointer over the border of the selection until the DRAG label appears.

3. Press and hold the Ctrl key, then begin dragging the selection to a new location. As you drag, the pointer label changes to COPY (see Figure 7.12) and the outline of the selection appears on the screen so you can see exactly where to place the selection.

4. Release the Ctrl key and the mouse button. The selection is copied to the new location.

 T I P You can use keyboard shortcuts Ctrl+C for Copy, and Ctrl+V for Paste in place of the menu commands or toolbar buttons.

CAUTION

Be sure the cells in the destination range are empty! If they contain data, they will be overwritten by the entries you copy.

Sometimes you might want to move selected spreadsheet data to a different location. The Edit, Cut command lets you remove data so it can be relocated to a separate range of cells, saving you the trouble of clearing data from one area and retyping the same information in another area. Just like when you copy data, you work with a source range and a destination range to move data.

To move data, follow these steps:

1. Select the cell or range of cells you want to move.

2. Choose Edit, Cut, and click the Cut button on the toolbar.

3. Click the first cell in the destination range.

4. Choose Edit, Paste, or click the Paste button on the toolbar. The selection is moved to the destination range of cells.

 T I P You can use the keyboard shortcut Ctrl+X for Cut in place of the menu command or toolbar button.

To use the drag-and-drop method to move data, do this:

1. Select the data to move.

2. Move the mouse pointer over the border of the selection until the DRAG label appears.

3. Press and hold the mouse button and begin dragging the selection to a new location. As you drag, the pointer label changes to MOVE (see Figure 7.13) and the outline of the selection appears on the screen so you can see exactly where to place the selection.

4. Release the mouse button. The selection is moved to the new location.

CAUTION

Be sure the cells in the destination range are empty! If they contain data, they will be overwritten by the entries you move.

FIG. 7.13

The selected cells are being dragged to the destination range.

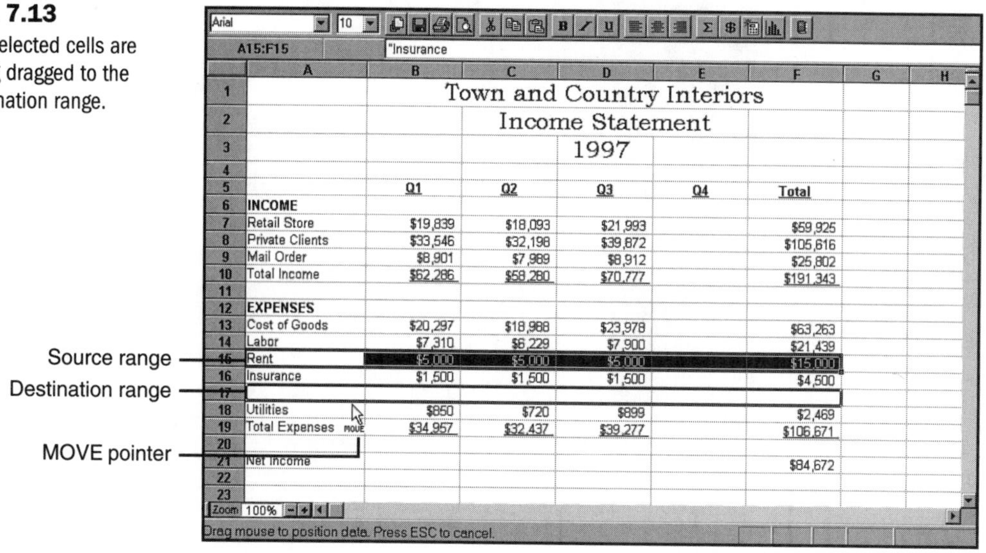

It's a good idea to check your spreadsheet carefully for errors immediately after you copy or paste data. It's possible to inadvertently overwrite existing data. If you find a problem, simply choose Edit, Undo Paste or press Ctrl+Z to undo the paste operation and try again.

▶ **See** "Undoing Changes," **p. 52**

Moving Rows and Columns

After you've created a spreadsheet, one of the most common changes is rearranging rows or columns, and *rearranging* is essentially *moving*. You usually rearrange to make a spreadsheet more readable or perhaps to place items in logical order.

Unlike when you move ranges of cells, when you move rows or columns in a spreadsheet, Works makes room for the moved data by *inserting* it. If you select column A to move it to column D, for example, Works doesn't overwrite column D. Instead, it inserts the data *before* column D and the remaining columns are shifted to the left to fill the void in column A. This process is easier to visualize than to describe in words. Figures 7.14 And 7.15 show the original spreadsheet and the results after moving column A.

When moving rows, Works operates the same way. The row you move is inserted above the new row you select, and the remaining rows are shifted to fill in the vacated row. It might seem

Ch

7

confusing that Works actually inserts rows or columns that you move, but the important thing to remember is that data is never overwritten when you move a row or column.

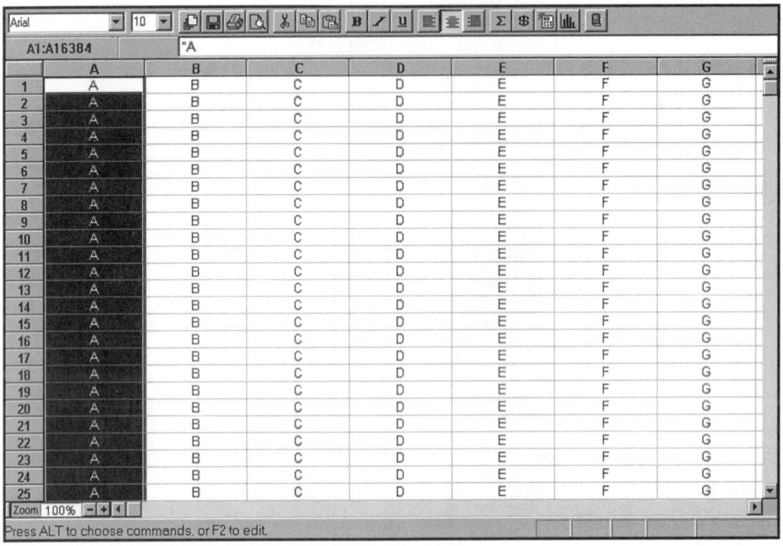

FIG. 7.14

Column A is selected to be moved to column D.

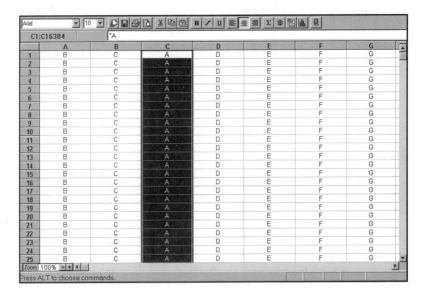

FIG. 7.15

Columns B and C are shifted to the left after column A is moved.

You can move rows or columns using these steps:

1. Select the row or column you want to move (or select all rows or columns you want to move).

2. Choose Edit, Cut; click the Cut button on the toolbar; or press Ctrl+X. Works removes the selected row or column from the spreadsheet and shifts the remaining rows or columns.

3. Select the cell at the beginning of the row or column where you want to move the data.

4. Choose Edit, Paste; click the Paste button on the toolbar; or press Ctrl+V. Works inserts the row above the row you select or the column before the column you select.

The drag-and-drop method is quicker and easier to visualize because Works gives you an on-screen cue in the form of a bold vertical or horizontal bar (see Figure 7.16).

FIG. 7.16
The column will be inserted to the left of the bold vertical bar.

Vertical bar

MOVE pointer

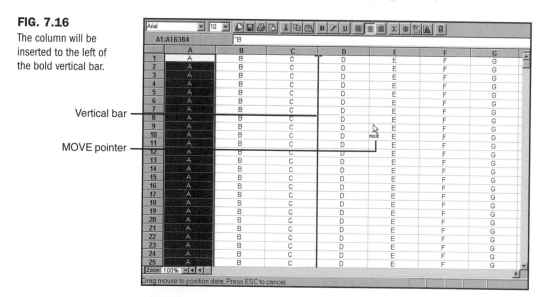

To use the drag-and-drop method to move rows or columns, follow these steps:

1. Select the row or column you want to move. To move multiple rows or columns, select all rows or columns you want to move at once.

2. Point to the selection border until the mouse pointer changes to an arrow labeled DRAG.

3. Press and hold the mouse button and drag the selection to its new location. The mouse pointer label changes to MOVE. As you drag, the bold vertical bar indicates where a column will be moved (see Figure 7.16); the bold horizontal bar indicates where a row will be moved.

4. Release the mouse button when the selection is properly positioned. Works shifts remaining rows and columns to fill the void left by the moved cells.

Inserting and Deleting Columns and Rows

As you build a spreadsheet, you often insert or delete rows or columns. When you insert a column, the existing columns are moved to the right; when you insert a row, Works moves the

Ch
7

existing rows of data down. Works automatically adjusts any formulas in the moved columns and rows.

To insert a row in a worksheet, follow these steps:

1. Select one cell or the entire row where you want to insert a new row.

2. Choose Insert, Insert Row. Works inserts a new row immediately above the row you selected in step 1.

To insert a new column in a worksheet, follow these steps:

1. Select one cell or the entire column where you want to insert a new column.

2. Choose Insert, Insert Column. Works inserts a new column immediately before the column you selected in step 1.

Deleting rows and columns in a spreadsheet is just as straightforward as inserting them. Here's how:

1. In the spreadsheet, select the row (or rows) or the column (or columns) to delete.

2. Choose Insert, Delete Row, or Insert, Delete Column. Works automatically deletes all selected rows or columns.

N O T E You can also use the Edit, Cut command or the Cut button on the toolbar to delete rows or columns. When you use Cut, the data is placed on the Clipboard so you can paste it in a different location if you like. When you use the Delete Row or Delete Column commands, the only way to retrieve the deleted data is to use Edit, Undo. ■

N O T E Deleting an entire row or column is different from deleting *data* in a row or column. To delete only the data in a column, simply select the cells, then press the Delete key. ■

Customizing the Spreadsheet Display

Works allows you to change some of the ways the spreadsheet behaves and is displayed to suit your personal preference. For example:

- You might not want zeros to be displayed when formulas result in zero.
- You might want to edit entries only in the cell rather than in the entry bar as well.
- You might choose to turn off drag-and-drop editing.
- You might want to change the default number of decimal places that are displayed in a spreadsheet when you enter numbers.

To configure Works with your spreadsheet preferences, choose Tools, Options, then click the Data Entry tab (see Figure 7.17).

In the Cell Data Entry Modes section of the dialog box you can choose the following options:

FIG. 7.17
You can control the behavior and appearance of many spreadsheet features in the Data Entry tab of the Options dialog box.

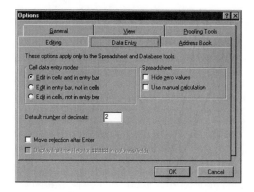

- *Edit In Cells And In Entry Bar* This option lets you edit the contents either in the cell or in the entry bar.

- *Edit In Entry Bar And Not In Cells* This option lets you edit only in the entry bar; the cursor is not available in the cell.

- *Edit In Cells And Not In Entry Bar* Choose this option if you prefer to edit an entry only in the cell. With this option, the entry bar is no longer displayed, which saves you some screen space.

In the Spreadsheet section, you can choose these options:

- *Hide Zero Values* When a formula result is zero, Works displays a 0 in the cell. To have Works display the cell as empty, choose this option.

- *Use Manual Calculation* In very large spreadsheets that contain a lot of formulas, the spreadsheet can begin to run very slow. This is because all formulas in the spreadsheet are recalculated each time you make a change like copying or moving. Use this option to temporarily turn off recalculation. You can recalculate at any time manually by pressing F9.

The following options are also available in the Data Entry tab of the Options dialog box:

- *Default Number Of Decimals* The default setting here causes Works to display two decimal places. If you typically work with spreadsheets that don't display decimal places, or display more than two decimal points, enter a different number here.

- *Move Selection After Enter* This is a timesaving device that automatically selects the cell below the current cell when you finish making an entry. (You can still click any cell to select it.)

- *Display First-Time Help For ##### In Columns/Fields* This option assures that the first time a numeric entry displays as ##### (because it is too long to display in the cell) a First-Time Help dialog box appears. In the dialog box you can get step-by-step instructions showing you how to display the number correctly.

A final option that controls several useful features is on the General tab in the Options dialog box. The Enable Drag-And-Drop Editing option, turned on by default, enables you to cut, copy, and paste by dragging the selection to a new location. If you prefer not to use this method, you can turn this feature off. (Note that turning off this feature also disables the Autofill feature.)

Ch

7

Printing a Spreadsheet

Chapter 2, "Getting Started with Works," includes an extensive section on printing Works documents. In general, all Works documents regardless of the type are printed the same way. That is, you set margins, paper source, paper size, print orientation, and starting page numbers using the File, Page Setup command (which displays the Page Setup dialog box). When all settings are correct, you preview the document, then print.

▶ **See** "Printing a Document," **p. 22**

The default margin settings (1 inch for top and bottom margins and 1.25 inches for left and right margins) are generally fine for most documents, but for some spreadsheets, you might want to change these settings in order to fit more data on a page. Also, when you print a range of cells that is smaller than a single page (see "Printing a Portion of a Spreadsheet"), you might want to change the margins to center the material on the page for a more pleasing appearance.

Another setting you're likely to change when printing a spreadsheet is the orientation. Often spreadsheets fit better and look better when printed "sideways" on a page, which requires you to change the standard orientation from *portrait* to *landscape*.

▶ **See** "Choosing Paper Source, Size, and Orientation," **p. 22**

Printing Special Features of a Spreadsheet

Spreadsheets contain two unique features that other documents don't have: gridlines and row and column *headers*, or labels. The printing of these two features is controlled by the Other Options tab in the Page Setup dialog box (see Figure 7.18).

FIG. 7.18
The Other Options tab displays useful print settings for spread-sheets.

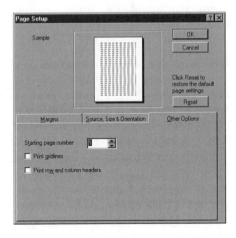

Works does not automatically print the gridlines that appear on the screen when you print a spreadsheet. However, gridlines can often make a spreadsheet easier to follow as you're reading. To print gridlines, select the Print Gridlines check box and then choose OK.

Printing row numbers and column labels (Works calls these headers) can also make a spreadsheet easier to read. This option is helpful when you are still making changes to a spreadsheet and printing draft copies as you work. The row and column headers can help you find the right cell when you go back to the screen to make corrections. To use this option, select the Print Row and Column headers check box, then choose OK.

Printing a Portion of a Spreadsheet

Often, you don't need to print an entire spreadsheet—only a portion of it. Printing a selected portion of a spreadsheet is a very useful feature, especially when a spreadsheet becomes rather large.

The portion of a spreadsheet that you print is called the *print area*. Normally, the print area includes all cells in the spreadsheet. When you want to print only a portion of a spreadsheet, however, you specify a different print area. To set the print area, use these steps:

1. Select the cells you want to include in the print area.
2. Choose Format, Set Print Area. Works displays a dialog box asking you to confirm the current selection as the print area.
3. Choose OK.

When you define a print area, Works assigns the range name `Print Area` to the cells you select. When you're ready to print the file, Works prints only those cells in the designated print area.

▶ **See**, "Listing Range Names," **p. 153**

To change the print area, you can either define a new print area using the previous steps or simply delete the current print area range name. To delete the print area range name, use the following steps:

1. Choose Insert, Range Name. Works displays the Range Name dialog box.
2. In the Select a name list, select Print Area and then choose the Delete button. Works removes Print Area from the list of range names.
3. Choose the Close command to close the Range Name dialog box.

Ch

7

Working with Formulas and Functions

Now that you've learned the ins and outs of a spreadsheet, you're ready to put it to work for you doing calculations. ■

Entering simple formulas that use basic math

These are some of the simplest calculations you'll make, but they are also the most common.

How formulas work and how to create them

Formulas calculate differently depending on the cells they reference. You'll learn how to specify the correct cell references.

Using AutoSum and Easy Calc to create formulas quickly and easily

As with all the tools in Works, the spreadsheet has its own time-saving tools. You'll learn to use AutoSum for quick addition and Easy Calc to help you build formulas when you're just starting out.

Moving, coping, and deleting formulas or data

You'll learn what happens in the spreadsheet as a result of these common editing changes.

Inserting functions in formulas

Functions save you the time of creating formulas from scratch and help ensure accuracy.

Naming a range of cells

Using familiar names for cell ranges makes formulas easier to work with and interpret.

Entering Simple Formulas

The power of spreadsheets is in their ability to perform mathematical calculations using *formulas*. A formula is an equation that performs a calculation on one or more values and returns a result. You use formulas to perform basic arithmetic calculations such as addition, subtraction, multiplication, and division. Or, using *functions*, you can perform more complex calculations. A function is a prepared equation designed to perform a specific task, such as calculating the periodic payment for a loan. Rather than creating the formula yourself, you use a function. You learn about using functions later in this chapter.

Figure 8.1 shows an example of a simple spreadsheet that doesn't include any formulas. Income and Expenses in columns B, C, and D need to be totaled.

FIG. 8.1

Enter formulas in cells B10:D10 and cells B18:D18 to sum the columns.

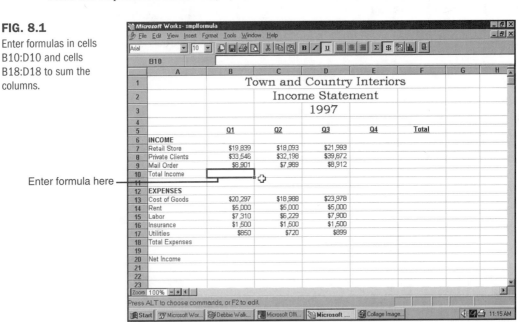

Works uses the equal symbol (=) to denote the beginning of a formula. You follow this symbol with a combination of values, cell references, and arithmetic operators including:

- plus (+) for addition
- minus (-) for subtraction
- slash (/) for division
- asterisk (*) for multiplication

The formula =B8*12 multiplies the value in cell B8 by 12 and displays the result in the cell where the formula is located (it could be located anywhere in the spreadsheet). In Figure 8.1, cells B10, C10, and D10 need formulas that will total the income figures for Q1, Q2, and Q3. The formula in cell B10 should read =B7+B8+B9.

You can create simple summation formulas using a variety of methods. You can type the cell references and operators—in this example, type **=B7+B8+B9** in cell B10. However, typing cell references can lead to errors. A faster and more accurate way to create the formula is to "point" to the cells using the arrow keys. Using this method, Works "reads" the values in the cells you point to. Here's how pointing works:

1. Select the cell where you want to create the formula and press the = key.

2. Using the up-arrow key, highlight the first cell you want added in the formula, then type a plus symbol. The highlight jumps back to the original cell and the address of the cell you selected is added to the formula.

3. Use the up-arrow key to highlight the second cell you want to add, then type a plus symbol. Again, the highlight jumps back to the original cell and the address of the cell you selected is added to the formula.

4. Repeat step 3 until all cells are included in the formula, then press Enter.

When you press Enter, the formula is complete and the result of the formula appears in the original cell (see Figure 8.2). The formula itself is shown in the entry bar rather than the calculated result.

FIG. 8.2

The result appears in the cell and the entry bar displays the formula.

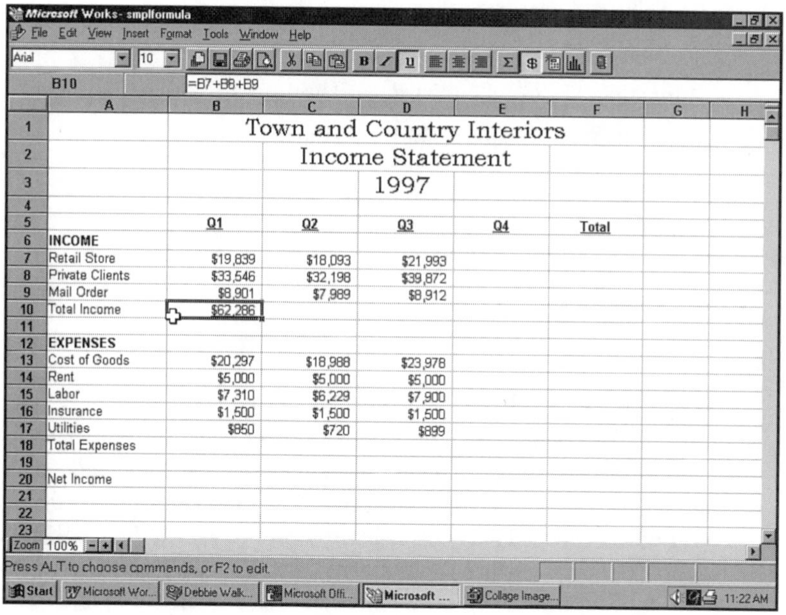

If you prefer, you can use the mouse rather than the arrow keys to point to the cells you want to include in a formula. Just follow the steps above but click the mouse on the cells you want to include in the formula instead of using the arrow keys.

Once entered in the spreadsheet, formulas are recalculated every time you make an entry or edit data in the spreadsheet. If you change values in the cells referenced by the formula, the formula recalculates and immediately displays the new result in the cell.

Spreadsheet formulas are often more complex than the simple summation formula you just saw. Formulas can contain many cell references, constant values, operators, and parentheses, such as in a formula like $=(3*4^3)-3*(D18*A4)+(3*E7)+25$. Granted, this formula is more complex than a simple addition formula, but the important thing to remember is that it is created in exactly the same way: either by typing cell references or pointing to them, then adding operators where appropriate.

Works uses standard algebraic rules to evaluate a formula, including evaluating values in parentheses first. For example, in the formula $=(C13+5)*35/E4$, C13+5 is evaluated before the rest of the formula. When parentheses are nested, the innermost set of parentheses is evaluated first. Operators are evaluated in the order shown in Table 8.1.

Table 8.1   Operators and Their Order of Evaluation

Operator	Order of Evaluation
- (negative) and + (positive)	First
^ (exponent)	Second
* (multiplication) and / (division)	Third
+ (addition) and - (subtraction)	Fourth
=, <>, <, >, <=, >=	Fifth
#NOT#	Sixth
#OR#, #AND#	Seventh

Using AutoSum

Because spreadsheets so often include formulas that sum columns of numbers, Works includes a handy toolbar button called AutoSum. It uses the SUM function, which automatically sums the values in the specified range of cells. The AutoSum button is intelligent; it looks for values near the current cell that look as if they could be added, then highlights them as the suggested cell range to sum. For example, if cells C5:C14 contain values, and you choose AutoSum in cell C15, it assumes you want to sum the values in the column (range C5:C14). If cells A2:A11 contain values and you choose AutoSum in cell A12, it assumes you want to sum the values in the row (A2:A11). An AutoSum function looks like this:

    =SUM(B7:B9)

Later in this chapter you learn about using other functions in Works in the section "Using Formulas and Functions."

You already know that the equal symbol denotes the beginning of the formula. The SUM part of the formula is the name of the function being used, and the cells referenced in parentheses are the range of cells whose values will be totaled.

To use AutoSum, follow these steps:

1. Select the cell where you want the formula result to appear.

2. Click the AutoSum button on the toolbar, or press Ctrl+M. Works highlights the range of cells it thinks you want to total and places a formula like =SUM(B7:B9) in the current cell. The cells referenced in the parentheses are the cells Works highlights (see Figure 8.3).

3. If the cell range is correct, press Enter or click the AutoSum button again to complete the formula. Works displays the result in the active cell and the formula appears in the entry bar.

To find the appropriate range to sum, AutoSum first looks above the current cell, then looks to the left. AutoSum works even if there are one or more blank cells between the highlighted cell and the range of values. If a range is not found, =SUM() appears in the cell and the entry bar. Enter the correct cell range in the parentheses to complete the formula.

FIG. 8.3
AutoSum highlights cells to sum and displays the formula in the current cell.

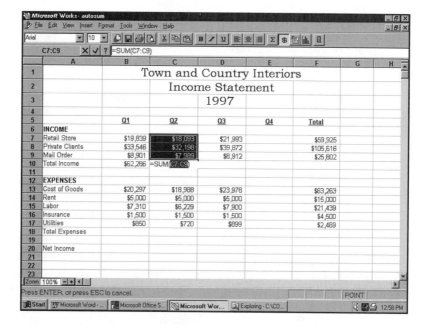

TIP If you get the message Missing Operand, your formula ends with an operator (such as +, -, *, /) instead of an operand. An *operand* is a number or a cell reference. To correct the error, remove the final operator from the formula, or add an operand following the operator.

Understanding Relative and Absolute Cell Addressing

Suppose cell D17 contains the formula =D14–D15, where the value in D15 is subtracted from the value in D14, and the result is displayed in D17. The cell references in this formula are called *relative* references because Works doesn't interpret them literally. What the formula actually means is "find the value in the cell two rows up and subtract it from the value in the cell three rows up, then display the result here."

A formula that uses relative addresses "follows directions" to find the values on which to calculate a result. It is this feature that allows you to copy a formula (such as the one above) across a number of columns and have it calculate correctly; that is, calculate on the correct cells in each column. For example, if you copy the formula **=D14-D15** from cell D17 to E17, Works automatically changes the formula to **=E14-E15** and calculates a result in cell E17 based on the values found in those cells.

Sometimes in a spreadsheet it's important that a formula calculate using values in specific cells. In this case, you create a formula with *absolute* references. Figures 8.4 and 8.5 illustrate why you need to use absolute cell references in some formulas.

The worksheet in Figure 8.4 lists a markup percentage (200%) in cell B4. Column B shows wholesale prices for the items listed in column A. The retail price (calculated by multiplying the retail price by a markup percentage) is displayed in column C. In cell C9, the formula is =B9*B4, which translates to $350*200%. This formula calculates the correct retail price in cell C9. For this cell, the formula really says: "find the value in the cell one column to the left ($350) and multiply it by the value in the cell one column to the left and five rows up (200%)." As you see in this example, when the formula is given the correct addresses for the values it operates on, it calculates correctly.

Now, suppose you copy the formula to C10, thinking it will multiply $59 (in B10) by 200% (in B4). The formula no longer calculates correctly (see Figure 8.5). With relative cell addressing, the formula in C10 now reads **=B10*B5**, which is incorrect. This formula really says: "Find the value in the cell one column to the left ($59) and multiply it by the value in the cell one column to the left and five rows up (cell B5)." Because there is no value in cell B5, the formula evaluates to zero.

If you copied the formula from C9 all the way through cell C16, it would start multiplying retail prices by retail prices rather than by the markup percentage—all because of the relative cell addresses. Formula errors like these can lead to disastrous results in a spreadsheet. You can correct this problem by using an *absolute* cell reference in the formulas. That is, you want to multiply *all* of the retail prices in Column B by the 200% markup percentage shown in cell B4, so the reference to cell B4 in all formulas must be an absolute reference.

FIG. 8.4

The formula in cell C9 calculates the correct result for the price of the merchandise.

Formula   Formula result

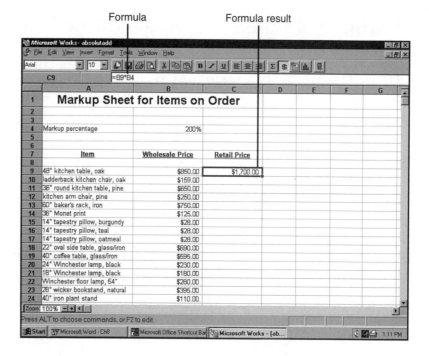

FIG. 8.5

When copied to C10, the formula from C9 is incorrect and evaluates to zero.

Formula is incorrect   Formula result is incorrect

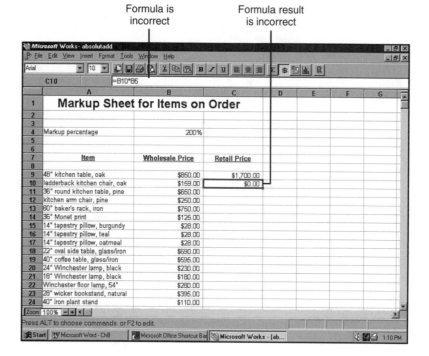

Creating Formulas with Absolute Cell References

To create a formula with absolute cell references, you must insert dollar signs preceding the column and row references. For example, to make the formula =B9*B4 *always* reference cell B4, the formula should read **=B9*B4**. The dollar sign preceding the B "locks" the cell reference to column B; the dollar sign preceding the 4 locks the reference to row 4. A locked cell reference is what Works refers to as an *absolute* reference. This means that if you copy the formula from cell C9 to cell C10, it now reads **=B10*B4**, which is exactly how you want it to read. If you copy the formula to C11, it reads **=B11*B4**. Now you can copy this formula from C10 through C16, and the retail prices will be calculated correctly. Figure 8.6 shows the results.

FIG. 8.6

An absolute cell reference causes all copied formulas to calculate correctly.

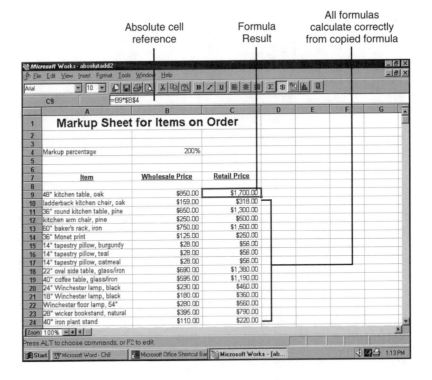

It is also possible to create a *mixed* cell reference, such as **$B4** or **B$4**. In a mixed cell reference, only one reference— either the row or the column—is absolute; the other is relative. For example, $B4 makes column B absolute but row 4 is still relative. The reference B$4 is just the opposite—column B is relative but row 4 is absolute.

You can create formulas with absolute or mixed cell references by typing the cell references, including the dollar signs. To be sure your cell references are accurate, however, it's often best to create a formula with relative references by pointing to the correct cells, and then adding the dollar signs when you edit the formula.

An alternative to typing dollar signs is to insert them using the F4 key. When you're creating a formula and point to a cell to reference it, such as C3, the cell reference is shown in the entry bar. Press F4 once to make the cell reference absolute. If you press F4 repeatedly, Works cycles through the following list of absolute, mixed, and relative references, creating them automatically for you:

Press F4 once	C3
Press F4 twice	C$3
Press F4 three times	$C3
Press F4 four times	C3

When you're sure all cell references are accurate, finish the formula by inserting operators and parentheses as you normally would.

Using the F4 key works only when entering the formula in the entry bar or when using Easy Calc, which is described later in this chapter. You cannot use F4 when editing a formula to change or add another cell reference.

Moving Formulas and Cells Referenced by Formulas

Unlike copying formulas, when you *move* a formula in a spreadsheet, Works does not change any of the cell references in the formula. This is based on the principle that you still want to perform the same calculations regardless of the location of the formula. If, for example, you move the formula =B10*B4 from cell C10 to cell K32, the formula still reads =B10*B4. You still want the formula to calculate a result on the same values, it's only the *location of the result* that you have changed.

However, when you change the location of *data* in a spreadsheet, Works changes the cell references in the formula if the references are to specific cells. Again, Works assumes that you still want to perform the same calculation, but the data is now located in a different cell, so the cell reference in the formula must also change. For example, if you move the value of 200% in cell B4 to cell B3 (refer to Figures 8.4 through 8.6), Works changes the reference in the formula from =B10*B4 to =B10*B3. This change ensures that the same calculation is performed now that the data (200%) is located in a different cell.

The exception to this is if the cells referenced in the formula are a *range* of cells. If, for example, the cell C11 contains the formula =SUM(C3:C10) and you move the contents of cell C7 to another location, Works does not change the cell range referenced in the formula; it assumes you still want to sum the values in cells C3 through C10. If, however, you move the data in C3 or C10—the cells that define the boundaries of the range—Works changes the formula. Check the original formula carefully to make sure any changes in the formula give correct results.

CAUTION

Whenever you move data or formulas in a spreadsheet, double-check all formulas and results carefully to make sure they are still accurate.

Copying Formulas and Cells Referenced by Formulas

When you want a formula to perform the same type of calculation on different data, you copy the formula from one location to another. In Figure 8.7, for example, you save yourself the trouble of recreating formulas if you copy the formula in cell B10, =SUM(B7:B9), to cells C10 through F10. Copying the formula to this range calculates total income for quarters 2, 3, and 4 as well as the yearly total. To get accurate results for each column, Works adjusts all relative cell references from the original formula in B10. Once copied, the formula in C10 reads =SUM(C7:C9); the formula in D10 reads +SUM(D7:D9), and so on.

Formula to copy

FIG. 8.7
When copied to C10 through F10, the formula in B10 calculates accurately.

Formula Result

Range to which formula will be copied

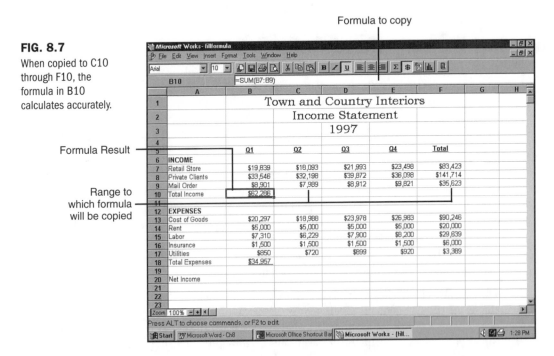

CAUTION

When you copy a formula that contains absolute cell references, such as C9*B4, the relative part of the formula (C9) is automatically adjusted, but the absolute portion of the formula (B4) remains unchanged.

Clearing and Deleting Cells That Are Referenced in a Formula

If you delete the contents of a cell, the value of that cell becomes zero. If that cell is referenced by a formula, the formula remains unchanged and calculates on the new value of zero. Deleting a value in a cell is no different than changing the value to 2 or 2000. Zero is a value just like any other value, and the formula, which remains unchanged, continues to calculate on the values referenced in the formula.

Removing a row or column from the spreadsheet, however, produces different results. If you delete a row or column that contains a cell specifically referenced by a formula, the formula displays ERR. Because the formula doesn't know where to find the cell—the original cell reference doesn't exist anymore— it can't calculate correctly. In the entry bar, the missing value is substituted with ERR as well, which helps you pinpoint the error quickly. You must edit or replace the ERR in the formula so it can calculate correctly.

When a formula refers to a cell *range* (such as =SUM(C2:C10)) rather than a specific cell, and you delete a row or column in that range, the formula itself does not change, nor is an ERR displayed. The formula simply recalculates based on the now absent data. In this case, Works assumes you still want the formula to calculate on the range, whether a column or row is deleted or not.

Using Easy Calc

In this chapter, you've seen how easy it is to create simple formulas when you remember to begin each formula with an equal symbol. You might appreciate some help creating more complex formulas, however. Until you become comfortable writing formulas, the Easy Calc Wizard is available to help you build formulas. Figure 8.8 shows the Easy Calc dialog box.

▶ **See** "Using TaskWizards," **p 31**

FIG. 8.8

In Easy Calc, you only have to choose the type of formula to create and provide the values.

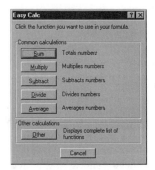

The Easy Calc dialog box provides buttons to Sum, Multiply, Subtract, Divide, or Average the values you want to use. For more complex calculations, you can choose <u>O</u>ther to use a function in your formula. (For more information on functions, see "Using Functions in Formulas," next in this chapter.)

To use Easy Calc to insert a formula in a spreadsheet, follow these steps:

1. Select the cell in which you want to display the result.
2. Choose <u>T</u>ools, <u>E</u>asy Calc or click the Easy Calc button on the toolbar. The Easy Calc dialog box in Figure 8.8 is displayed.
3. From the Common Calculations list, choose <u>S</u>um, <u>M</u>ultiply, S<u>u</u>btract, <u>D</u>ivide, or <u>A</u>verage.
4. Follow the instructions provided on the screen.

N O T E   If the Easy Calc dialog box is in your way, move the dialog box by dragging the title bar to a different location on the screen. ■

5. Choose <u>F</u>inish. Works displays the formula's result in the current cell.

Using Functions in Formulas

You already know that *functions* are prepared equations designed to make it easier for you to create formulas in a spreadheet. Functions perform common tasks like finding the sum of a range of numbers (SUM). They can also perform complex tasks like finding the net present value of an investment based on constant future cash flows (NPV). Save yourself the trouble of creating a complex formula by inserting a function in your spreadsheet. Works contains 76 built-in functions. You select functions from the Function dialog box (see Figure 8.9), which is displayed when you choose <u>I</u>nsert, <u>F</u>unction. The available functions cover a broad range of categories, including financial, logical, statistical, mathematical, and trigonometric.

Functions have two parts: the function name, and one or more *arguments*. Arguments represent the values upon which the function operates. You replace the arguments in a function with one of the following:

■ a constant
■ a reference to a cell that contains a value
■ a reference to a cell that generates a value
■ a range of cells
■ a named range (named ranges are discussed later in this chapter)

When you insert a function in a spreadsheet, Works inserts an equal sign, the function name, then the arguments enclosed in parentheses. Arguments are separated by commas and no spaces. For example, the present value function, before you replace the arguments, looks like this:

PV(payment,rate,term)

After you substitute the arguments with values or cell references, the formula might look like this:

=PV(25000,7.75%,4)

Or this:

=PV(C2,C6,C3)

N O T E   A few functions, such as PI and NOW, do not accept arguments; however, the open and close parentheses still follow the name of the function. When you use one of these functions, leave the parentheses empty. ■

If you know the required arguments for a function, you can type them in the cell, but the easiest way to insert a function in a spreadsheet is to use the Insert, Function command, which displays the dialog box shown in Figure 8.8. The dialog box displays a list of function categories. The Choose a Function list box lists specific function names and their arguments. If you're not sure what a function does, check the Description box, which gives a brief description of the purpose of the function that's currently selected.

To insert a function in a spreadsheet, follow these steps:

1. Select the cell where you want the function result to be displayed.

2. Choose Insert, Function, or click the Easy Calc button, then choose Other. The Insert Function dialog box in Figure 8.9 is displayed.

FIG. 8.9

The Choose a Function list box shows an alphabetized list of functions for the selected Category.

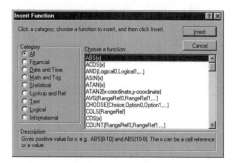

3. From the Category list, choose a category.

4. In the Choose a Function list box, highlight the function you want to use.

5. Click the Insert button. Works inserts the function, including all of its arguments, in the current cell. The equal symbol precedes the function. In the cell, the first argument is highlighted.

6. Replace each argument with a value or cell reference, then press Enter or click the Enter button in the entry bar. Works displays the function result in the current cell.

 TIP You can highlight subsequent arguments automatically by entering the value or cell reference for the first argument, then pressing Enter twice. The first time you press Enter an error message appears, the second time you press Enter, Works highlights and the next argument so you can replace it. Repeat this process for each argument name until you replace all arguments.

If you make an error as you enter a function, Works displays an error message. When you click OK or press Enter, Works highlights the error in the entry bar so you can correct it.

Using and Creating Range Names

Works allows you to assign a *range name* to a cell or range of cells. Using a range name, you can identify cells by a familiar name rather than a cell reference like C14:F18 or K37. This allows you to create more "natural language" types of formulas. You can include a range name in a formula just like you use cell references. Using range names makes a formula easier to create as well as interpret. The formula =Total Income-Total Expenses is much more descriptive than the formula =F10-F18. In the spreadsheet shown in Figure 8.10, you might consider naming cells B7:B9 "Q1 Income" and cells B13:B17 "Q1 Expenses." Or you might name cells B10:E10 "Total Income" and cells B17:E17 "Total Expenses."

FIG. 8.10

A number of ranges in this example can be named to simplify creating formulas.

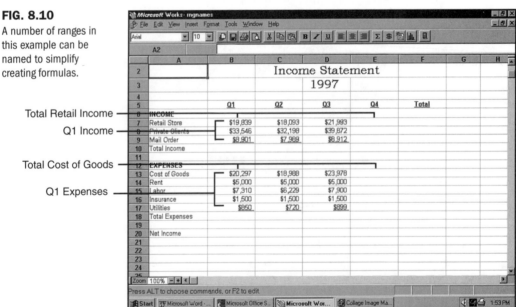

When you have defined range names, Works recognizes them when you use functions such as AutoSum. For instance, the formula in B10 (see Figure 8.11) is =SUM(Q1 Income). Without the range name Q1 Income, Works would insert B7:B9 in the formula. With a range name defined, Works automatically inserts the range name rather than the cell range.

FIG. 8.11

Formulas that use range names are easier to interpret than those with cell references.

Range name used in formula

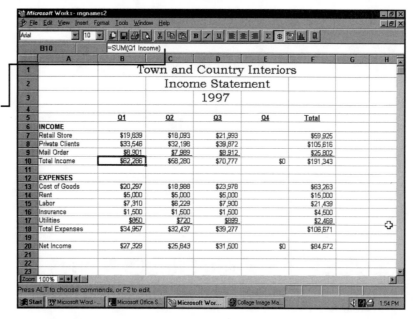

There are other advantages to naming ranges:

■ If you type a *range name* incorrectly in a formula, Works displays an error message. But if you reference the wrong *cell* in a formula, Works doesn't know the difference and has not way to alert you to the error.

■ Using the Edit, Go To command, you can move to a range name quickly when you want to find it.

You can name a single cell or any range of cells in a worksheet. Range names can be up to 15 characters and can include any combination of letters, numbers, spaces, and other symbols like *, #, and +. You can also use any combination of upper- and lowercase letters.

CAUTION

Avoid using the symbols +, -, *, and / in a range name. Because these symbols are operators for formulas, they could cause errors in a formula.

To name a range of cells, follow these steps:

1. Select the cell or cell range you want to name.

2. Choose Insert, Range Name. The Range Name dialog box in Figure 8.12 is displayed.

3. In the Name box, enter a name for the selected cell or range.

4. Choose OK. Works adds the new name to the Select A Name list and closes the dialog box.

FIG. 8.12
Use the Range Name dialog box to list all existing names and create new ones.

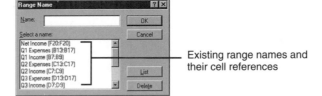

Existing range names and their cell references

 TIP If you need to print portions of a worksheet, consider naming each area so you can set the print area easily. Refer to Chapter 7, "Creating, Saving, and Printing a Spreadsheet."

Changing and Deleting Range Names

Occasionally you might name the wrong range of cells. You can change the range of cells that the name refers to by following these steps:

1. Select the new cell or cell range you want to use for an existing named range.

2. Choose Insert, Range Name. The Range Name dialog box in Figure 8.12 appears.

3. In the Select a Name list box, highlight the named range you want to change.

4. Click OK. Works automatically adjusts the cell reference for the named range.

If the cell range is correct but you want to change the range name, use these steps:

1. Select the cell range you want to rename.

2. Choose Insert, Range Name. The Range Name dialog box in Figure 8.12 appears.

3. In the Select a Name list box, highlight the named range you want to change.

4. In the Name box, edit the range name.

5. Click OK. Works automatically renames the range without changing the cell references.

If you make extensive changes to the data in a spreadsheet, you might find that you no longer need some of the named ranges you created.

You can delete a range name at any time using these steps:

1. Choose Insert, Range Name. The Range Name dialog box in Figure 8.12 appears.
2. In the Select a Name list box, highlight the named range you want to delete.
3. Click Delete. Works deletes the range name and removes it from the list.

NOTE You can't use Edit, Undo to, restore a deleted name. ■

NOTE If you delete a range name, formulas that used that range name still calculate correctly. Works automatically replaces the range name in the formula with the actual cell reference. ■

Listing Range Names

When you begin to recognize the value of naming cell ranges, you might find yourself creating many range names in a single spreadsheet. You can use a blank area of your spreadsheet in which to list range names. If you want a printed copy of range names and the cells they reference, you can print that area of the spreadsheet.

To create a list of range names, do this:

1 Choose a blank area of the spreadsheet where the list will fit without overwriting other data in the spreadsheet. Select the cell where you want the list to begin.
2. Choose Insert, Range Name, then click the List button. Works inserts a two-column list like the one in Figure 8.13.

NOTE If the area you choose contains data, Works displays an error message asking if it's okay to overwrite the existing data. If not, choose Cancel, then select a new area of the spreadsheet in which to list range names. ■

FIG. 8.13

Use the List button in the Range Name dialog box to paste a list of range names into your spreadsheet.

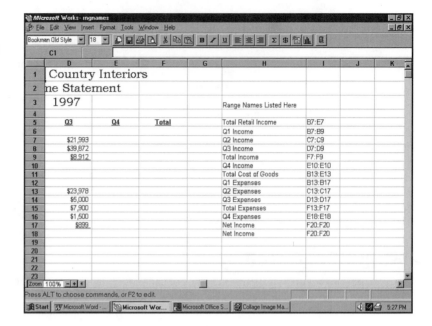

CHAPTER 9

Searching, Sorting, and Changing the Look of a Spreadsheet

Searching a spreadsheet

Just as in the word processor, in the spreadsheet you can search for specific entries that you might want to replace.

Sorting a spreadsheet

You can sort a spreadsheet in many different ways to make the data useful for the particular task you're currently performing.

Formatting numbers and aligning data

These are important features in a spreadsheet that make it much easier to read and interpret.

Choosing enhancement features for your spreadsheet

Fonts, styles, colors, borders, and patterns contribute significantly to the overall appearance of a spreadsheet as well as its readability.

Add headers and footers

Just as in word processor documents, the top and bottom of spreadsheet pages can include a title, file name, date, page number, or other useful information.

Now that you've mastered entering and editing data and creating formulas in spreadsheets, you're ready to perform certain functional tasks, such as searching and sorting. These tasks allow you to find and work with data in ways that are most useful to you. You also discover how to use formatting characteristics to enhance a spreadsheet, making it easier to read, easier to find and distinguish information, as well as making it more polished and professional-looking. ■

Finding and Replacing Entries in a Spreadsheet

In Chapter 4, you learned how to search for text in a word processor document and replace it with new text. You can use this same feature in the Spreadsheet tool to find text or a specific value, or to find cells, cell ranges, or range names referenced in a formula. When you find the information you're looking for, you can replace it with new information if you choose.

Use Edit, Find to locate specific text or a value in a spreadsheet. Use Edit, Replace to find the text or value you specify and replace all occurrences or the occurrences you select with a new entry. Both the Find and Replace commands give you the option of searching a spreadsheet by rows or by columns. When you choose to search by rows, Works searches left to right through the spreadsheet one row at a time. If the entry you're looking for is located near the top of the spreadsheet, choose to search by rows. When you choose to search by columns, Works searches a spreadsheet from top to bottom, one column at a time. If the entry you're looking for is located in the first few columns of the spreadsheet, choosing the columns option may help you find the information more quickly.

In the Find dialog box (see Figure 9.1), you choose whether you want Works to search the formulas of a spreadsheet or its values. Choose the Look In Formulas option if you're looking for any of the following items:

- a specific formula, such as =SUM(B2:B9)
- a cell reference used in a formula (such as B2:B9 in the formula =SUM(B2:B9))
- a range name used in a formula, such as =Total Income-Total Expenses

In all cases, Works finds the *cell* where the formula is located, where the cell reference is used in a formula, or where the range name is used in a formula. Works *does not* find a cell range or a range name and highlight the range. To find and highlight a cell range, use the Edit, Go To command.

▶ **See** "Using Go To," **p. 116**

To find a value or text in a spreadsheet, choose the Look In Values option in the Find dialog boxes. If you're looking for a number like 10,398 that is formatted with a comma, be sure to include the comma in your search; otherwise, Works won't find the entry. (You don't need to include other formatting such as dollar signs.)

You don't have to type the complete entry; you can enter only part of a value or formula and Works will still find the entry. For example, if you enter **10,3** instead of 10,398, Works will highlight the cell where 10,398 is located. If your spreadsheet contains the formula =SUM(Q1 Income) and you enter **(Q1 Inco**, Works will find the cell that contains the formula. Or, if you enter **Town and**, Works will find Town and Country Interiors.

To find text, a value, or a cell or range reference in a spreadsheet without replacing it, follow these steps:

1. Select the range of cells you want to search (or select no cells to search the entire spreadsheet).

FIG. 9.1

Find any text or value in a spreadsheet's cells or formulas using the Find dialog box.

Ch

9

2. Choose Edit, Find, or press Ctrl+F. The Find dialog box shown in Figure 9.1 is displayed.

3. In the Find What text box, type the text, value, or cell reference to search for.

4. Under Search options, choose By Rows or By Columns.

5. From the Look In options, choose Values or Formulas.

6. Choose OK. Works finds the first occurrence in the spreadsheet.

When Works finds the formula or value you're looking for, it highlights the first cell where the formula or value is displayed and closes the Find dialog box. If Works doesn't find the value, it displays the message *Works did not find a match*.

N O T E   If there are multiple occurrences of an entry and you want to find each one (whether you want to replace them or not) use the Edit, Replace command, which keeps the dialog box open and allows you to keep searching the spreadsheet using the Find Next command. ▪

When you want to find an entry and replace it, choose the Edit, Replace command, which displays the Replace dialog box shown in Figure 9.2. In this dialog box, you specify the text or value you're looking for as well as the replacement text or value. If Works finds the text or value you specify, it highlights the first occurrence. (The Replace dialog box remains open on the screen so you can continue searching and replacing.) You can choose to replace all occurrences of the text you're looking for (using the Replace All button), you can select specific occurrences to replace (using the Replace button), or you can skip the occurrence and go on to the next (using the Find Next button). If you change your mind about using Replace, choose Cancel.

FIG. 9.2

Use the Replace dialog box to specify the text or value to find as well as the replacement text or value.

To replace text or a value in a spreadsheet, follow these steps:

1. Select the range of cells you want to search, or select none to search the entire spreadsheet.

2. Choose Edit, Replace, or press Ctrl+H. The Replace dialog box shown in Figure 9.2 is displayed.

3. In the Fi<u>n</u>d What text box, type the text, value, or cell reference to search for.

4. In the Replace With text box, type the replacement information.

5. From the Search options, choose R<u>o</u>ws or <u>C</u>olumns.

6. Choose the <u>F</u>ind Next button. Works finds the first occurrence.

T I P   When you use the <u>F</u>ind Next button, you might need to drag the Replace dialog box to a different location on the screen to see the cell that is highlighted.

7. If you want to replace all occurrences in the spreadsheet, click the Replace <u>A</u>ll button. If you want to replace only the current occurrence, click the R<u>e</u>place button. If you want to find the next occurrence without replacing the current one, click the <u>F</u>ind Next button.

8. Repeat step 7 until you are finished searching and replacing.

9. Close the Replace dialog box by choosing the Clos<u>e</u> button. (The Cancel button becomes the Close button when Works is finished replacing.)

▶ **See** "Finding and Replacing Text in a Document" **p. 53**

Using Wild Cards in a Search

When you're not sure of the exact text or value you're searching for, you can insert a question mark as a wild card to represent any single character. For instance, if you search for *?00*, Works finds *100, 300,* and *500*. If you enter 1???3, Works finds all five-digit numbers that begin with 1 and end with 3, or entries like 1SRV3, such as a possible part number or inventory control number. To use the question mark wild card in the Find or Replace dialog box, type a question mark for *each unknown character* you are searching for in the Fi<u>n</u>d What text box.

You use the asterisk wild card to replace more than one character in a search. For example, if you search for 1*6, Works finds 146, 1236, 13498756, or any other text entries such as 1RLQ6 . Similarly, you can search for 12* and Works will find all entries that begin with 12. If you enter *12, Works finds entries of any length that end with 12. To use the asterisk wild card in the Find or Replace dialog box, type an asterisk for any number of unknown characters you are searching for in the Fi<u>n</u>d What text box.

▶ **See** "Finding and Replacing Text in a Document" **p. 53**

Sorting a Spreadsheet

As you build a spreadsheet, you often enter data in random order. Often the information can be easier to work with if you sort it for the particular type of task you're working on. For instance, you can rearrange entries in a spreadsheet alphabetically or numerically in ascending or descending order.

Works sorts all types of entries, whether they are names, dates, times, descriptions, part numbers, dollars, and so on. When you sort in ascending order on entries that contain both text and numbers, Works lists text entries first, then numbers. When you sort in descending order, numeric entries appear first and text entries follow.

In Figure 9.3, the spreadsheet contains data regarding employees and hours worked; this information is entered randomly. Individual employees appear in rows. You could conceivably sort this spreadsheet by any of the columns, such as last name, department, hourly rate, or number of hours worked.

FIG. 9.3

Employee data entered randomly in a spreadsheet could be sorted by any column heading.

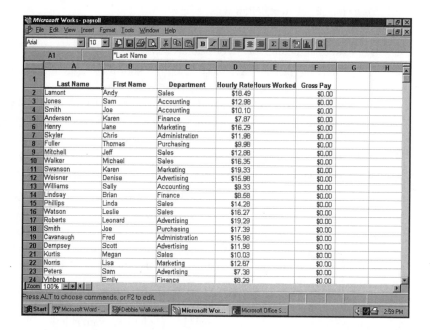

If you want to sort the entire spreadsheet, it isn't necessary to select rows before sorting. However, if your spreadsheet includes report titles, column headings, or other descriptive information that isn't part of the spreadsheet's raw data, you'll want to select specific rows to sort. For instance, in Figure 9.3, you would *exclude* row 1 so that the column headings are not included in the sorted information. After you select the rows to sort, choose Tools, Sort, which displays the Sort dialog box shown in Figure 9.4.

N O T E As a safeguard, Works has you select entire rows to sort. This ensures that all the information in a row (that is, across all columns) is sorted together. It is possible, however, to sort selected rows in only one (or several) columns. If you select only part of a row, then choose Tools, Sort, Works displays a message asking you to confirm that this is what you really want to do. ■

FIG. 9.4

In the Sort dialog box, choose the column by which you want to sort selected rows.

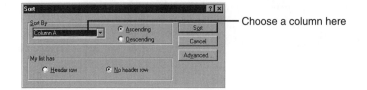

Choose a column here

To sort a spreadsheet, follow these steps:

1. Select the rows you want to include in the sort. (Don't include rows that contain titles, subtitles, column totals, or blank cells.)

2. Choose Tools, Sort. The Sort dialog box shown in Figure 9.4 is displayed. (If the First-Time Help dialog box is displayed, you can choose to see a demostation on one of the listed topics or click the Don't Display This Message In The Future box and choose OK.)

3. From the drop-down list in the Sort By box, choose the column (A, B, C, or other column) by which you want to sort. Select Ascending or Descending for the sort order.

4. If you have included column labels in the selection and want them to remain at the top of the columns, choose Header Row from the My List Has options.

5. Choose Sort. Works sorts the selection in the order you specify.

You can also sort a spreadsheet by columns or sort a portion of a spreadsheet. When you highlight several columns or a selection of cells and then choose the Sort command, Works displays a message box asking you to choose whether to sort the selection only or the entire spreadsheet. Choose one option, then click OK. The Sort dialog box is displayed.

To sort information by one, two, or three columns in ascending or descending order, choose the Advanced button in the Sort dialog box (see Figure 9.4). When items in the first column you specify match, Works sorts items based on the second column. When items in the first and second column match, Works sorts items based on the third column. This concept is illustrated in Figure 9.5. In the figure, a payroll spreadsheet lists employees by last name, first name, department, hourly rate, hours worked, and total. The spreadsheet is sorted by last name, first name, and department.

To first sort the payroll list by last name, which is displayed in column A, you choose Column A from the Sort By drop-down list in the Sort dialog box (see Figure 9.6). To then sort the payroll list by first name, you choose Column B from the Then By drop-down list. In this example, two employees are named Joe Smith. Because their last and first names match, you must use a third column to determine the order in which these two names are sorted. To sort by department, choose Column C from the second Then By drop-down list. This final sort by department ensures that Joe Smith in Accounting is displayed in the list before Joe Smith in Purchasing.

FIG. 9.5

Sorting on three columns sorts two Joe Smiths correctly.

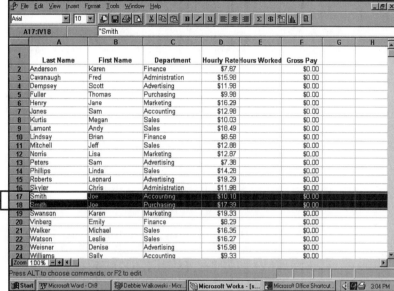

Sorting by department determines which Joe Smith is displayed first

FIG. 9.6

Choose the Advanced button to display this Sort dialog box to sort on one, two, or three columns.

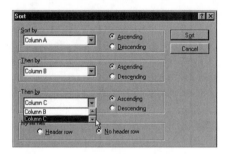

To sort a spreadsheet by more than one column, follow these steps:

1. Select the entries you want to include in the sort. For example, don't include report titles, column totals, or blank rows.

2. Choose Tools, Sort. The Sort dialog box shown in Figure 9.4 is displayed.

3. To sort on multiple columns, choose the Advanced button to display additional sort criteria in the Sort dialog box (shown in Figure 9.6).

4. Choose the column (A, B, C, or other column) you want to sort from the Sort By drop-down list. Select Ascending or Descending for the sort order.

5. To sort on two columns, select another column from the first Then By drop-down list and choose Ascending or Descending order.

Ch

9

6. To sort on three columns, select another column from the second Then By drop-down list and choose Ascending or Descending order.

7. If you included a row with column labels in the selection to sort, choose Header Row from the My List Has options at the bottom of the dialog box.

8. Choose Sort. Works sorts the spreadsheet in the order you specify.

Sometimes you want to retain a spreadsheet in the random order in which data was entered rather than sorting it. You could make a backup copy or store a copy under a different name, but another way to preserve the original spreadsheet is to add a column that sequentially numbers items as they were originally entered. For example, in Figure 9.7 the payroll spreadsheet now has an inserted column (Column A) which contains sequential numbers for each row of data in the spreadsheet. Now you can use Column A to restore the original spreadsheet if you sort incorrectly or by mistake, Just select the rows to sort, then sort on column A in ascending order. Works re-sorts the spreadsheet in its original order.

FIG. 9.7

A column that sequentially numbers entries enables you to re-sort data in the original order.

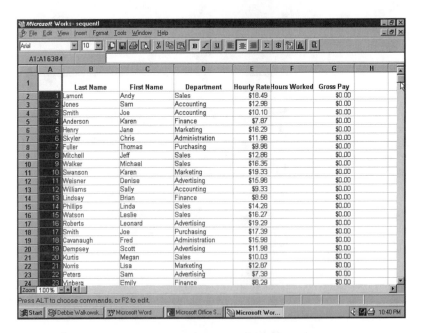

You can easily create a column of sequential numbers using the AutoFill feature you learned about in Chapter 7. Insert a new column, then type the number 1 in the cell in the first row of data. Move down one cell and type the number 2. Highlight these two cells, then move the mouse pointer over the AutoFill box in the lower-right corner of the selection. The FILL label appears on the mouse pointer. Now drag the AutoFill box to the last row of data in the spreadsheet. Works automatically fills the column with sequential numbers.

▶ **See** "Using Autofill" **p. 122**

> **CAUTION**
>
> Take care when using the Sort command. A simple error in selecting cells could result in some data being separated from its companion data. Review the results of Sort immediately and choose Edit, Undo Sort if necessary. To safeguard against errors, number the rows as just described and *always* save the file just before beginning the Sort.

Using AutoFormat

If you don't have time to format a spreadsheet yourself, you can have Works do it for you. Works includes more than a dozen predefined format styles that are available in the AutoFormat dialog box, displayed when you choose Format, AutoFormat (see Figure 9.8). Choose a style from the list. The Example area shows how the selected style will look when applied to your spreadsheets. Each format applies a special font, size, and style to text and numbers and adds borders, colors, and shading to make the spreadsheet more attractive. You can choose to have Works format the last row or column of data you select in a special way to make it stand out as a Total.

FIG. 9.8

You can choose a spreadsheet format from the AutoFormat dialog box.

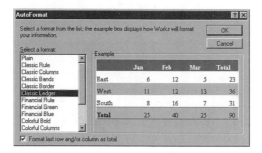

To apply an AutoFormat to a spreadsheet, follow these steps:

1. Select the entire range of cells you want to format.

2. Choose Format, AutoFormat. Works displays the AutoFormat dialog box shown in Figure 9.8.

3. In the Select a Format list box, highlight a format style. The Example area illustrates the style you choose.

4. To have Works add special formatting to the last row or column of data selected, choose the Format Last Row and/or Column as Total check box.

5. When you find a format you want to use, choose OK. Works applies the format to the selected cells in the spreadsheet.

When you apply an AutoFormat to a spreadsheet, all selected cells are changed. Be aware, also, that some cells you *didn't* select might also be changed, because some AutoFormats adjust column width. Works also changes any formatting that you applied previously to selected cells. After an AutoFormat is applied, you can also add or change any formatting features individually. If you decide the format you chose is not appropriate, choose Edit, Undo to restore the previous formatting.

Applying a Number Format to Selected Cells

Works automatically right-aligns all numbers in spreadsheet cells and left-aligns text. It does not automatically apply any other notations, such as dollar signs, commas, percent symbols, and so on. These and other notations are called number *formats*.

To change cells from the default General format to another format, you use the Format, Number command, which displays the Number tab of the Format Cells dialog box (see Figure 9.9). Most number formats offer display options, such as the number of decimal places to display, or a style, such as the way the day, month, and year appear in a date format. Formats and options are described in Table 9.1.

FIG. 9.9

Choose a number format from the Number tab of the Format Cells dialog box.

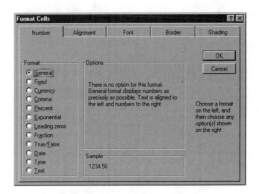

Table 9.1 Number Formats

Format	Effect
General	This option is the Works default format. Text is left-aligned and numbers are right-aligned. It uses scientific notation when a number is too long to be displayed in a cell.
Fixed	This choice rounds the display of numbers to the number of decimal places you specify. If you specify two places, for example, 34.2391 is displayed as 34.24. Negative numbers are preceded by a minus (–) symbol.
Currency	Here, numbers are preceded by a dollar symbol ($); large numbers use commas as thousands separators. Use this format to choose the number of decimal places and to display negative numbers in red.

Format	Effect
Comma	This format inserts commas as thousands separators. Negative numbers appear in parentheses rather than with a minus (–) symbol, or choose to display negative numbers in red.
Percent	This option places a percent symbol (%) after a number. If you enter .081 in a cell with this format, Works displays 8.1%. You can specify the number of decimal places to use.
Exponential	Use this format to display numbers using scientific notation. If you enter 7898.23, Works displays 7.90E+03. You can specify the number of decimal places to use.
Leading zeroes	This selection displays the number you enter with leading zeroes such as 00043. You specify the number of digits (up to 8) to display. Use this format when you want to display leading zeroes of invoice numbers, part numbers, and so on.
Fraction	Use this option to display numbers as fractions, rounded to the fraction you specify (1/2, 1/3, 1/8, 1/10, 1/16, 1/32, 1/100), or you can choose to display all fractions. If you enter 2.781 and choose the 1/4 setting, works displays 2 3/4.
True/False	This choice displays numbers as logical values, either TRUE or FALSE. All zeroes that appear are displayed as FALSE. All non-zero numbers are displayed as TRUE.
Date	This option displays entries in the date format you specify. Choose from three numeric formats, such as 3/20/98, or four text formats, such as March 20, 1998.
Time	Use this format to display entries in the time format you specify. Choose 12- or 24-hour format, and whether to include seconds in the display.
Text	This choice formats the entry as text rather than as a number.

To apply a number format, do this:

1. Select the cell or range of cells you want to format. (Note that you can also select empty cells; when you enter data, the data will automatically be formatted with the format you specify.)

2. Choose Format, Number, or right-click and choose Number from the shortcut menu. The Number tab in the Format Cells dialog box is displayed.

3. From the Format area, select one format.

4. In the Options area, specify the appropriate option for the format chosen (such as 2 decimal places or MM/DD/YY for a date format).

5. Click OK.

Ch
9

When you specify a number of decimal places for a particular format, only the display is affected. Works stores the complete number as you entered it. The full number is displayed in the entry bar and is used in calculations. To display a number with more precision, increase the number of decimal places in the number format.

 T I P Because dollars are a common entry in a spreadsheet, Works includes a currency toolbar button. When you click this button, Works formats the selected cells with dollar signs, commas (if applicable), and two decimal places. If you don't want two decimal places, use the Format, Number command to specify the number of decimal places for the Currency format.

Aligning Entries Within Cells

Works automatically applies the General format to all entries you make in a spreadsheet. With this format, Works left-aligns text and right-aligns numbers in a cell. You might want to change the alignment of entries to improve the overall appearance of a spreadsheet or make data easier to read.

To align entries horizontally, you can left-align, right-align, or center an entry in a cell; fill a cell; or center an entry across a selection of columns. These options are available in the Alignment tab of the Format Cells dialog box, which appear when you choose Format, Alignment (see Figure 9.10).

FIG. 9.10

Choose an alignment style from the Format Cells dialog box.

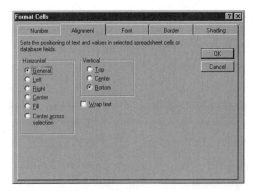

To change the horizontal alignment of entries in a cell or cell range, follow these steps:

1. Select the cell or cell range for which you want to align entries.
2. Choose Format, Alignment. The Alignment tab of the Format Cells dialog box shown in Figure 9.10 is displayed.
3. Under the Horizontal options, choose an alignment style.
4. Choose OK.

TIP Left, center, and right alignment buttons are available on the spreadsheet toolbar. To use these buttons rather than the Format Cells dialog box, select the cell or cells for which you want to change the alignment, and then click the appropriate toolbar button.

When you choose Left alignment, both text and numeric entries are left-aligned. When you choose Right alignment, text and numbers are right-aligned. Center alignment centers an entry within the width of a cell. If the centered entry is too long to display within the borders of the cell, a text entry fills the cells immediately to the left and right of the current cell, provided those cells are empty. If both the cells to the left and right contain data, the centered entry appears to be cut off on both the right and left edges of the cell. You can view the entire entry by selecting the cell and then checking the entry bar. If appropriate, you can also extend the width of the column to display the entire entry.

The Fill option duplicates the characters entered in the cell as many times as possible until the cell is filled. For instance, if you type the pound sign (#) in a cell and use the Fill option, Works fills the cell up with pound sign (#) characters. If you type **ABC** in a cell formatted with the Fill option, Works displays ABCABC in the cell until the cell is filled. You might use this option to create a placeholder in a cell.

Use the Center Across Selection option to center a title or other information across several columns in a spreadsheet (see Figure 9.11). In the figure, the title "Examples of Alignment Options" is entered in cell 2D but is centered across columns C, D, an E.

FIG. 9.11

Examples of horizontal and vertical alignment within a cell.

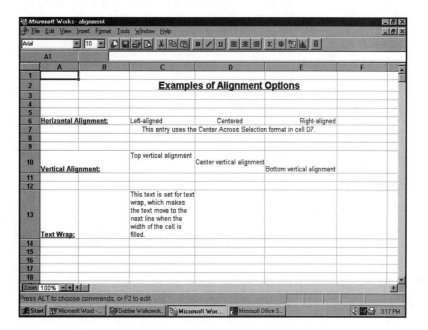

Ch

9

Although you might not think of spreadsheet cells two-dimensionally, all cells have height as well as width. When you enter data into cells, Works automatically aligns entries along the bottom edge of a cell. Generally, you don't notice this because the default row height is appropriate for the height of the current font. However, in some cases, particularly when you increase the height of a row or use an especially tall special font, you might want an entry to be vertically aligned along the top of a cell or through the horizontal center of a cell. Examples of each style are shown in Figure 9.11. To change the vertical alignment of an entry, choose Format, Alignment to open the Format Cells dialog box, then choose the Top, Center, or Bottom option in the Vertical section of the Alignment tab.

As you saw earlier in this chapter, when a cell contains a long entry, it "spills over" into the next cell if it's empty. But sometimes you want your text entries to be formatted more like a paragraph rather than strung across columns. To solve this formatting problem, use the Wrap Text option on the Alignment tab in the Format Cells dialog box. This option wraps a long text entry to the next line in the same cell by increasing the row height while maintaining the column width. Wrapping text within a cell is commonly used for column headings (see Figure 9.12). Works automatically wraps existing text within the cell and adjusts row height as necessary.

FIG. 9.12
Wrapped column headings allow reasonable column widths in a spreadsheet.

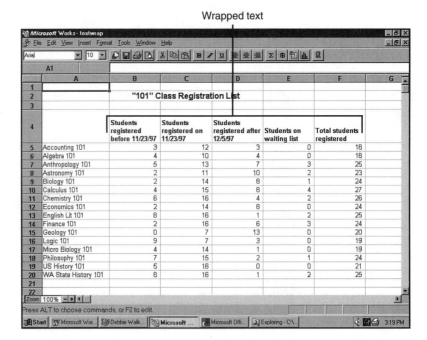

Adjusting Row Height

When you open a new spreadsheet file, Works uses the standard row height of 12 points. Because the default font is Arial 10, a row height of 12 adequately accommodates all new entries you type. If you change the font or point size, Works automatically adjusts the row height as well. For example, if you change the font throughout your spreadsheet to Times New Roman 12, Works automatically sets the row height throughout the sheet to 15. (The three extra points allow for spacing.) If you enter a title on row 1 in Arial 16, Works adjusts the row height of row 1 to 18 points.

You don't have to use the row height Works suggests for the font you're using. You can specify an exact row height by selecting the row or rows you want to adjust and then choosing Format, Row Height. The Format Row Height dialog box in Figure 9.13 is displayed. In the Row Height text box, type a number in points. If you choose the Best Fit button, Works automatically adjusts the row height for the largest font used in the row. If you select multiple rows that use different fonts, the Best Fit option assigns different row heights to each row in the selection. To return to the default row height, choose the Standard button.

FIG. 9.13

Use the Format Row Height dialog box to specify an exact row height or best fit.

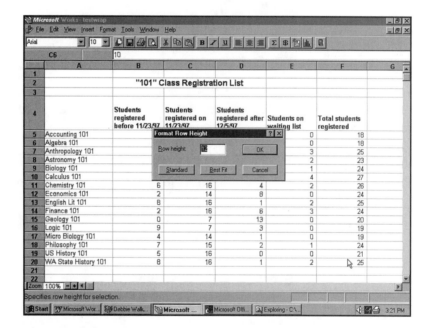

In Chapter 7, you learned how to adjust column width by dragging a column border. The same method works for adjusting row height. When you point to the bottom border of a row label (see Figure 9.14), the mouse pointer changes to an up/down arrow labeled ADJUST. Hold down the left mouse button then drag the border down to increase the row height; drag the border up to decrease row height. Release the mouse button when the row is the height you want.

▶ **See** "Adjusting Column Width," **p. 124**

FIG. 9.14
Drag the bottom border
of a row up or down to
adjust row height.

Point here to
adjust row height

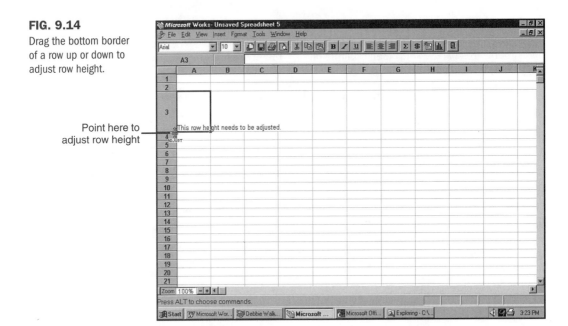

Choosing a Character Font, Size, Color, and Style

One of the best ways to emphasize data, draw attention, and make a spreadsheet more visually appealing, is to choose a different font, size, color, and style for different areas of the spreadsheet. To apply these characteristics, you can use menu commands, toolbar buttons, or keyboard shortcuts. When using menu commands, choose Format, Font and Style, which displays the dialog box shown in Figure 9.15.

FIG. 9.15
In the Font tab of the
Format Cells dialog box
you can choose a
different font, change
the size, choose a style,
and even select other
colors.

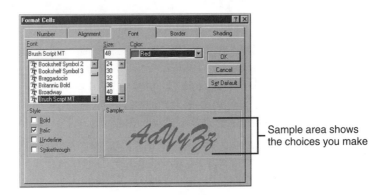

Sample area shows
the choices you make

In the dialog box shown in Figure 9.15, you see settings for the font, size, color, and style. These attributes are described in the following list:

- ■ *Font*   A font refers to a specific style or design for a set of characters. Each font has a particular thickness, size (apart from point size), style, weight, as well as a "feel" or "attitude" it conveys that distinguishes it from other fonts.

- ■ *Size*   Fonts are available in a variety of sizes and are generally measured in *points*. (A point is equal to 1/72 of an inch.) The most common point sizes for use in the body of a spreadsheet are 10 or 12. Other elements in a spreadsheet, such as titles or row and column labels, often appear in larger sizes, such as 14, 16, 18, or 24 points.

- ■ *Color*   If you have a color monitor, you can display selected cells in a variety of colors. If you have a color printer, you also can print the colors that you display in your spreadsheet.

- ■ *Style*   In Works, a text *style* refers to bold, italic, underline, or strikethrough. Bold, Italic, and Underline are the most common styles used for emphasis. Strikethrough prints a line through an entry, marking it for deletion, but the entry itself is still readable.

In the Font tab of the Format Cells dialog box, you can choose font, size, color, and style for selected cells. The Sample area of the dialog box displays the choices you make and is especially helpful for previewing the unique design of a particular font and the relative size of characters.

To apply a character style to cells that contain data or to empty cells, follow these steps:

1. Select the cells to which you want to apply a character style.
2. Choose Format, Font and Style, or right-click and choose Format from the shortcut menu. The Font tab of the Format Cells dialog box in Figure 9.15 is displayed.
3. Select one option from any of the Font, Size, and Color lists.
4. From the Style options, choose as many styles as you want to apply to the selected cells.
5. When the text shown in the Sample area is displayed as you want, choose OK. Works automatically reformats the selected cells.

If you prefer to use the toolbar to apply a character style, buttons are available for font and size, as well as for bold, italic, and underline (see Figure 9.16).

Click here to display the
font drop-down list   Bold   Italic   Underline

FIG. 9.16

Choose a character
style from the
spreadsheet toolbar.

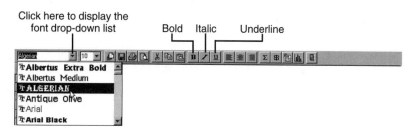

You can quickly choose font and point sizes using the Font and Size toolbar buttons To change a font or size for selected cells, choose a font or size from the drop-down lists. You can also quickly add bold, italic, or underline to cell entries, by selecting the cells first, then clicking the appropriate toolbar button.

 T I P You can quickly determine the format of a cell by selecting it, then checking the toolbar to see the name of the font and the point size—and whether any style or alignment buttons are selected.

Works provides keyboard shortcuts for the character styles shown in Table 9.2. To use a keyboard shortcut, select the cells you want to format and then press the appropriate key sequence.

Table 9.2 Keyboard Shortcuts for Character Styles

Key Sequence	Character Style
Ctrl+B	Bold
Ctrl+U	Underline
Ctrl+I	Italic
Ctrl+Space bar	Plain text (remove all character styles)

N O T E If you want to change the *color* of text, you must use the Font tab in the Format Cells dialog box shown in Figure 9.15. No toolbar buttons or keyboard shortcuts are available for color. ▉

Attributes that you *add to* entries (such as bold, italic, underline, and strikethrough) toggle on and off, regardless of the method you use to apply them. To remove any of these character styles individually, select the affected cells and then select the dialog box option, the toolbar button, or the keyboard shortcut again to remove the attribute.

When a cell contains several attributes and you want to remove *all* the attributes, the quickest way is to select the text then press Ctrl+Space bar. This keyboard shortcut changes the format of all selected cells back to plain text, eliminating the task of removing each attribute individually. If you changed the font used in the selected cells, Works restores the default Arial 10 font.

Adding Borders and Patterns to Cells

It is very common to want to draw the reader's attention to a particular area of a spreadsheet. In an income statement, for example, you might want to emphasize Net Income so the reader instantly focuses on "the bottom line." One way to make a cell or cell range stand out is to place a border around it. You can add a border to cells using a variety of line styles and add a color if you like.

We generally think of a border as something that completely surrounds an object. In Works, this type of border is called an *outline border*. But you can also create *partial* borders that appear on the top, bottom, left, or right sides of a cell, or you can use any combination of these four.

To add a border and define its style and color, you use the Border tab in the Format Cells dialog box, which is displayed when you choose Format, Border (see Figure 9.17).

FIG. 9.17

Use the Border tab of the Format Cells dialog box to choose a border, style, and color.

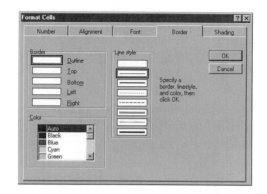

Ch

9

To add a border to spreadsheet cells, follow these steps:

1. Select the cell or cell range you want to border.

2. Choose Format, Border, or right-click and choose Font from the shortcut menu, then click the Border tab. The Format Cells dialog box is displayed with the Border tab selected (refer to Figure 9.17).

3. From the Border options, choose the Outline option to create an outline border. Or choose any of the Top, Bottom, Left, and Right border styles to create a partial border.

4. From the Line Style options, select a line style to apply.

5. Select a color from the Color list box.

N O T E Unless you have a color printer, the color is visible only on-screen. However, colors will print in varying shades of gray on a black-and-white printer. ∎

6. Repeat steps 3 through 5 to add a border to more than one side of the cell if you want a different line style or color for other sides of the cell.

7. Choose OK. Works adds the specified border to the selected cells.

To remove a border, use the preceding steps but select the blank line style box to clear all borders from the Outline, Top, Bottom, Left, and Right options.

You can also call attention to particular cells by adding a pattern to them. A pattern shades the background of a cell. (If you choose a dark pattern, consider changing the text color to white so the entry is still readable.) You can add a pattern to individual cells or to a range of cells by choosing a pattern style, a foreground color, and a background color from the Shading tab of the Format Cells dialog box (see Figure 9.18). To open this dialog box, choose Format, Shading. When you choose the solid pattern (the first choice on the pattern drop-down list), the selected cells display only the foreground color. All other patterns in the list have a foreground color and a background color. The foreground color defines the lines and dots that make up the pattern; the background color fills in the inside are of the cell that is typically white. The Sample area in the dialog box shows an example of the pattern and colors you choose.

FIG. 9.18

Choose cell pattern and colors in the Shading tab of the Format Cells dialog box.

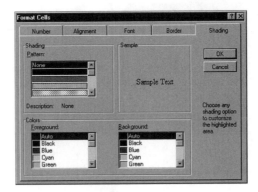

Use the following steps to add a pattern to a cell or cell range. As you make choices in the dialog box, be sure to check the Sample area, which illustrates the choices you make.

1. Select the cell or cells to which you want to apply a pattern.
2. Choose Format, Shading or right-click and choose Format from the shortcut menu, then click the Shading tab. The Shading tab of the Format Cells dialog box is displayed (refer to Figure 9.18).
3. In the Pattern list box, select a pattern style.
4. (Optional) In the Foreground list box, select a color for the pattern foreground.
5. (Optional) In the Background list box, select a color for the pattern background.
6. When you create a pattern you like, choose OK.

N O T E   Many black-and-white printers print shades of gray for the colors you define. Experiment with color selections and your printer to find printed output that works with your data. ■

To switch a pattern back to its previous colors, select the cells you want to change and choose Format, Shading. In the Foreground and Background list boxes, choose the Auto option; this restores the default settings. To remove a pattern entirely, choose None as the option in the Pattern list box. Works removes pattern and colors from the selected cells.

Ch
9

Adding Headers and Footers to a Spreadsheet

Repetitive text displayed at the top of each spreadsheet page is called a *header;* repetitive text at the bottom of the page is called a *footer*. Before printing a spreadsheet, you might want to add a header or footer that includes a title, page number, date, or other information.

Headers and footers print within the top and bottom margin areas of a spreadsheet. Unlike in a word processor document, in a spreadsheet, headers and footers are restricted to a single line of text. You can insert special codes that automatically print the current date, current time, page numbers, file name, and so on, but you cannot change the font or add effects such as bold, underline, or italic. In a multi-page spreadsheet, you can choose to eliminate the header or footer from the first page. After you create a header or footer, it is visible only on the Print Preview screen.

▶ **See** "Creating a Header or Footer," **p. 82**

To create a header, footer, or both, follow these steps:

1. Choose <u>V</u>iew, <u>H</u>eaders and Footers.
2. In the H<u>e</u>ader box, type the text you want to use for the header.
3. In the <u>F</u>ooter box, type the text you want to use for the footer.
4. To eliminate a header or footer on the first page of your document, choose the <u>N</u>o Header on First Page or N<u>o</u> Footer on First Page check boxes.
5. Choose OK.

Formatting Headers and Footers and Adding Special Text

Works automatically centers all headers and footers. To align the text differently, insert special codes, as shown in Table 9.3, into the header or footer text in the View Headers and Footers dialog box. Some codes align text and other codes insert special text such as a page number, file name, or current date. For codes that align text, you enter the code immediately preceding the text. For example, you can specify that Works right-align your header or footer text by entering **&r** immediately preceding the text that you want right-aligned. For codes that insert text, you simply type the code, such as **&f**, which prints the file name in the header or footer. You also can combine codes, where appropriate. If you want Works to insert the file name of the current document and right-align it, type **&r&f**. The codes can be typed with either upper- or lowercase letters.

TIP When inserting codes, you can put a space between separate codes to make them easier to read but be careful not to put a space within a code itself. If you type **& f** for *&f*, the header will read & f instead of printing the file name.

Table 9.3 Format and Alignment Codes

Code	Function
&l	Left-aligns the text that follows the code
&r	Right-aligns the text that follows the code
&c	Centers the text that follows the code
&f	Prints the file name
&p	Prints page numbers
&t	Inserts the time at the time of printing
&d	Inserts the date at the time of printing (such as 3/2/98)
&n	Inserts the long form date at the time of printing (such as 2 March 98)
&&	Prints an ampersand (&)

Changing or Deleting a Header or Footer

You can change the content of a header or footer, as well as the alignment or any special text that you insert. To change or delete a header or footer, simply recall the View Headers and Footers dialog box and then make the appropriate changes. To delete a header or footer entirely, delete the entries in the Header and Footer text boxes. ●

CHAPTER 10

Creating, Enhancing, and Printing Charts

A chart is a graphical representation of numeric data. It is used to contrast and compare data visually, to identify and quantify the parts of a whole, to show relationships between two or more numbers, and to identify trends among data. Because its visual impact is often immediate, a chart can usually convey information quicker than data presented in the form of a spreadsheet.

In Works, charts are directly dependent upon data in a spreadsheet. You tell Works which data to use to create the chart, and Works creates the chart. When you change the data in your spreadsheet, Works automatically updates the data in the chart. ∎

The basic chart types and their characteristics

Works includes a dozen chart types, each designed to convey information in a different way and with a different emphasis.

The elements of a typical chart

Most types of charts have (or can have) several common elements, including a title, scale, legend, gridlines, labels, and so on.

How Works plots charts

You need to know how Works "reads" spreadsheet data to be charted so that you select the correct data.

How to create, name, delete, and duplicate a chart

These are the basic tasks you learn before you change or enhance a chart.

Enhancing the appearance of a chart

Add color, patterns, and other visual pointers to make a chart easier to interpret and more attractive to look at.

Printing a chart

While there are some special options for printing charts, the printing process is just like printing a spreadsheet or any other Works document.

Reviewing Chart Types

Works include 12 basic chart types. These include area and 3-D area, bar and 3-D bar, line and 3-D line, pie and 3-D pie, stacked line, X-Y (scatter), radar, and combination. Each chart type has a unique purpose and characteristics. For each of the 12 chart types, you can choose from a variety of style variations. Review the figures and descriptions throughout this chapter to choose the chart type that best illustrates your particular data.

Area charts are designed to show how each part contributes to a whole over a span of time. Because data is depicted over a period, an area chart shows how an item changes over time. In Figure 10.1, for example, the area chart shows how each category of income contributed to total income throughout the year.

FIG. 10.1

Area charts emphasize the relative contribution of items in a category.

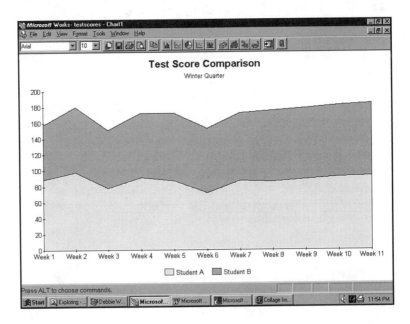

 Bar charts compare different items and emphasize their relationship to one another at distinct points in time. Rather than depicting a continuous flow, a bar chart is like a series of snapshots of data taken at regular intervals. Positive values are charted above the horizontal axis (the x-axis); negative values appear below. Figure 10.2 illustrates 1997 expenses for Town and Country Interiors at four intervals: Q1, Q2, Q3, and Q4. One variation lets you stack bars on top of one another, showing the percentage that each item contributes to the whole (100%).

 Line charts illustrate trends among data items. The x-axis usually represents time (days, months, quarters, years, and so on). Each line in the chart represents a distinct data item; markers on the line pinpoint the exact values charted. In Figure 10.3, the five types of expenses that are charted include Cost of Goods, Rent, Labor, Insurance, and Utilities.

FIG. 10.2
A bar chart compares
distinct items over a
period of time.

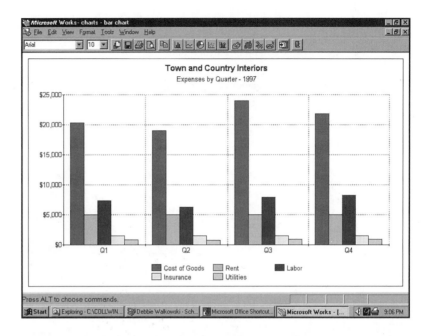

FIG. 10.3
Line charts illustrate
trends among data
items.

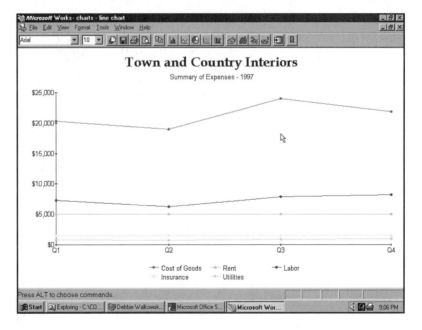

 Pie charts illustrate how individual parts contribute to a whole. Each pie slice corresponds to a specific value in a category of data; the entire pie corresponds to the sum of the category. Unlike area, line, and bar charts, pie charts are like a single snapshot that pinpoints data at a specific point in time. Works provides pie chart variations that let you explode slices. In Figure 10.4, the total income of Town and Country Interiors for 1997 is shown using a pie chart. The Retail Store slice is exploded for emphasis.

FIG. 10.4

The pie chart illustrates how parts contribute to the whole.

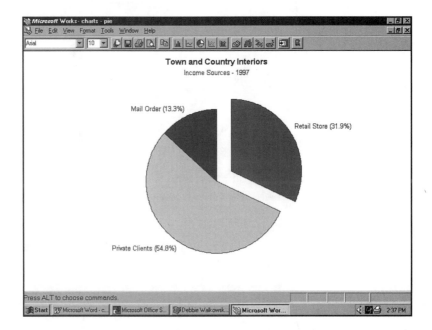

Stacked line charts are similar to line charts except that the lines are stacked to show the total of all items shown. Works adds the values of the first line to the second line, the second line to the third line, and so on. The stacked line chart illustrates the flow of data over time unlike an area chart, which indicates the volume of data over time. Figure 10.5 shows three categories of income for the year 1997 in a stacked line chart.

 An *X-Y chart*, sometimes called a *scatter* chart, is designed to depict the relationship between two related items, such as temperature and relative humidity. This type of chart illustrates how a change in one value affects the other. In Figure 10.6, the x-y chart shows how the number of consecutive hours worked affects employees' productivity.

A *radar chart* compares two or more sets of data on an equivalent scale. Each set of data is graphed on a scale that radiates from a center point outward. The resulting graph resembles a spider-web shape. Figure 10.7 shows a comparison of data on two separate cars. For each car, five criteria (purchase price, options, horsepower, reliability, gas mileage, and cost of maintenance) are ranked on a scale of 1 to 10.

FIG. 10.5

A stacked line chart depicts the total of all items shown.

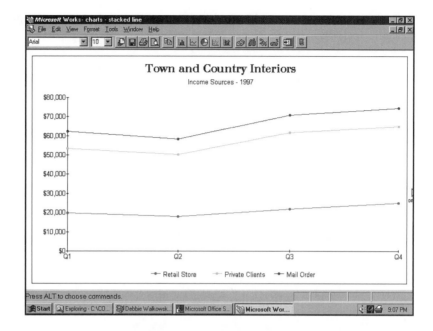

FIG. 10.6

An x-y chart shows the correlation between two related values.

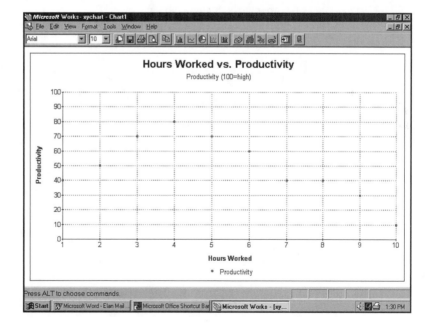

FIG. 10.7

A radar chart compares two sets of data on an equivalent scale.

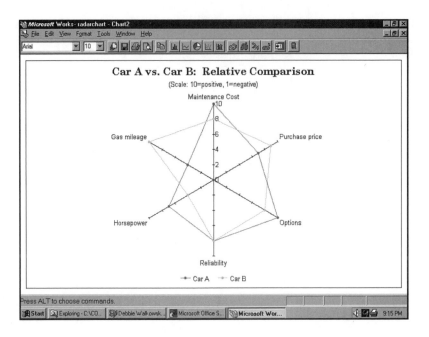

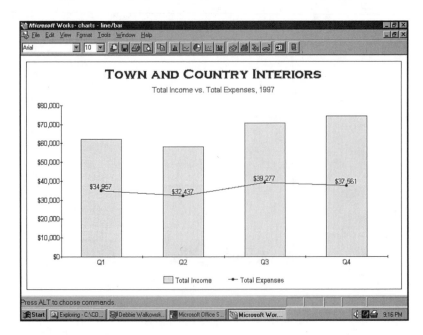

Combination charts are charts that mix bars and lines. The mixture of these two elements allows these charts to depict pinpoint data (via the bars) as well as trends in the same data (via the lines). The chart in Figure 10.8 displays total income as bars and total expenses as a line.

FIG. 10.8

In this combination chart, a line overlays bars.

3-D area, 3-D bar, 3-D line, and 3-D pie charts are similar to their 2-D counterparts but they add depth to the areas, bars, lines, and pie slices. Although it does not add any new information, the 3-D variation adds interest and can help emphasize data better than a 2-D chart. In addition, 3-D area and bar charts let you to depict each data item separately rather than stacked. For instance, instead of stacking three types of income on top of one another, as shown in the area chart in Figure 10.1, a 3-D area chart enables you to show each type of income as a distinct 3-D area (see Figure 10.9).

FIG. 10.9
This 3-D variation shows each data item separately.

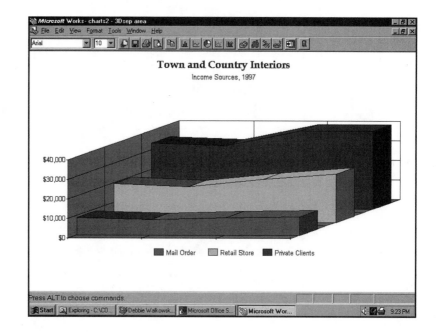

You can use a *3-D bar chart* to depict distinct data items separately rather than side-by-side or stacked. Figure 10.10 depicts the 1997 expenses for Town and Country Interiors in a 3-D bar chart. Refer to the same data charted in a 2-D bar chart in Figure 10.2.

3-D line charts are essentially the same as 2-D line charts except that they represent lines of data as ribbons. This style is especially effective for displaying lines of data that cross one another. Figure 10.11 illustrates the test scores of two different students across a nine-week period.

There is very little difference between 3-D pie charts and 2-D pie charts. The primary difference is in the depth that is added to the slices in the 3-D version. This depth gives the chart more visual impact. Figure 10.12 shows the same data from Figure 10.4 charted as a 3-D pie with slices exploded.

FIG. 10.10

A 3-D bar chart depicts distinct data items separately.

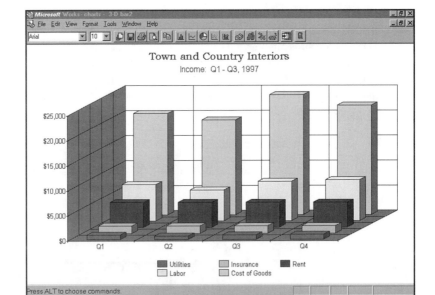

FIG. 10.11

In a 3-D line chart, individual data items are represented by ribbons.

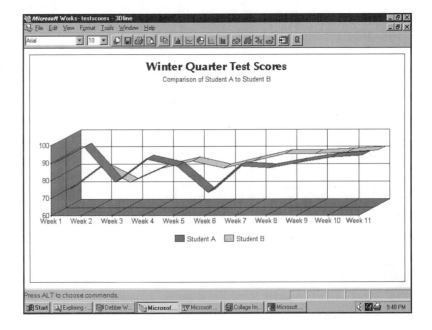

FIG. 10.12
A 3-D pie chart illustrates how parts contribute to a whole.

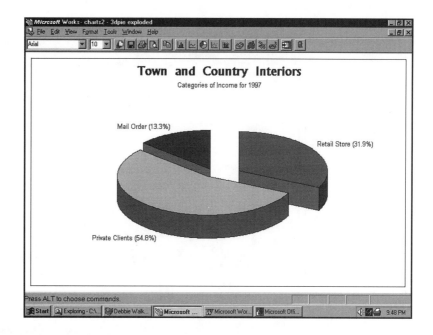

Identifying the Elements of a Chart

Every chart has some common elements (see Figure 10.13). Some are standard while others ae optional features you can add or remove. You can include in a chart any or all of the elements described in the following list.

- *Axes*   With the exception of pie charts and radar charts, most chart types have two axes. The horizontal axis, or *x-axis*, often represents dates or the passage of time. The vertical axis, or *y-axis*, often represents percentages or a quantity such as dollars. *Tick marks* indicate the intervals along an axis. Some chart types allow you to add a right y-axis to make the data on the far right side of a chart easier to read.

- *Scale*   A scale depicts units of measure (such as dollars, or months in a year) along an axis. Based on the data you select to chart, Works automatically determines the maximum number, the minimum number, and the interval used in the scale.

- *Chart Titles*   The chart title identifies the content and purpose of a chart. You can create a one-line title or you can include a subtitle. You can also format a chart title individually using any font or point size. The font or size you choose for a chart subtitle is applied to all other text in a chart. To make a chart more readable, you can also add titles to the horizontal and vertical axes of a chart. (We would probably refer to these as axis *labels*, but Works calls them axis *titles*.)

- *Legend*   A legend appears at the bottom of a chart and identifies the bars, lines, pie slices, or other markers that represent data.

FIG. 10.13
This bar chart shows the common elements of a chart.

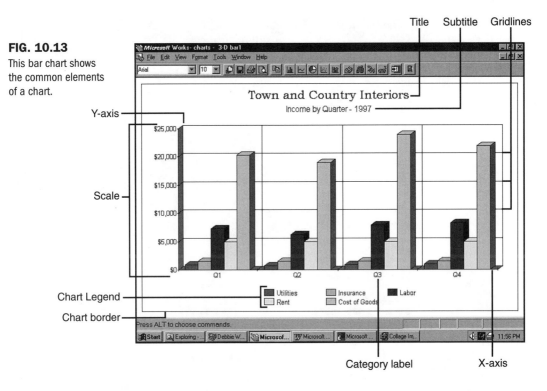

■ *Gridlines*   Horizontal gridlines mark the intervals along the x-axis; vertical gridlines mark the intervals along the y-axis. Gridlines can make a chart easier to read by allowing your eye to track data across a chart or up and down.

■ *Category labels*   Category labels identify categories of data represented in a graph. In Figure 10.13, Q1, Q2, and Q3 are category labels for each quarter.

■ *Data labels*   Data labels mark the exact value or percentage represented by a data point. When a chart contains a lot of data, data labels can make the chart look very cluttered, so use them with care. In Figure 10.12, data labels identify exact percentages of the pie slices.

■ *Border*   To give a chart a more polished, professional appearance, add a border, which surrounds the chart data, title, and legend.

Understanding How Charts Are Plotted

Creating a chart in Works is a straightforward task because the data already exists in the spreadsheet; you simply select the range of cells to be charted. Works creates a bar chart automatically from the cell range you select, so it's important to understand how Works interprets the content of the selected cell range. The example shown in Figure 10.14 helps to illustrate the process.

Works create a chart based on the shape of the cell range you select and the data contained in the range. When the cell range contains more columns than rows—which is often the case—Works translates the column heads into *categories* and places them along the x-axis. In Figure 10.14, cells A6 through E9 are selected. Because there are more columns than rows in this selection, the column titles in cells B6 through E6 are translated into categories or, the *x series*.

FIG. 10.14
Works translates a selection of cells into a chart.

X-series categories

Y-series categories

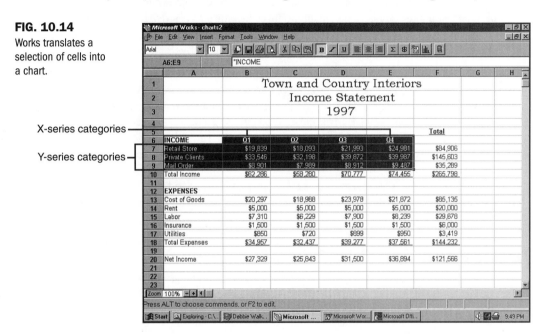

Each row of data in your selection represents a distinct *data item* (such as Retail Store, Mail Order, and Private Clients). A row of cells that represents a particular data item is referred to as a *y series*. Works plots the *data points*, or values, for each y series along the y axis. You can include up to six y-series data ranges in a chart. The chart produced from the spreadsheet shown in Figure 10.14 includes three y-series ranges: Retail Store, Private Clients, and Mail Order taken from rows 7, 8, and 9.

If you include both row and column headings in your cell selection, Works translates the column headings into category labels along the x-axis and translates row headings into a legend at the bottom of the chart. In Figure 10.14, the row headings Retail Store, Private Clients, and Mail Order make up the chart legend. The category labels, Q1, Q2, Q3, and Q4, are taken from cells B6:E6. (The "Income" label in cell A6 is ignored.)

Selecting Spreadsheet Data to Chart

You've just seen how Works translates data if your selection contains more columns than rows. If the range you select contains more rows than columns, Works interprets and transfers the data to the chart in exactly the opposite order: Row headings transfer to the x-axis as categories and values in columns are used to plot data points on the y-axis. Regardless of the shape of the range, however, when the selection contains row and column headings, Works automatically creates a chart legend and adds category labels to the chart.

Because pie charts can only show one data item at a time, you must select only one y-series cell range when creating a pie chart. For instance, to use the data shown in Figure 10.14 to create a pie chart, you must choose only one of the three income sources (B7:E7, B8:E8, or B9:E9), or choose the total income (B10:E10) as the y-series range. If you mistakenly select more than one y-series range, Works charts the first range and ignores the remaining ranges.

Because Works interprets data automatically based on the shape of the cell range you select, it is important to remove any unnecessary blank rows or columns from the body of a spreadsheet before you create a chart. Notice in Figure 10.14 that the selection does not include any blank rows or columns. Blank rows and columns in the spreadsheet cause blank categories and bars in a chart. For the same reason, do not select entire rows or entire columns when you select a cell range to be charted because they invariably contain blank cells.

N O T E   If it isn't possible to remove blank rows or columns from a spreadsheet, you can still plot a chart. Refer to the section "Changing X- and Y-Series Cell Ranges" later in this chapter. ■

Creating and Viewing a Chart

When you create a chart, it appears in a separate window but it is actually part of the active spreadsheet. You can create up to eight charts for each spreadsheet. Each chart you create is given an individual name and is printed from the chart window.

To create a new chart, first select the range of cells to be charted, and then choose Tools, Create New Chart or click the New Chart button on the toolbar. The New Chart dialog box appears with the Basic Options tab selected (see Figure 10.15). In the What Type of Chart Do You Want? box, Works highlights the Bar chart type by default and a sample bar chart showing the data you selected in your spreadsheet appears in the Your Chart area. This preview of your chart gives you the perfect opportunity to check whether you selected the correct cell range before actually creating a chart. If you include column and row headings in your selection, a legend appears under the sample chart.

 T I P   If the First-Time Help dialog box is displayed, you can choose to see a demo on one of the listed topics or click the Don't Display This Message In The Future box and choose OK.

The Finishing Touches area of the dialog box lets you add a chart title, and include a border and gridlines in your chart. If you don't select these options now, you can add a title, border, and gridlines to the chart later.

See "Adding a Title, Subtitle, and Axis Titles," and "Adding a Border, Gridlines, Droplines, and 3-D Effect," later in this chapter.

FIG. 10.15
Choose a chart type
that will most effectively
display the selected
information.

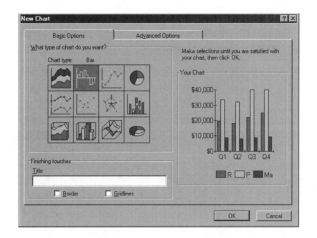

If Works misinterprets the cell range you selected (that is, confuses the x-series range with
y-series ranges), you can change the way the data is interpreted by editing the cell ranges. In
the New Chart dialog box, choose the Advanced Options tab (see Figure 10.16). Based on the
cell range you select, Works fills in the options in the How Is Your Spreadsheet Data Organized
area. The following list explains these options:

- The first step asks `Which Way Do Your Series Go, Across or Down?` If your data items
  appear in rows, Works chooses the Across option. If your data items appear in columns,
  Works chooses the Down option.

- The second step, `First Column Contains Legend Text or A Category`, refers to the
  content of the entries in the first column. If the first column describes data items, Works
  creates a legend from the entries. If the first column describes categories of data, Works
  creates category names from the entries.

- The third step, `First Row Contains Category Labels Or A Value (Y) Series`, refers
  to the content of the entries in the first row. If the first row describes categories of data,
  Works creates category names from the entries. If the first row describes data items,
  Works creates a legend from the entries.

To create a new chart, follow these steps. (Be sure to delete all blank rows and columns, if
possible, before beginning.)

1. In the spreadsheet, select the range of cells you want to chart. Select row and column
   headings as well if you want Works to create category labels and a legend.

2. Choose Tools, Create New Chart command; or click the New Chart button on the
   toolbar. The New Chart dialog box appears (refer to Figure 10.15).

3. From the examples in the What Type of Chart Do You Want area, choose a chart type.

4. To add a title to your chart, type the title text in the Title text box.

5. To add a border or gridlines to a chart, select the Border or Gridlines check boxes.

Ch
10

6. (Optional) To change the way Works interprets and charts the selected data, choose the Advanced Options tab (see Figure 10.16). Change any of the options in the How Is Your Spreadsheet Data Organized area.

7. Check the sample chart to make sure that the chart is correct, then click OK. Works displays your chart in a separate window on-screen. Your spreadsheet window, still open, is located under the chart window.

FIG. 10.16
In the Advanced Options tab, you change the way Works charts data.

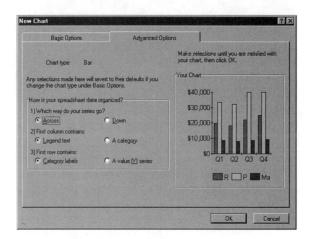

Using the Charting Toolbar

As you learned in Chapter 1, "Introduction to Works 4.5," each of the Works programs has a unique toolbar. After you create a chart using spreadsheet data and the chart window is active, the spreadsheet toolbar changes to the charting toolbar shown in Figure 10.17.

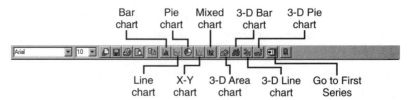

FIG. 10.17
Use buttons on the charting toolbar to speed up your work.

The first seven buttons and the last button on the toolbar are familiar. The remaining 10 buttons let you choose different chart types or switch you back to the spreadsheet window with the first set of data (the data series) highlighted. When you click a chart type button, Works displays a dialog box showing the variations for a particular chart type. When you select a variation from the dialog box, Works switches the current chart to the chart type you select.

To switch quickly back to the spreadsheet window and highlight the cells that represent the first y-series, click the Go to First Series button on the toolbar.

Naming and Saving a Chart

As you learned earlier in this chapter, you can create up to eight charts per spreadsheet in Works. Works names the first chart Chart1, the second chart, Chart2, and so on, through Chart8. You can use the chart names that Works assigns, or you can assign a unique names to a chart, such as 1997 Income Sources. Works displays chart names in the title bar of a chart window, on the Window drop-down menu when a chart is open, and in the Charts dialog box when you choose View, Chart.

Follow these steps to rename a chart:

1. From either the spreadsheet or chart window, choose Tools, Rename Chart. The Rename Chart dialog box appears.

2. All existing charts for the current spreadsheet are shown in the Select a Chart list box. Highlight the name of the chart you want to rename.

3. In the Type a Name Below text box, type a new name of no more than 15 characters. The name can include spaces if you like.

4. Click the Rename button and the new chart name is added to the list.

5. Repeat steps 2 through 4 to rename additional charts.

6. When you finish renaming charts, choose OK.

Because charts are tied to spreadsheet data, they are saved with the corresponding spreadsheet. When you choose File, Save or File, Save As for your spreadsheet, Works saves the chart along with any changes to the spreadsheet itself. If you create a chart after saving a spreadsheet, you must save the spreadsheet file again to save the chart.

Viewing a Chart and Its Spreadsheet

As you work with your spreadsheet and create new charts, you might find it helpful to switch back and forth between the chart window and the spreadsheet window. If the two windows are not maximized, you should be able to see at least a portion of each window on-screen and click the window you want. When the two windows are maximized, you can switch back to the spreadsheet window from a chart window by choosing View, Spreadsheet. Or you can choose Window and then choose the spreadsheet's file name in the list at the bottom of the menu. If you want to return to the first y-series in the spreadsheet, you can click the Go to First Series button on the toolbar (refer to Figure 10.17).

 T I P If you want to see all the open charts and spreadsheets at once, choose Window, Tile.

To switch back to a chart from a spreadsheet, choose Window and then choose the chart name from the bottom of the menu. On the Window menu, click the chart name listed at the bottom of the menu. To view a different chart (one that is not currently open), choose View, Chart. When the New Chart dialog box appears, highlight the chart you want and click OK.

Viewing a Saved Chart

To view a saved chart, you must first open the spreadsheet, then open the chart by choosing View, Chart, which displays the View Chart dialog box. In the Select a Chart list box, highlight the chart you want to recall, then click OK. Works opens the chart in its own window on top of the spreadsheet window.

Changing X- and Y-Series Cell Ranges

Because Works automatically determines x- and y-series ranges based on the shape of the cells you select, you sometimes might want to change the x- or y-series ranges. If you add data to a spreadsheet, or if you originally selected the wrong cell range, you'll certainly need to change the defined ranges.

Before you change a range reference, check your spreadsheet and make note of the new ranges you want to define. Then define choose Edit, Series, which displays the Edit Series dialog box shown in Figure 10.18.

FIG. 10.18

The Edit Series dialog box displays existing x- and y-series cell ranges.

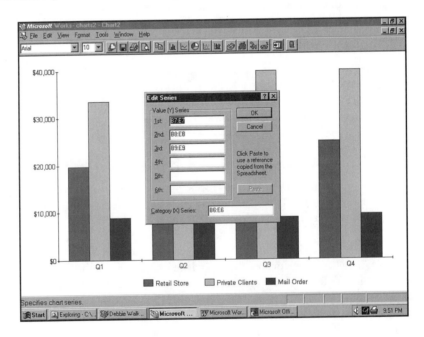

Use the following steps to add or change existing series ranges:

1. In the active window, display the chart for which you want to change series ranges.

2. Choose Edit, Series to display the Edit Series dialog box shown in Figure 10.18.

3. To add a range or adjust existing y-series ranges, type the correct cell range in the 1st, 2nd, 3rd, 4th, 5th, or 6th boxes.

4. To adjust the x-series range, type the correct cell reference in the Category (X) Series box.

5. When you have entered the new ranges correctly, choose OK. Works redisplays your chart reflecting the new series ranges you specified.

 T I P If you select and copy the correct range of cells before you choose Edit, Series, you can click the Paste button in step 3 to insert the correct cell range.

Duplicating and Deleting a Chart

When you want to create several charts using the same or similar data, it's often easier to duplicate an existing chart rather than to create a new chart from scratch. For example, suppose you want to create a chart that depicts expenses for 1997, but you want a bar chart as well as a line chart. The data series, titles, and legend are the same for both charts, so it's quicker to duplicate the first chart, changing only the chart type for the second chart.

After you duplicate a chart, you can change any of the data, titles, or other features, if necessary. When you duplicate a chart, Works assigns the new chart the next available chart name.

Use the following steps to duplicate a chart:

1. From either the spreadsheet or chart window, choose Tools, Duplicate Chart. The Duplicate Chart dialog box appears.

2. In the Select a Chart list box, highlight the name of the chart you want to duplicate.

3. In the Type a Name Below text box, type a name of no more than 15 characters for the duplicate chart. The name can include spaces if you like.

4. Click the Duplicate button. Works adds the new name to the list of chart names.

5. Repeat steps 2 through 4 to duplicate additional charts.

6. When you finish duplicating charts, choose OK.

Because Works can store only eight charts with a spreadsheet, it's important to delete charts that you no longer use or need. When you try to create a chart in a spreadsheet that already has eight charts, Works tells you to delete a chart to make room for another.

To delete a chart, follow these steps:

1. From either the spreadsheet or chart window, choose Tools, Delete Chart. The Delete Chart dialog box appears.

2. All existing charts for the current spreadsheet are shown in the Select a Chart list box. Highlight the name of the chart you want to delete.

3. Click the Delete button. A message is displayed asking you to confirm that you want to delete the chart. Choose OK. The chart is removed from the list of charts.

4. Repeat steps 2 and 3 to delete additional charts.

5. When you finish deleting charts, choose OK.

Ch

10

When you delete a chart, Works displays a warning that says you cannot undo this action. Choose Cancel if you don't want to delete the chart.

Adding a Title, Subtitle, and Axis Titles

If you don't specify a chart title when you create a new chart, you can add a title to an existing chart by choosing Edit, Titles, which displays the Edit Titles dialog box shown in Figure 10.19. You also use this dialog box to specify a chart subtitle and horizontal and vertical axis titles.

FIG. 10.19

Use the Edit Titles dialog box to add a title, subtitle, and axis titles to a chart.

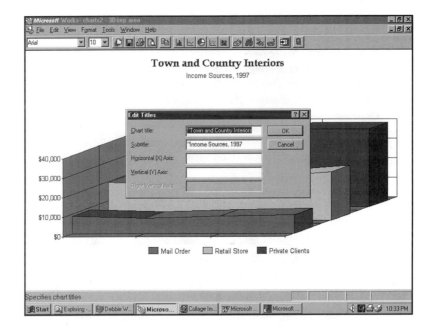

Works automatically centers a chart title at the top of a chart. If you add a subtitle, it is centered as well, just beneath the chart title. When you add a title such as "Dollars" to the vertical axis, the title appears alongside the scale. A title for the horizontal axis appears just below the axis (and above the legend, if the chart includes one). Some chart types enable you to add a right vertical axis to a chart. When you use a chart of this type, you can add a title to the right vertical axis as well.

To add titles to a chart, use the following steps:

1. In the active window, display the chart to which you want to add titles.

2. Choose Edit, Titles. The Edit Titles dialog box shown in Figure 10.19 opens.

3. Type text for the titles in the appropriate text boxes.

4. Choose OK. Works returns to your chart and inserts the titles you specify.

To remove a title from a chart, open the Edit Titles dialog box and clear the text box that contains the title you want to remove.

Choosing a Character Font, Size, Color, and Style

In Chapters 5 and 9 you learn how to enhance word processor and spreadsheet documents by using the Format Font and Style dialog box. In this box, you can change the font, size, color, and style of text. You use this same dialog box to change these characteristics in a chart.

In a chart, you can change the text format of the title independent of any other text in a chart. If you change the format of any other text (subtitle, data labels, and so on) *all* other text is changed as well. The Format Font and Style dialog box for a chart title is shown in Figure 10.20. Notice the name in the dialog box specifically states `Format Font and Style - Title`. If you select the subtitle to change its text format, the title in the dialog box reads `Format Font and Style - Subtitle` and the options in the dialog box are identical. When you select any other text to format (such as a data label), the title changes to `Format Font and Style - Tick Labels, Data Labels`, and so on. The Sample area of the dialog box displays sample text using the settings you choose. Remember to check this area to preview your choices before closing the dialog box.

FIG. 10.20

Use the Format Font and Style dialog box to change font, size, color, and style of text in a chart.

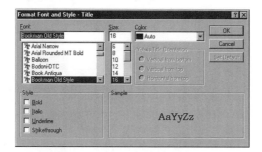

To change the text format of a chart's title, use the following steps. (Note that it isn't necessary to change all available settings, just choose the ones you want to change.)

1. Click the chart title; Works highlights the title by surrounding it with a box with handles.
2. Choose Format, Font and Style, or right-click and choose Format from the shortcut menu. The Format Font and Style - Title dialog box opens.
3. In the Font box, select a font for the title.
4. In the Size box, select a point size for the title.
5. In the Color box, select a screen-display color for the title text.
6. In the Style area, choose the Bold, Italic, Underline, or Strikethrough options to add these features to the title.
7. When all settings are correct, choose OK. Works reformats the title using the settings you specified.

To change the text format of the subtitle, axis titles, or any other text in the chart, click that part of the chart, then choose Format, Font and Style and follow steps 2 through 7. Works displays the appropriate Format Font and Style dialog box in which you can choose new settings.

Choosing Colors, Patterns, and Markers

When you create a new chart, Works automatically assigns colors to the bars, lines, areas, and pie. For the y-series data ranges 1 through 6, Works uses red, green, blue, yellow, cyan, and magenta as the default colors. You can changes these colors if you choose. Colors you see on the screen are translated to shades of gray on a black-and-white printer. Sometimes, this translation results in bars or slices that don't provide enough contrast.

Patterns are designs that fill bars, areas, or slices of a pie, or they can also be line styles (dashed, dotted, or dot-dash, and so on) used in a line chart. You can use a pattern to differentiate bars, areas, pie slices, or lines in a chart. Figure 10.21 shows an example of pattern style used in a pie chart.

FIG. 10.21

Various pattern styles appear in the slices of this pie chart.

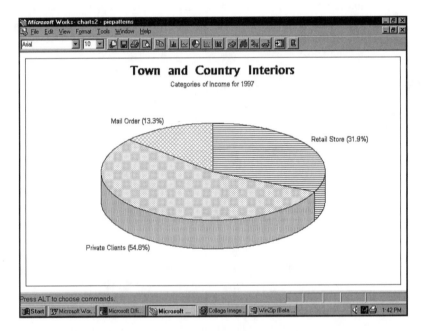

When you create a line chart or an x-y scatter chart, Works uses *data markers* for each data item. Data markers pinpoint the locations in the chart that represent actual values from the spreadsheet. The default data marker is a filled circle, but you can change the style of the data markers for each y-series range. Data marker styles include a filled circle, filled box, filled diamond, asterisk, hollow circle, hollow box, hollow diamond, dot, or dash.

To change the color, pattern, or data markers used in a chart, you use the Format Shading and Color dialog box shown in Figure 10.22. (Note that the Markers box is available only for line and x-y scatter charts. (Note that if the active chart is a pie chart, the dialog box displayed is slightly different than the one shown in Figure 10.22.) The patterns available in the Patterns list box vary depending on the type of chart you are using.

FIG. 10.22

Use the Format Shading and Color dialog box to customize the colors, patterns, and markers in your charts.

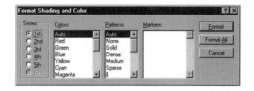

To change colors, patterns, or markers in an existing chart, use the following steps:

1. In the active window, display the chart you want to change.

2. Choose Format, Shading and Color to display the dialog box shown in Figure 10.22.

3. From the Series list, select one y-series range.

4. In the Colors, Patterns, and Markers list boxes, highlight the option you want to use.

5. To assign the current choices to the selected y-series range, click the Format button. Or to assign the current choices to all y-series ranges, choose the Format All button.

N O T E   If the dialog box obscures your view of the chart, drag the dialog box to another location on the screen. ▓

6. Repeat steps 3, 4, and 5 to select a color, pattern, or marker for other y-series ranges.

7. When all settings are correct, choose the Close button. Works returns to your chart and assigns the colors, patterns, and markers you specified.

Adding a Border, Gridlines, Droplines, and 3-D Effect

If you didn't add a border to your chart when you created it, you can add a border later. First, display the chart in the active window then choose Format, Border. Works shrinks the chart slightly and adds a border. A check mark appears next to the Border command on the Format menu. To remove a chart's border, choose Format, Border again to remove the check mark.

Gridlines help your eye track horizontally or vertically through a chart. Gridlines also help you pinpoint exact values depicted in a chart. If you add gridlines to a new chart using the New Chart dialog box, Works automatically adds both horizontal and vertical gridlines. If you don't add gridlines when you create a chart, you can add horizontal or vertical gridlines separately later.

To add gridlines to an existing chart, use the following steps:

1. In the active window, display the chart to which you want to add gridlines.

2. To add horizontal gridlines, choose the Horizontal (X) Axis command from the Format menu.

3. In the Format Horizontal Axis dialog box that appears, select the Show Gridlines check box, then choose OK.

Ch

10

4. To add vertical gridlines, repeat steps 2 and 3, choosing the Vertical (Y) Axis command rather than the Horizontal (X) Axis command.

Droplines are vertical lines that extend from data points to the x-axis to help emphasize the data points along the x-axis for each of the data items in the chart. They are especially helpful in 2-D and 3-D area charts. Notice in Figure 10.23 how the droplines make the data points for each quarter easier to distinguish.

FIG. 10.23

In area charts, you can add droplines that extend from data points to the x-axis.

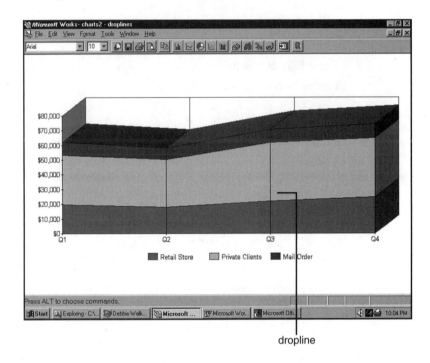

dropline

To add droplines to an area or 3-D area chart, display the chart in the active window then choose Format, Horizontal (X) Axis. In the dialog box, select the Show Droplines check box then choose OK. To remove droplines from a chart, remove the check mark from the Show Droplines check box in the Format Horizontal Axis dialog box.

N O T E   Sometimes droplines can be difficult to see if the data items in your chart are shown in a dark color. To make droplines visible, choose a lighter color for data items. (Refer to the previous section "Choosing Colors, Patterns, and Markers.") ∎

The Format menu includes a handy command, 3-D, that lets you change a 2-D chart into a 3-D chart instantly. When you choose this command, Works switches the area, bar, line, or pie chart displayed in the current window to a 3-D version of the same chart and retains the current chart variation. Using this command, you avoid having to re-create or duplicate the chart. To switch back to a 2-D version of the same chart variation, choose Format, 3-D again to remove the check mark.

TIP You can rotate a 3-D bar chart five degrees at a time right, left, up, or down by pressing Ctrl and any arrow key. Rotating a chart often makes the data more readable. Press Ctrl+Home to return the chart to its original position.

Adding a Chart Legend

When you create a new chart using the New Chart dialog box, Works automatically creates a chart legend if you select row and column headings. If your chart doesn't include a legend, you can add one later.

To add a legend, choose Edit, Legend/Series Labels, which displays the dialog box shown in Figure 10.24. In the Series Labels section, you enter the cell address for the label of each y-series data range. For instance, if your first y-series range in cells A9-3:E9 is mail order income and cell A3 contains the label *Mail Order*, enter A9 in the 1st Value Series text box.

Follow these steps to add a legend to an existing chart:

1. In the spreadsheet, note the cell range that contains the descriptions for each y-series range.

2. Display the chart for which you want to add a legend.

3. Choose Edit, Legend/Series Labels. The Edit Legend/Series Labels dialog box shown in Figure 10.24 opens.

Ch
10

FIG. 10.24
Use the Edit Legend/
Series Labels dialog
box to add a legend
to an existing chart.

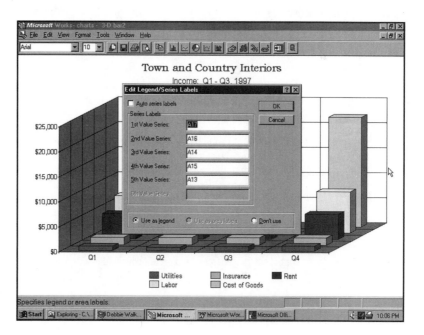

4. In the 1st Value Series box, type the cell reference for the description of the first y-series data range.

 TIP If your label in the spreadsheet isn't descriptive enough, you can type a new label in each Value Series box.

5. Repeat step 4 for all y-series ranges, entering references in the 2nd and 3rd Value Series box, and so on.

6. Choose the Use as Legend option at the bottom of the dialog box, then choose OK. Works adds a legend to your chart.

N O T E If you select the Auto Series Labels check box in the Edit Legend/Series Labels dialog box, Works inserts *Series 1*, *Series 2*, *Series 3*, and so on as the legend text for the y-series ranges in your chart. Because these labels are not very descriptive, use them only as placeholders until you replace them with more descriptive labels. ■

To remove a legend from a chart, delete the contents of each Value Series in the Edit Legend/Series Labels dialog box.

Adding Data Labels

When it's important to show precise values in a chart, you can add *data labels*. Data labels pinpoint exact values used to plot a y-series range in a chart. Works inserts the labels at the top of each bar in a bar chart, next to the points plotted in a line or area chart, or to the side of each slice in a pie chart.

An example is shown in Figure 10.25. In the Figure, you clearly can see that expenses for Q1, Q2, Q3, and Q4, respectively, are $34,957, $32,437, $39,277, and $37,561, but the exact values might be difficult to determine without the use of data labels.

You can add data labels for all y-series ranges in a chart or just to selected y-series ranges. (Notice in Figure 10.25 that data labels were added to the expense data points but not the income bars.) It's wise to use data labels sparingly as they can make a chart look cluttered. Note that data labels are not available for 3-D charts.

To add data labels to a chart, you choose Edit, Data Labels, which displays the dialog box shown in Figure 10.26. In this box, you specify which cells to use as data labels.

 TIP To add data labels to all y-series ranges, select Use Series Data in the Edit Data Labels dialog box. Works reads the correct cell ranges from the selected cells and inserts the correct data labels.

FIG. 10.25

Data labels pinpoint
exact expense amounts
for Q1, Q2, Q3, and Q4.

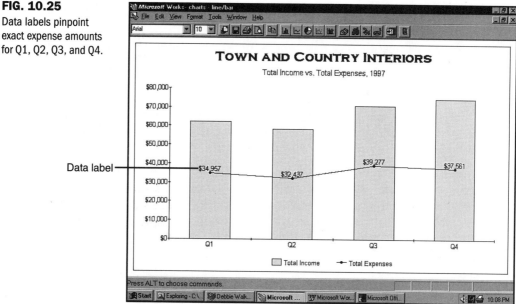

Data label

FIG. 10.26

Use the Edit Data
Labels dialog box to
add data labels to a
chart.

Use the following steps to add data labels to a chart:

1. In the spreadsheet, note the cells that contain the values you want to use as data labels for y-series ranges. (If you are adding data labels to only a single y-series range, you can select the cell range then choose Edit, Copy.)

2. Display the chart for which you want to add data labels.

3. Choose Edit, Data Labels. The Edit Data Labels dialog box shown in Figure 10.26 opens.

4. Click the Value (Y) Series box (1st, 2nd, 3rd, and so on) for which you want to add data labels. Type the correct cell range in the Value (Y) Series box, or select the Use Series Data check box. If you copied a cell range from the spreadsheet in step 1, choose the Paste button to automatically insert the correct range.

5. Type the correct cell range in all other Value (Y) Series boxes for which you want to add data labels.

6. When all ranges are entered, click OK. Works returns to your chart and adds data labels.

Changing the Chart Type

When you begin working with charts, experiment with different chart types until you find the one that is most appropriate for your data. The more you work with charts, the more familiar you become with the unique features of each chart type.

To see a sample of chart variations, choose Format, Chart Type or click one of the chart buttons on the charting toolbar. (Note that the Chart Type command appears on the Format menu only when the active window contains a chart.) With the 3-D bar chart selected in the Basic Types tab of the Chart Type dialog box, the Variations tab shows examples of the 3-D bar chart variations (see Figure 10.27). Each of the six bar chart variations is slightly different, as the following list shows:

■ The first variation in the top row is the standard 3-D bar chart that Works creates automatically.

■ The second variation in the top row stacks the bars on top of one another, illustrating the combined total of data items.

■ The third variation in the top row also stacks the bars but shows each value as a percentage of the whole (100%).

■ The first variation in the second row creates a separate bar for each data series

■ The second variation in the second row creates separate bars for each data series and adds vertical gridlines.

■ The third variation in the second row is like the previous one but adds horizontal gridlines as well.

FIG. 10.27

Works offers six 3-D bar chart variations in the Variations tab of the Chart Type dialog box.

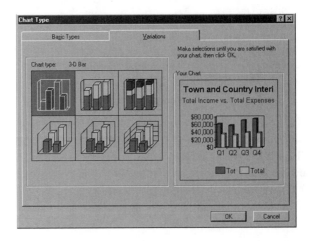

There are variations for each type of chart. Most charts offer variations that add data labels and gridlines. Some variations are unique, appropriate to the particular chart type. For instance, pie chart variations include exploded slices, and 3-D area and bar charts enable you to show the x- and y-axis in 3-D.

When you change a chart type, the x- and y-series cell ranges are not affected *unless* you change from a chart that depicts multiple y-series ranges (such as a bar chart) to a chart that depicts only one y-series range (such as a pie). In this case, Works charts only the first y-series you selected. To adjust x- or y-series cell ranges, refer to the "Changing X- and Y-Series Cell Ranges" section in this chapter.

To select a new chart type or a variation of the same chart, follow these steps:

1. In the active window, display the chart you want to change.
2. Choose Format, Chart Type to display the Chart Type dialog box.
3. Select the basic type of chart you want to switch to then choose the Variations tab. Works displays the dialog box showing the available chart variations for the basic type you selected.
4. Choose the variation you want to use, then choose OK. Works redisplays your chart using the new variation or chart type you selected.

Ch 10

Setting a Preferred Chart Type

If you don't select a chart type in the New Chart dialog box, Works always creates a bar chart. If you seldom use bar charts or most often create a different type of chart, you can change the default chart type by following these steps:

1. Create a new chart of the type you want to use as a default.
2. When the new chart appears on-screen in its own window, choose Format, Set Default Chart. Works sets the current chart type as the preferred chart type.

The next time you create a new chart, the chart type you specified as the default chart is highlighted in the New Chart dialog box. You can redefine the preferred chart type at any time using the preceding steps.

Printing a Chart

Chapter 2, "Getting Started with Works," includes an extensive section on printing Works documents. In general, all Works documents regardless of the type are printed the same way. That is, you set margins, paper source, paper size, print orientation, and starting page numbers using the File, Page Setup command (which displays the Page Setup dialog box). When all settings are correct, you preview the document, then print.

▶ **See** "Printing a Document," **p. 22**

One setting you might change when printing a chart is the orientation. Often a chart fits better and looks better when printed "sideways" on a page, which requires you to change the standard orientation from *portrait* to *landscape*.

▶ **See** "Choosing Paper Source, Size, and Orientation," **p. 22**

The Other Options tab in the Page Setup dialog box (see Figure 10.28) lets you specify the size you want to print a chart. When you choose the Screen Size option, Works prints a chart as closely as possible to the size that is displayed on-screen. The Full Page, Keep Proportions option prints the chart as large as will fit on the page at its correct height-to-width proportions. The third option, Full Page, also prints the chart as large as will fit on the page but Works adjusts the height-to-width proportions.

FIG. 10.28

The Other Options tab lets you specify the print size for a chart.

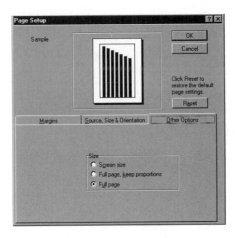

CHAPTER 11

Creating a Simple Database

A database is a record-keeping system for a collection of related information. Most of us use a database in one form or another almost every day—a phone book is a good example. With Works, you can create a database easily using a TaskWizard. The TaskWizard performs most of the chores involved in designing a database form and printing reports. And, with Works, you can choose from several predesigned databases, such as mailing lists, inventories, or even an address book. ■

Create a database using a TaskWizard

By far, the quickest and easiest way to create a commonly-used database, such as an address book, inventory, or list of suppliers, is with the help of a TaskWizard. If the database isn't exactly how you want it, start here anyway. You can modify it after Works creates it for you.

Creating a database file from scratch

Based on your planning, you build the structure of the database when you create the file. Go this route if your database or the information you're tracking is unique.

Using Form and List views

Depending on the task you want to perform, you can view the database in several different ways. Here you'll learn the usefulness for Form and List views.

Using the database toolbar

Learn which toolbar buttons are unique to the database and what each is used for.

Entering and editing data

You'll find this an easy task, especially in List view, because the format is so similar to a spreadsheet.

Creating a New Database Using a TaskWizard

Using a TaskWizard, there are several preformatted databases Works can create for you instantly: an address book, phone list, customer/client list, employee profile, sales contacts, suppliers, and vendors, to name a few. If you don't have a specific layout in mind for your database form, or if your needs are fairly simple (such as a generic address book), your best choice is to use a TaskWizard because much of the planning and layout of the database form have already been done. After you create the basic design with a TaskWizard, you can modify it to suit your particular needs.

▶ **See** "Using TaskWizards," **p. 31**

All databases consists of *records*. One record contains all the information about one company, one client, one product, and so on. Records consist of multiple *fields*. A field is one piece of information in a single record. For example, fields in an address book record might include first name, last name, address, city, state, ZIP code, and phone number. The TaskWizard inserts many fields automatically, and gives you the opportunity to add fields if you wish.

In the following steps, you create an address book using the Address Book TaskWizard:

1. Choose File, New or click the Task Launcher toolbar button. The Works Task Launcher dialog box is displayed With the TaskWizard tab selected.

2. In the TaskWizard list, the first category of wizards is called "Common Tasks." Double-click the first wizard in this category, called Address Book. (If you don't see a list of wizards under the Common Tasks category, click Common Tasks to expand the list.)

3. In the dialog box that appears, choose Yes, Run The TaskWizard. Works displays the screen shown in Figure 11.1. The wizard offers six different types of address books.

4. Click the Personal address book option, then click Next. The screen shown in Figure 11.2 is displayed.

5. Click Next. You will see the screen shown in Figure 11.3. The screen includes three buttons for adding fields; an example of the database form, as it is currently set up, is shown on the right side of the screen.

6. (Optional) To include additional fields in the database, click the Additional Fields button. The screen shown in Figure 11.4 is displayed.

7. To add fields for extended phone numbers (work, mobile, e-mail, fax, and pager), personal information (such as nicknames, spouse and children's names, birthdays, and so on), or notes, click the appropriate box. As you click any of these options, notice the example database form on the right side of the screen change to include additional fields. When you're finished adding fields, click OK. The wizard displays the screen shown in Figure 11.3 again.

8. (Optional) To create additional fields, click the Your Own Fields button. The screen shown in Figure 11.5 is displayed.

FIG. 11.1

The Address Book TaskWizard offers six types of address books.

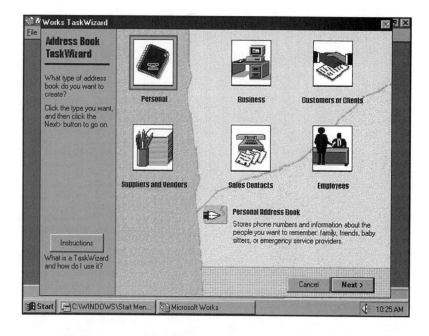

FIG. 11.2

This screen displays "general information" and "address" fields that will automatically be included in the address book.

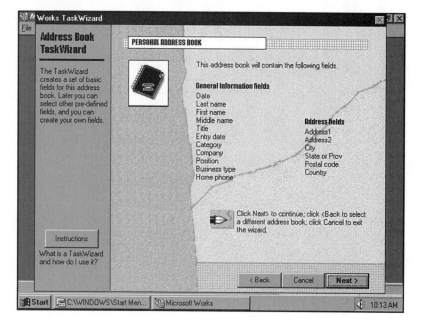

Ch
11

FIG. 11.3
This screen displays three buttons that allow you to modify the database.

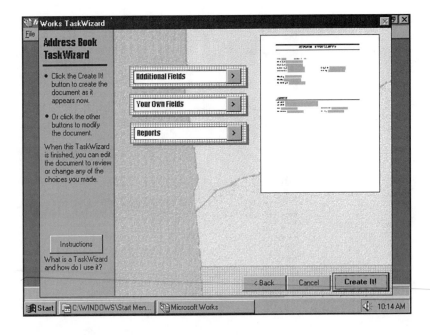

FIG. 11.4
This screen shows additional field options.

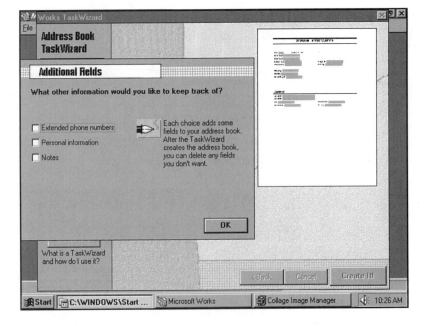

9. To add a field, click in the Field 1 box, then enter a name for the field (up to 14 characters). Repeat this step using Fields 2, 3, and 4, if desired. Notice, again, the sample database form on the right changes to include the fields you add. When you are finished adding fields, click OK. The screen shown in Figure 11.3 is displayed again.

FIG. 11.5

The Wizard lets you add up to four additional fields in the database.

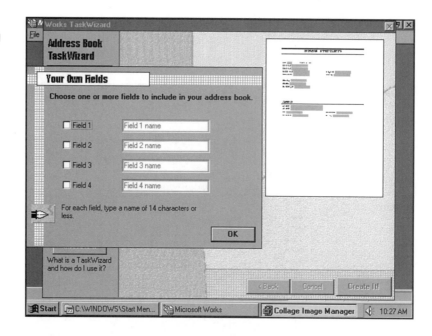

10. (Optional) To choose custom reports, click the Reports button. The screen shown in Figure 11.6 is displayed.

Ch
11

FIG. 11.6

The wizard will create an alphabetized or categorized address book at your request.

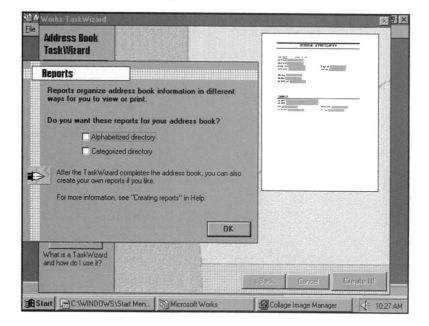

11. If you want to be able to print an alphabetized directory or a categorized directory, click the appropriate box, then click OK. The Checklist screen shown in Figure 11.7 is displayed. It summarizes the choices you have made for your database.

FIG. 11.7
The Checklist screen lists all the choices you made for your address book.

If you don't request additional fields, this box shows <<None>>

If you don't request reports, this box shows <<None>>

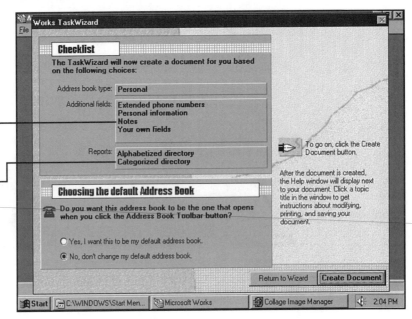

12. To change any of the choices you made for your address book, click the Return To Wizard button.

To use this address book as your default address book (the one that opens when you click the Address Book toolbar button), choose the Yes, I Want This To Be My Default Address Book option.

When you're satisfied that the address book is complete, click the Create Document button. The wizard creates your address book and displays it as the active document (see Figure 11.8).

 TIP Now would be a good time to choose File, Save to save your new address book database.

In Figure 11.8, a shaded box appears next to each database field. This is where you type *field entries*, the actual information that makes up a record; in this case, personal and address information about a friend or business colleague.

NOTE Even when you use a wizard to create a database, you can still modify the database (add or remove fields) later. See Chapter 12. ■

FIG. 11.8
Your new address book is displayed on the left; the Help window is open on the right.

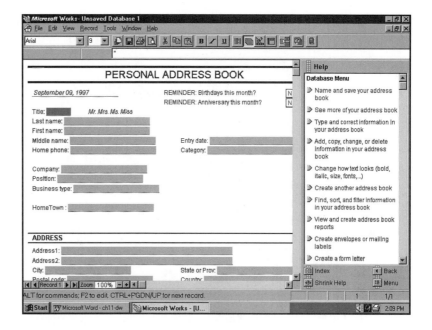

Creating a New Database from Scratch

Ch
11

Creating a database from scratch gives you the freedom to choose your own fields, but it does require some planning as well. Without the wizard offering suggested field names, you must think about all the fields you want to include in each record, the pieces of information that are most important to you, and the information that is *not* necessary. Although it's possible to add fields once a database is created, you want to avoid this task, especially after you have already added information (field entries) to the database. When planning a database, consider these factors:

- Logical Order of Fields   Create fields in a logical order (Title, Name, Address, City, State, ZIP Code, and so on) so you can enter information quickly and smoothly.

- Which Fields Are Most Important?   Enter your most important fields up front and move those fields that are not as important or might be left blank to the end of your list so you can skip over them easily as you're entering information.

- Are There Fields You're Not Sure You'll Use?   Include them now so you don't have to add them later! Leaving some unused fields blank is less trouble than having to add fields to a database later.

- Will Other People Use the Database?   Include examples of required format (such as MM/DD/YY), or consider using Note-It to annotate the database form.
  - ▶ **See** "Using Note-It," **p. 282**

To create a database from scratch, you'll use the Create Database dialog box shown in Figure 11.9. This dialog box is displayed when you click the Task Launcher toolbar button, then click the Works Tools tab, then choose the Database button.

FIG. 11.9

In the Create Database dialog box, Works leads you through the process of creating the database fields.

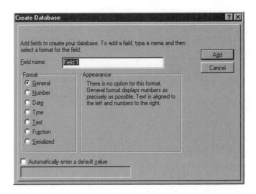

For each database field you create, you'll need to select a format, much like you select formats for cells in a spreadsheet. Table 11.1 describes the various formats available for database fields.

Table 11.1 Database Field Formats

Format	Description
General	This is a generic format you can use if you aren't sure what kind of data you'll be entering in the field. General is the default format. Numbers are displayed as precisely as possible and aligned to the right; text is aligned to the left.
Number	Use this format for numeric-only entries. Select a sample style from the Appearance list and choose the number of decimal places in the Decimal Places box.
Date	Use this format when the field contains a date. Choose a style from the Appearance list.
Time	Choose this format to display all entries in the field in a time format that you choose.
Text	Use this format to format any type of entry as text (left-aligned), including numbers that contain non-numeric characters (like telephone numbers with parentheses, slashes, or hyphens).
Fraction	This format converts a decimal number to the nearest fractional equivalent that you choose. For instance, if you choose $1/2$, then enter 1.123 in the field, Works formats the entry as 1. But if you choose $1/8$ for the fraction format, Works displays the entry as 1-$1/8$.

Format	Description
Serialized	A useful format for automatically numbering records, this format increments its value each time you enter a new record. Using this format, Works automatically numbers the first record *1*. When you enter the second record, Works automatically numbers it *2*, and so on (you can't type a number in a serialized field). If you want Works to begin numbering with a number other than 1, enter that number in the Next Value box. If you want Works to increment each record by a value of more than 1, enter that number in the Increment box.

N O T E The difference between General and Text formats is subtle. Both formats display symbols, numbers, and letters the same way. But General displays numbers as concisely as possible, and Text displays the number exactly as you entered it. For instance, the number 6.000 appears exactly like that in Text format, but it appears as 6 in General format. ▪

N O T E You can select the Do Not Reduce check box to make sure Works does not round off fractions to a lower number. This option is useful when it is important not to underestimate an amount but a slight overestimation is acceptable. ▪

To create a new database file, use these steps:

1. Choose File, New or click the Task Launcher toolbar button. The Works Task Launcher dialog box is displayed.

2. Click the Works Tools tab.

3. Choose the Database button. The Create Database dialog box opens, as shown in Figure 11.9. The first field is named Field 1.

N O T E The first time you click the Database button, you see the First Time Help dialog box. Just click the button labeled To Create a New Database, and then proceed with step 3. ▪

4. Type a new name to replace the default in the Field Name box. You may use spaces in the name.

5. From the Format options, select a format for this field (refer to Table 11.1). If applicable, also select an appearance option.

6. Click Add to add the field to your database.

7. Repeat steps 4 through 6 to add more fields as needed.

8. Click Done when you're finished adding fields. Your new database appears on-screen, as shown in Figure 11.10.

When you create a database from scratch, Works displays it in List View, which looks much like a spreadsheet. (You'll learn more about working in List View and Form View later in this chapter.) The field names you entered appear as column headings. When you're ready to enter data, you'll type all the field entries for one record in each row.

Ch
11

FIG. 11.10
The fields you created appear as column headings.

Field names ⟶

Each row is a record ⟶

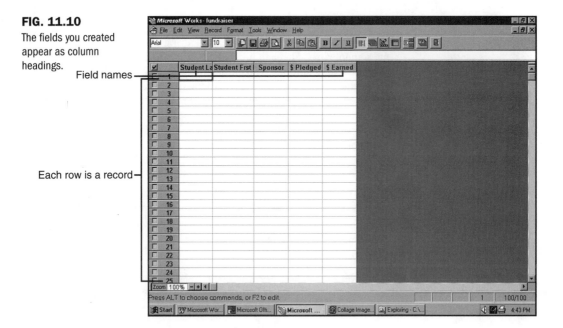

At this point the database doesn't look very impressive. The column width is automatically selected, and some of the field names aren't entirely visible. You'll learn how to modify the database in List view (as well as Form view) in Chapter 12.

▶ **See** "Modifying a Database Form," **p. 220**

▶ **See** "Modifying a Database in List View," **p. 227**

 Don't forget to choose File, Save to save the new database you just created.

Using the Database Toolbar

As you've seen in previous chapters, some buttons on the toolbar are common among all Works applications. The first 12 buttons on the database toolbar should be familiar to you (Font, Size, Task Launcher, ...Bold, Italic, Underline) The remaining buttons are unique to the database tool and are described in Table 11.2. Note that some buttons might require you to select data prior to clicking the button.

Table 11.2 Buttons Unique to the Database Tool

Database Buttons	Purpose
	Switches to List view.

Database buttons	Purpose
	Switches to Form view.
	Switches to Form Design view.
	Switches to Report view.
	Inserts a new record.
	Opens the Filter dialog box, where you can create or apply a filter.
	Opens the database that you have defined as your address book.

Viewing the Database

As you work with a database file, you have the option of viewing and displaying it in several different ways. The view you choose depends on the type of task you are performing. The four views include:

- List view
- Form view
- Form Design view
- Report view

List view displays your database very much like a spreadsheet (see Figure 11.11). Each column represents a field; each row represents a record. You'll probably use List view most often when working with a database, especially when you are entering a large number of records all at once. When you create a database from scratch, Works automatically displays the database in List view. Just like in a spreadsheet, a "cell" is located at the intersection of a row and column. The cell is where you type field entries for records in the database. The field entry for the active cell is also displayed in the entry bar.

Notice in Figure 11.11 that the status bar in List view displays the number of the active record—4—and the number total number of records—100. The number 100 is repeated, as in 100/100, to indicate that all 100 records are shown on the list.

Form view is designed to mimic a form you might fill out on paper or an index card in a paper filing system. As such, it displays only a single record at a time (see Figure 11.12). When you're looking up information (as opposed to entering new records) it's often best to use Form view so you only see the information that applies to the particular record you want.

FIG. 11.11

A database in List view shows many records at one time.

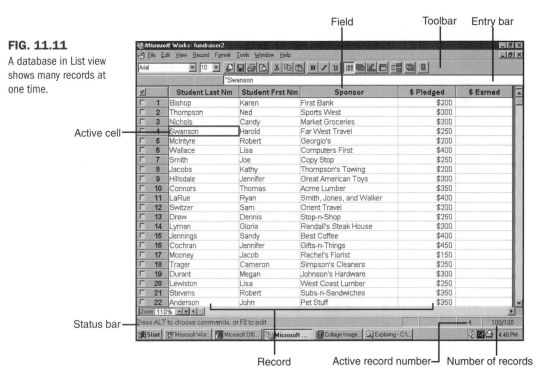

FIG. 11.12

A database displayed in Form view shows only one record at a time.

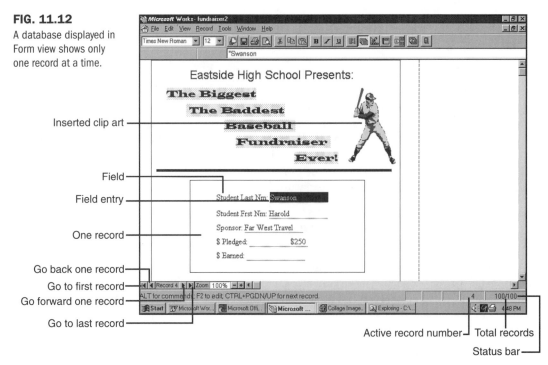

T I P As you're entering or editing entries in a database file, you'll often switch between Form view or List view. To switch quickly between these two views, press F9 (for Form view) or Shift+F9 (for List view); or click the Form view or List view button on the toolbar; or choose the Form or List command from the View menu.

Form Design view is nearly identical to Form view, except you use it to change how the form looks (rearrange fields, add borders, shading, clip art, and so on) rather than to browse records. You'll work with Form Design view in Chapter 12.

Report view enables you to view and print reports. You'll work with Report view in Chapter 13.

Entering and Editing Data

Because a database in List view is nearly identical in structure to a spreadsheet, you move around in the database and enter data the same way you do in a spreadsheet. Use the Tab key or right and left arrow keys on the keyboard to move from field to field (columns), or the up and down arrow keys to move from record to record (rows). Or, simply click the cell where you want to move. If you're looking for a particular record, you can so also use the Edit, Find and Edit, Replace commands. To enter data, move to the appropriate cell and begin typing. To edit an entry, click the cell, then retype the contents, or click in the entry bar and position the cursor, then correct the entry.

▶ **See** "Moving Around the Spreadsheet," **p. 116**

▶ **See** "Entering Text," **p. 118**

▶ **See** "Entering Numbers," **p. 119**

▶ **See** "Finding and Replacing Entries in a Spreadsheet," **p. 156**

Form view contains many of the same window elements as List view, including the toolbar, the entry bar, and the status bar. You move from field to field within one record by pressing the arrow keys or the Tab key on your keyboard. You move from record to record by clicking the arrow buttons in the lower-left corner of the screen. If you're looking for a particular record, you can so also use the Edit, Find command.

▶ **See** "Finding and Replacing Entries in a Spreadsheet," **p. 156**

To enter data in Form view, click in the field entry area and begin typing. For most databases created using a TaskWizard, the field entry area appears in gray. If you create a database from scratch, the field entry area is noted by a blank line; when you click it to enter data, Works highlights the field entry area. An example of this is clearly seen in the database shown in Figure 11.5. Press Tab to move forward from one field entry area to the next, or Shift+Tab to move backwards. ●

Ch
11

CHAPTER 12

Editing, Sorting, and Printing a Database

In Chapter 11 you learned how to create a simple database, either from scratch or by using a TaskWizard. The TaskWizards are a great tool to get you started because they automatically determine the layout of the database form for you. In this chapter you learn how to change the layout of a database form to suit your particular preferences. You can move, add, or delete fields, change a field name or its width, rearrange fields, and add artistic elements (such as clip art or word art) to the database form to give it a professional look. You also learn how to sort database information in different ways to make it most useful. And you learn about your options for printing database information. ■

Modifying the database form

You can change field names, field widths, add and delete fields, and rearrange fields on the database form to make it more useful.

Adding special touches to a database form

Because you can insert objects from other Works tools, you can dress up a database form to make it look truly professional.

Changing elements of a database in List view

Because List view is so different from Form view, you use different methods for changing field names, field widths, adding and deleting fields, and rearranging fields.

Sorting your database

One of the advantages of cataloging information in a database is that the data can be sorted in different ways. You learn all the ins and outs of sorting.

Printing database records

For the most part, you've mastered printing at this point. Here you learn some of the fine points of printing database files that differ from word processor documents and spreadsheet files.

Modifying a Database Form

As you learned in Chapter 11, "Creating a Simple Database," the database form resembles a paper form. It is intended to be the "attractive" view of a database record. Once the fields are entered, you are free to rearrange fields, add spacing and alignment, choose from a variety of fonts and sizes, and add graphic elements (lines, rectangles, and clip art). These creative touches not only make the form more visually appealing, but make the information easier to find. You aren't changing the content of the database, you're only redesigning the layout of the form.

To design a database form, you use Form Design view. This view is nearly identical to Form view, except that each element in the form is outlined by a dotted line. The dotted lines let you see exactly where each element is positioned in the form (see Figure 12.1). They also allow you to select and drag an element to a new location or alter it in some other way. (If you try to alter a form in Form view, you discover that you can't select elements of the form.) The following sections show you how you can modify the database form in Form Design view.

Changing Field Width in Form Design View

When you create a database using a TaskWizard, it automatically determines the width of each field in Form view. For example, the Address Book wizard assigns 10 characters as a width to the Title field, 35 characters as a width for fields like Last Name, First Name, Middle Name, Home Phone, Company, and 70 characters as a width for the Address1 and Address2 fields. These widths are built into the TaskWizard as a size that's likely to hold all the information you will enter. When you create a database using a TaskWizard, its unlikely you'll need to change a field width.

When you create a database from scratch, however, Works automatically assigns a field width of 20 characters to each field in Form view. For many entries, this width is adequate, but for some, you might want to change the width.

N O T E   Field widths in Form view and List view are not correlated. If you change a field width in Form Design view, the corresponding column width in List view doesn't automatically change. You change the width of a column in List view independently of Form Design view. ■

The easiest way to resize a field is with the mouse. Follow these steps to change the size of a field in Form Design view:

1. If you're not already in Form Design view, click the Form Design button or choose View, Form Design.

2. Select the field entry you want to resize. (Be sure to select the *field entry*, not the *field name*.)

   When you select the field entry, it turns black, and sizing handles appear around it (see Figure 12.1).

3. Move the mouse pointer onto one of the field sizing handles at the right edge of the field until the pointer changes to a box with an arrow labeled RESIZE.

N O T E When you add a field, the *tab order* changes automatically based on where you position the new field. As you press Tab to move from field to field, it always moves the cursor from top to bottom on the form. When two fields are side-by-side, the left field is selected first, then the field to the right. If you want to set a different tab order, see the section "Changing Tab Order" later in this chapter. ■

When you switch from Form Design view to List view, the new field appears at the end of the database (the right-most column) regardless of where you placed it in the database form. To change the position of the column in List view, see "Moving Fields in List View" later in the chapter.

N O T E If you have already entered records into your database when you add a field, the new field is blank in all the records. You need to go back and enter data into the new field for each record. ■

Deleting a Field in Form Design View

If you're sure you no longer want to use a field in a database, you can delete it. Deleting removes the field, the field's name, and all the data and formatting. When you delete a field in Form Design view, all views are affected. *The deleted fields are completely removed from the database.* This is an action that Edit, Undo cannot reverse, so use this command carefully! The only way to recover a deleted field is to close the file without saving changes. (Of course, any other unsaved changes to the file are lost, as well.)

To delete a field from the entire database using Form Design view, follow these steps:

1. Highlight the field name you want to delete.
2. Choose Edit, Delete Selection or press the Delete key.

   Works prompts you to confirm the deletion and warns that you cannot undo this operation (see Figure 12.4).
3. Choose OK to confirm the deletion. Works deletes the field and all its data from the record.

FIG. 12.4
Make sure you really want to delete the field from every record in this database.

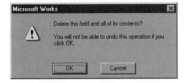

If you delete a field in List view, you can undo the deletion using Edit, Undo. To use this method, refer to the section "Deleting a Field in List View," later in this chapter.

 If Works won't delete a field, the field is probably *protected*. (Databases that you create with TaskWizards often contain protected fields.) To unprotect a field, choose Format, Protection, and then deselect the Protect Form check box and choose OK.

Ch
12

Rearranging Fields in Form Design View

After creating a database, you might decide that you want to arrange the fields differently in the database form. You can easily move fields around in Form Design view. Just click the field you want to move (click the field name or field entry part—it doesn't matter which, for this action). The word DRAG appears below your mouse pointer when you point at the selected field.

To move the selected field, drag it to any new location on-screen. If you want several fields to appear side-by-side, drag them into position—you can have as many columns of fields across a form as will fit on the screen.

> **N O T E**   The rearranging you do in one view does not affect the other views. For instance, the changes you make in Form Design view affect only Form view, not List view, and vice versa. ■

If you want to move several fields at one time, you can save time by holding down the Ctrl key while you click each field, or by drawing a *lasso* around them to select them. To lasso a block of fields, just click above one corner of the block, then drag the mouse to the opposite corner and release the mouse button. Works highlights all the selected fields. Now drag the selected fields as a group. This method is especially helpful if you have created a new field that you want to insert in the middle of a group of existing fields. For example, in Figure 12.5, all the fields below Address2 are dragged down a bit to make room for a new Address3 field.

FIG. 12.5

You can select a single field or multiple fields, then drag the selection to a new position on-screen.

Mouse pointer shows that you're dragging

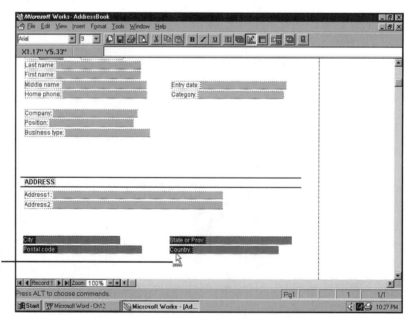

> **TIP**   You can undo a move by choosing Edit, Undo immediately after you move.

Another way to reposition a field (or several fields) is to use the Position Selection command:

1. Select the field(s) you want to move. (To select multiple fields, hold down the Shift key as you click each one.)

2. Choose Edit, Position Selection. The mouse pointer becomes an arrow with the word DRAG under it.

3. Use the arrow keys or the mouse to move the field to the new position. You don't need to hold down the mouse button.

4. Press Enter or click when the field is repositioned.

N O T E If you're trying to reposition a field and its position keeps shifting, you're experiencing the Snap To Grid feature at work. An invisible grid exists in Form Design view, with lines .08" apart. Whenever you move a field, it aligns with one of those invisible grid lines. This feature is meant to keep your screen tidy, but you can turn it off by choosing Format, Snap To Grid. ■

Adding Artistic Elements to a Database Form

Figure 12.6 shows a database form that includes some objects that make the form more attractive and easier to read. The curved title at the top of the form is a Word Art element, the baseball player is a Clip Art object, and the bold horizontal line is a Microsoft Draw object. You'll learn more about how to use Word Art, Clip Art, and Draw in Chapter 14, "Using the Works Tools Together."

▶ **See** "Using Clip Art," **p. 273**

▶ **See** "Using Word Art," **p. 275**

FIG. 12.6

This database form includes rectangles, Clip Art, and Word Art that dress up the form.

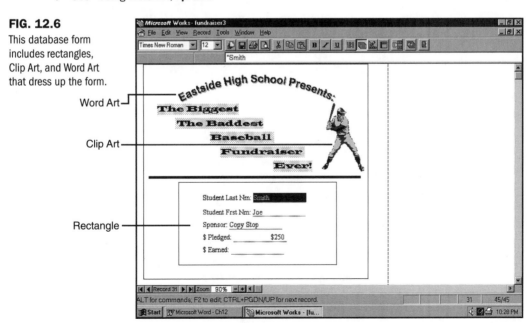

Ch
12

The rectangles that border the database record information and the entire form give the form some structure and continuity. To add rectangles to a database form, choose Insert, Rectangle. Works inserts a small rectangle near the location of the cursor. The rectangle is automatically selected, noted by the resize handles visible at the corners and sides of the rectangle. If you point inside the rectangle, the DRAG label appears on the mouse pointer, allowing you to move the rectangle. If you point to a resize handle, the RESIZE label appears on the mouse, allowing you to change the size and shape of the rectangle. These are the same mouse pointer labels you saw in Figure 12.1 for resizing a field.

To resize the rectangle, point to any handle until the RESIZE label appears, then drag until the rectangle is the size you want it to be. To move the rectangle, point inside of the rectangle until the DRAG mouse label is visible, then drag the rectangle to a new location.

 If you try to select a particular object (field name, field entry, rectangle, clip art) and Works keeps selecting a different object, you might need to rearrange the order in which objects are "layered" on the form. Try using the Format, Send to Back command on the object Works keeps selecting by mistake. This will rearrange the order in which objects are "stacked" on the form. (Think of them as a stack of papers on your desk; the Send to Back command moves the selected object to the bottom of the stack.)

Changing Tab Order

When you press the Tab key in a database form, the cursor follows a standard tab order as it moves through the form. The cursor always moves from top to bottom and left to right. For example, in the Address Book database shown in Figure 12.7, the cursor moves from Title, to Last Name, to First Name, to Middle Name, *then across to Entry Date*, then to Home Phone, and so on when you press the Tab key. When two or more fields are arranged side by side (as are Middle Name and Entry Date), the cursor moves left to right.

Figure 12.7 illustrates the tab order Works uses when you use the Task Wizard to create an Address Book.

When you rearrange fields on a database form, Works automatically rearranges the tab order to follow the top-to-bottom and left-to-right motion. You don't have to use this tab order, however. You might find that entering data in a different order is quicker. For instance, in the Address Book shown in Figure 12.7, you might decide it makes more sense to move from Middle Name down the list to Home Phone, Company, Position, Business Type, *then* move across the column to Entry Date and Category.

Set up a tab order that is most useful to you using these steps:

1. Choose Format, Tab Order. The Format Tab Order dialog box appears (see Figure 12.8), with your fields listed.

2. Select the field you want to move in the tab order.

Fifth   Seventh

FIG. 12.7
Tab order runs from
top to bottom and
right to left.

First
Second
Third
Fourth
Sixth
Eighth
Ninth
Tenth

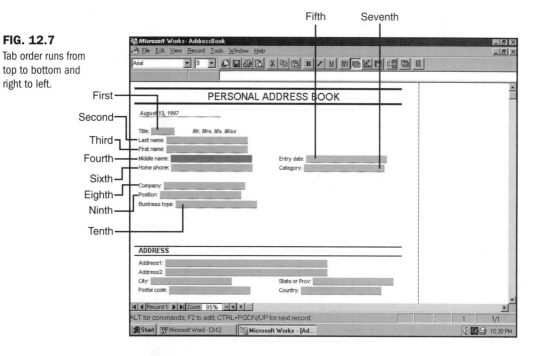

FIG. 12.8
Change the tab order
from the normal
top-to-bottom with
this dialog box.

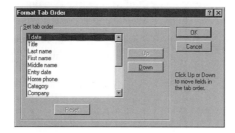

Ch
12

3. Choose the Up or Down button as many times as necessary to move the field to a new position in the list.

4. When you're satisfied with the field's position, repeat steps 2 and 3 to move another field, or click OK to finish.

Now press Tab repeatedly to move through your fields. The new tab order is in effect.

Modifying a Database in List View

As you've seen in the first part of this chapter, many of the changes you make in Form Design view do not affect the database in List view. For instance, it would be nice if field width automatically applied in both views, but it doesn't. You must change field width separately in each view. The following sections outline the changes you can make in List view. Changes that affect both views are noted.

Changing a Field Name

Just as you can in Form view, you can change a field name in List view at any time. You might decide to change a field name, perhaps to be more precise or more descriptive. No matter which view you use to change a field name, the name change appears in all views.

To change a field name in List view, follow these steps:

1. If you're not already in List view, click the List View button on the toolbar or choose View, List.
2. Select the column heading for the field whose name you want to change.
3. Choose Format, Field.
4. Type a new name in the Field Name box.

   Field names can contain up to 15 characters, and cannot begin with a single quotation mark (').
5. Click OK.

Changing Field Width in List View

In List view, Works displays fields as columns, just like in a spreadsheet. All the columns start out the same width (10 characters), but you can easily resize them in a number of ways. The easiest way is to simply drag the column border:

1. Position your mouse pointer to the right of the column heading for the column you want to resize. The mouse pointer changes to read ADJUST (see Figure 12.9).
2. Drag the column divider to the left or right to increase or decrease the width of the column. All the columns to the right of the current column are shifted to allow for the change.

The more precise way to resize a column in List view is to use the Field Width dialog box:

1. Select the column heading for the field you want to change.
2. Choose Format, Field Width to open the Field Width dialog box, shown in Figure 12.10.
3. Take one of the following steps:
   - Type an exact width in the Column Width box.
   - To create a field wide enough to display the longest data currently in the field, choose Best Fit.
   - To reset the field to its standard width (usually 10 characters), click Standard.
4. Choose OK.

N O T E Field width in List view can be 0 to 79 characters. If you set width to 0, you hide the field. ■

ADJUST mouse
pointer

Dotted line shows
new position

FIG. 12.9
You can adjust a
column's width by
dragging the column
heading.

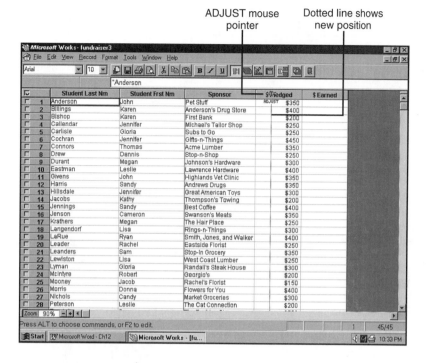

FIG. 12.10
Set a precise field
width with the Field
Width dialog box.

The Best Fit option is only useful after you enter records in a database because it uses the
width of the longest entry to judge the best fit. If you haven't entered any records in your database yet, Best Fit does nothing.

 If a particular field contains a lot of text, consider turning on Text Wrap instead of widening the field to
make it all fit.

Adding a Field in List View

In List view, you can add new fields to the database in any position. Because List view is similar
to a spreadsheet, you actually insert a column when you add a field.

To add a field in List view, follow these steps:

1. Select the field name (column) next to where you want the new field inserted. (You can
   place the new field on either side of the selected field.)

2. Choose Record, Insert Field. From the submenu that appears, choose 1 Before (to place the new field to the left of the selected one) or 2 After (to place the new field to the right).

3. The Insert Field dialog box appears (see Figure 12.11). It is the same dialog box you saw in Figure 12.3 when you first created the fields. Type a name in the Field Name box.

4. Select a field type from the Format list.

5. If any appearance options appear in the Appearance area, select the ones you want.

6. Choose the Add button.

7. Repeat steps 3 through 6 to insert another field, or click Done.

FIG. 12.11

Type a name for the new field in the Insert Fields dialog box.

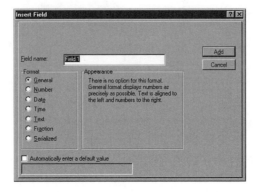

When you add a field in List view and then switch to Form view, the new field appears at the bottom of the Form. You can move the field anywhere on the form; see "Rearranging Fields in Form Design View" earlier in this chapter.

Deleting a Field in List View

As you saw earlier in this chapter, you can delete a field in Form view as well as List view. Deleting a field removes the field and all of its contents from the entire database. The advantage of deleting in List view is that the Edit, Undo command will reverse the deletion if you make an error. In Form View, Edit Undo will *not* undo a deletion.

Follow these steps to delete a field in List view:

1. If you're not already in List view, click the List View button on the toolbar or choose View, List.

2. Highlight the field you want to delete by clicking its name.

   You can delete several adjacent fields at one time. To select the fields, click the first field and drag to the last field name in the series; or hold down the Shift key and click the first and last fields in the series.

3. Choose Record, Delete Field.

4. When asked to confirm, click OK.

T I P If you delete a field by mistake, and have already made other editing changes before selecting Edit, Undo, the only way to recover the deleted field is to close the file without saving changes. Of course, any other unsaved changes will be lost as well.

Moving Fields in List View

When you want to move a field in List view, you actually rearrange columns. To move a field, just click the column heading (the field name) to select the entire column. The DRAG label appears on the mouse pointer. Drag the column to a new position (when you begin dragging, the mouse pointer changes to MOVE). As you drag, a bold line appears between columns to show where the column will be inserted (see Figure 12.12). Release the mouse button when the line appears between the two columns where you want to move the field.

FIG. 12.12

Drag a column to rearrange fields in List view.

Mouse pointer shows that you're moving

Another way to move a field in List view is with the Edit, Cut and Edit, Paste commands. Follow these steps:

1. Select the field (column) you want to move by clicking the column heading.
2. Choose Edit, Cut or click the Cut button. Works asks if you want to permanently delete this information.
3. Click OK. (You aren't really permanently deleting your field, you're just cutting the column to the Clipboard.)
4. Select the column to the left of the position where you want to move the column you cut.
5. Choose Edit, Paste or click the Paste button.

N O T E One limitation of Works is that you can't drag a column to the right-most position in List view. To get around this problem, just drag the column to the next-to-rightmost position, then drag the right-most column one place to the left. ■

Sorting Database Records

Often the order in which you enter records in a database is not the most useful order. The *sort* function arranges the records in a database in alphabetical, numerical, or date or time order, by any field you like. For more precise sorting, you can sort on up to three fields, in ascending order (1, 2, 3... or A, B, C...) or descending order (100, 99, 98... or Z, Y, X).

For instance, if you choose three fields to sort by (such as Student Lst Nm, Student Frst Nm, and Sponsor), Works sorts by the primary field (Student Lst Nm) first. All records that have identical entries in the primary field are sorted by the second field (Student Frst Nm). Finally, all the records with identical entries for the first and second fields are sorted according to the third field (Sponsor). Works sorts all records without regard to capitalization.

Figure 12.13 shows a database in List view sorted by Student Lst Nm, Student Frst Nm, and Sponsor in ascending order. Notice that the two people with the same Student Lst Nm of Joe Smith have different sponsors. These records were sorted by Sponsor, because their entries for both Student Lst Nm and Student Frst Nm were identical. (Had you requested descending order, the entries would be reversed.)

FIG. 12.13

This database is sorted first by Student Lst Nm, then by Student Frst Nm, then by Sponsor.

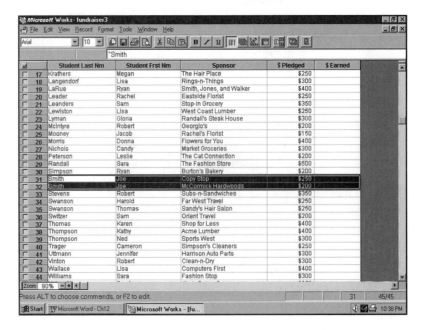

To sort a database, follow these steps:

1. With the database displayed in Form view or List view, choose <u>R</u>ecord, <u>S</u>ort Records. Works displays the Sort Records dialog box (see Figure 12.14).

FIG. 12.14

Use the Sort Records dialog box to sort up to three fields at a time.

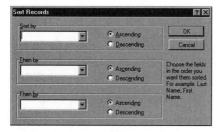

2. From the <u>S</u>ort By drop-down list, select the name of the field to sort by, then choose <u>A</u>scending or <u>D</u>escending.

3. Optionally, select the names of up to two more fields to sort by in the Then By boxes, selecting Ascending or Descending for each.

4. Choose OK.

   Works sorts your records on-screen according to the criteria you specified.

 To undo a sort, choose <u>E</u>dit, <u>U</u>ndo Sort; or press Ctrl+Z. You must choose <u>U</u>ndo Sort before performing any other tasks.

If you add data to the database after a sort, you can repeat the sort quickly within the same Works session using the same sort criteria. Here's how:

1. Choose <u>R</u>ecord, <u>S</u>ort Records.

   Works displays the Sort Records dialog box with the sort options you chose previously.

2. Choose OK.

Works resorts the database using the same sort criteria.

 If you need to sort your database on more than three fields, sort the database twice, using the three least important criteria in the first sort. For example, suppose you want to sort on Amount Due, Credit Rating, Last Name, First Name, ZIP. If you determine that Amount Due and Credit Rating are the two most important fields (in that order), sort the database first on Last Name, First Name, and ZIP. Then sort the database again and specify Amount Due in the <u>S</u>ort By text box and Credit Rating in the first <u>T</u>hen By text box.

Ch

12

Printing Database Records

Chapter 2, "Getting Started with Works," includes an extensive section on printing Works documents. In general, all Works documents, regardless of the type, are printed the same way. That is, you set margins, paper source, paper size, print orientation, and starting page numbers using the File, Page Setup command (which displays the Page Setup dialog box). When all settings are correct, you preview the document, then print.

▶ **See** "Printing a Document," **p. 22**

The default margin settings (1 inch for top and bottom margins and 1.25 inches for left and right margins) are generally fine for most documents, but for some databases, you might want to change these settings in order to fit more data on a page.

Another setting you're likely to change when printing a database is the orientation. Databases, like spreadsheets, often fit better and look better when printed "sideways" on a page. To accomplish this effect, you need to change the standard orientation from *portrait* to *landscape*.

▶ **See** "Choosing Paper Source, Size, and Orientation," **p. 22**

 Using List view, you can hide records that you don't want to print. See "Hiding Records" in Chapter 13.

Inserting and Deleting Page Breaks in List View

Before you print, you can save time and paper by checking where page breaks occur. When using List view, Works automatically prints as many records on a page as it can on a page. But sometimes the pages break awkwardly, leaving half a record dangling between pages. To solve this problem, you can insert horizontal page breaks exactly where you want them. You can also insert *vertical* page breaks, (which let you determine how many fields will print on a page) because a database in List view often can span multiple pages in *width* as well as length.

To insert a horizontal or vertical page break in List view, follow these steps:

1. Highlight any field in the record below which you want a horizontal page break.

   or

   Highlight any field entry in the field to the right of where you want a vertical page break.

2. Choose Format, Insert Page Break.

   The Insert Page Break dialog box appears (see Figure 12.15).

3. Choose Record to insert a horizontal page break, or Field to insert a vertical one.

4. Choose OK.

   Works inserts a dashed page break line above the record or to the left of the field.

FIG. 12.15

Choose which type of page break you want: horizontal (Record) or vertical (Field).

You can also insert page breaks in List view *without* using the Insert Page Break dialog box:

1. To insert a horizontal page break, highlight the entire record below which you want the page break.

   or

   To insert a vertical page break, highlight the entire field to the right of where you want the page break.

2. Choose Format, Insert Page Break.

   Works inserts a page break above the record or to the left of the selected field.

To delete a page break in List view, follow these steps:

1. Highlight the record below or the field to the right of the page break.

2. Choose Format, Delete Page Break.

   Works removes the page break.

Setting Other Page Options

Like spreadsheets, databases printed in List View contain two unique features that other documents don't have: gridlines and record and field labels (in spreadsheets, these are called row and column headers, or labels). Printing of these two features is controlled by the Other Options tab in the Page Setup dialog box (see Figure 12.16).

Ch

12

FIG. 12.16

When you view a database in List view, the Other Options tab in the Page Setup dialog box is almost identical to the one used for spreadsheets.

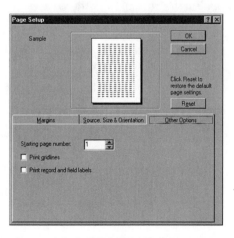

Works does not automatically print the gridlines that appear on the screen when you print a database in List view. However, just like for spreadsheets, databases are often easier to read when gridlines are printed. To print gridlines, select the Print Gridlines check box and then choose OK.

Printing record and field labels in List view can also make a database file easier to read. To use this option, select the Print Row and Column headers check box, then choose OK.

When you display the database in Form view, the Other Options tab in the Page Setup dialog box changes slightly to look like the one shown in Figure 12.17. In it you can specify options that pertain to the way a *database form* (as opposed to the database *list*) is printed.

FIG. 12.17

When Form view is active, the Other Options tab in the Page Setup dialog box offers different options than the one shown in Figure 12.16.

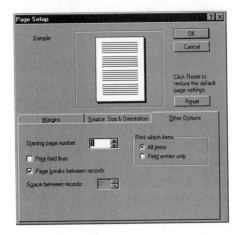

Table 12.1 describes the settings on the Other Options tab in the Page Setup dialog box when Form view is active.

Table 12.1   Print Options When Printing in Form View

Setting	Description
Starting Page Number	If you want a number other than 1 for the first printed page, enter it here.
Print Field Lines	Prints horizontal lines under each field
Page Breaks Between Records	Prints a single record per page
Space Between Records	Lets you specify in inches the amount of blank space you want between records.
All Items	Print field names as well as data.
Field Entries Only	Print only data, eliminating field names.

N O T E   To print a single record, display the record you want in Form view, choose File, Print, then choose Current Record Only. ■

CHAPTER 13

Expanding Your Database Skills

Get ready to go to work; you're going to learn some advanced features of the database tool. You've mastered creating the database file and customizing the database form, now you're ready to use some of the more powerful features. ■

Discover how to use formulas and functions in the database

You can use formulas and functions in a database field just like you do in a spreadsheet to perform calculations on database data.

Learn how to protect data

It's important to "lock" portions of your database so that other users can't inadvertently delete or change data.

Find and replace data

Just like in a word processor document or spreadsheet, you can use the Find and Replace features of Works in a database file.

Work with filters

A filter lets you zero in on specific database records based on the criteria you specify.

Create reports

Aside from cataloging information, databases are most often used to generate reports on selected data. In this chapter you learn how to create standard and customized reports.

Creating a Simple Formula in a Field

Just like in a spreadsheet, Works enables you to perform math calculations on numbers in database fields. When Works performs the calculation you specify, it inserts the result in the field that contains the formula. For example, Figure 13.1 shows a database form with two calculated fields.

FIG. 13.1
Works calculates a result when you type information in fields the formula references.

Formula in TotalAmtDue field

Calculated result

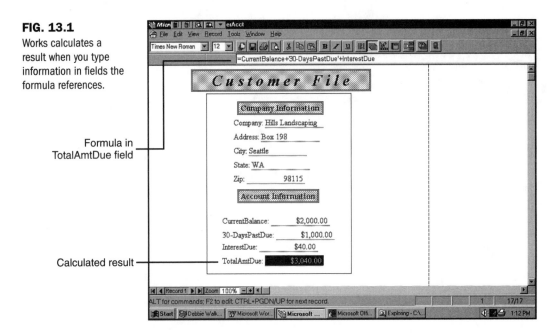

The first calculated field is TotalAmtDue. In Figure 13.1, this cell is highlighted and the formula used to calculate the amount due appears in the entry bar:

```
=CurrentBalance+'30DaysPastDue'+InterestDue
```

The second calculated field in Figure 13.1 is the InterestDue field. It contains the formula ='30DaysPastDue'*.04. So, when you type a value in 30DaysPastDue, Works automatically calculates the interest, then uses it to calculate the result in the TotalAmtDue field.

The primary difference between entering a formula in a spreadsheet and a database is that, in the database, the formula is automatically copied to the same field in every other record. You don't need to re-enter the formula for each new record. This is a great time saver and it also ensures accuracy in the database.

> **CAUTION**
> When you enter a formula in a field, it replaces all existing data in that field for all records.

You can create a formula in either Form view or List view. Follow these steps to enter a formula:

1. Highlight the field where you want to create a formula.

2. Type an equal sign (=) then type the formula. Or you can point to the cells you want to use in the formula, inserting operators where appropriate.

   As you type, the formula appears in the field and in the entry bar.

3. Press Enter. (You can also press Tab or an arrow key if you prefer.)

   Works calculates the formula and inserts the results in the field. After you create a formula, Works calculates the formula in the field for each record you display.

▶ **See** "Entering Simple Formulas," **p. 138**

 T I P To perform math calculations on more than one record, use a database report. For example, you can use a report to calculate the sum of all the entries in the TotalAmtDue field in a database. See "Creating a Database Report," later in this chapter.

Using a Formula to Fill Fields

You can use a formula to fill in identical entries in a field. For example, if you know that most of the entries in the City and State fields will be *Seattle* and *WA*, you can use a formula to insert these words in the fields automatically. If, for some records, the city and state are not *Seattle* and *WA*, you can simply type over these entries in the appropriate record.

Follow these steps to create a formula that inserts the same data in a field:

1. Highlight the field where you want to insert the formula.

2. Type = (equal sign) followed by the entry you want to appear in the field.

   For example, in the City field, type **="Seattle"**, and in the State field, type **="WA"**.

3. Press Enter.

   In each record of the database, Works inserts the entry in the selected field.

N O T E When entering text as a formula, you must enclose the text in double quotes, as shown. You don't need to enclose numbers, dates, or times in double quotes. ■

When using List view, you can also fill fields using the <u>E</u>dit, Fill Do<u>w</u>n command.

▶ **See** "Filling Cells," **p. 120**

Using a Function in a Field

As you learned in Chapter 8, Works contains 77 built-in mathematical formulas, called *functions*, that you can insert into spreadsheet cells. You can also apply these functions to field entries in a database.

Ch
13

Functions perform calculations or enter data without requiring you to type complex formulas or long text. For example, you can use the AVG (average) function to calculate the average of the contents of the fields Distance1, Distance2, and Distance3. In the field where you want Works to insert the average, type **=AVG(Distance1,Distance2,Distance3)**. When you enter data in the distance fields, Works calculates the average and inserts the results in the field where you typed the formula with the AVG function.

N O T E Unfortunately, you cannot browse a list of the available functions from within the database tool like you can in the spreadsheet tool. To see a list of functions, open a blank spreadsheet and choose Insert, Function or Tools, EasyCalc. For more detailed information, see Chapter 8, "Working with Formulas and Functions." ▪

To enter a function in a database field, follow these steps:

1. Highlight the field where you want to enter the function.
2. Type = (equal sign) followed by the name of the function you want to use.

   For example, type **=avg**. You may use uppercase or lowercase letters when you type function names.

3. In parentheses, type the names of the fields you want the function to use, separated by commas.

   Your line should look something like this:

   =avg(Distance1,Distance2,Distance3)

4. Press Enter.

▶ **See** "Using Functions in Formulas," **p. 148**

Protecting Your Data

A user generally has access to alter a form design or data contained in a database. To prevent either deliberate or accidental changes to your database, protect your fields. You can protect a single field or all fields from changes. When field protection is on, it isn't possible to change, delete, or clear data from protected fields, or to rearrange the tab order in the form. (You still can copy and sort protected fields.)

N O T E You can't protect a single record—protection applies to fields and their data. ▪

You can protect fields using either List View or Form Design view; the procedure is the same for both. To protect a field and its data, use these steps:

1. Highlight the field(s) you want to protect.
2. Choose Format, Protection.

The Format Protection dialog box appears (see Figure 13.2).

3. Select the Protect Field check box to protect the field(s).

4. Choose OK.

FIG. 13.2

The Format Protection dialog box enables you to turn field protection on or off.

 To quickly protect all fields, select an entire record before applying the protection command.

When changes to a protected field are necessary, you can unprotect a field by following the same previous steps, removing the check mark from the Protect Field box in step 3.

Hiding Records and Fields

Hiding records is useful when you don't want to display or print selected records.

1. In Form view, display the record you want to hide.

   or

   In List view, highlight the record(s) you want to hide.

2. Choose Record, Hide Record.

   Works hides the selected record(s).

 After you hide records, the status bar tells you the total number of records displayed and the total number of records in the file. For example, if the status bar reads 95/100, 5 records are hidden.

To redisplay hidden records, choose Record, Show, 1 All Records. Works redisplays all the hidden records. In certain circumstances, it's also useful to hide fields. For instance, if your database contains 15 fields of information about clients but you're only concerned with 10 of those fields, you can hide the remaining fields. This makes it easier to find and focus in on the information you're interested in.

To hide a field or fields, do this:

1. Select the field or fields you want to hide.

2. Choose Format, Field Width. The Field Width dialog box is displayed.

3. In the Column Width box, type **0**, then click OK. The field and all of its data still exists but it isn't visible on the screen.

Ch

13

T I P   If you want to hide just one field, you can select the column and drag the column border until the column width is 0.

To redisplay hidden fields, use these steps:

1. Choose Edit, Go To. The Go To dialog box is displayed.
2. From the Select a Field list, highlight the field you want to display, then click OK.
3. Choose Format, Field Width. The Field Width dialog box is displayed.
4. In the Column Width box, type a number for the field width, or choose Standard or Best Fit.
5. Click OK.
6. Repeat steps 2-5 for all hidden fields you want to redisplay.

Finding and Replacing Data

The easiest way to locate information in a database is with the Edit, Find command. This command can help you move quickly through all occurrences of a word, phrase, name, or number in your database. You learned in Chapters 4 and 9 how to use this feature in word processor documents and spreadsheets. The command works in much the same way in the database tool.

To find text in either List view or Form view, use these steps:

1. To search selected fields, highlight those fields. To search the entire database, place the cursor on any field.
2. Choose Edit, Find. Works displays the Find dialog box in Figure 13.3. The Next Record option is selected in the Match area of the dialog box.

FIG. 13.3
Type the word, phrase, or number you want to find.

3. In the Find What box, type the characters you want to find.
4. Choose OK. Works closes the dialog box and highlights the first occurrence in the database.
5. To find the next occurrence, press Shift+F4. You can continue pressing Shift+F4 to find all occurrences in the file.

▶ **See** "Finding and Replacing Text in a Document," **p. 53**
▶ **See** "Finding and Replacing Entries in a Spreadsheet," **p. 156**

A variation of the Edit, Find command allows you to find all records that match the characters you type in the Find What box and automatically hide all others. This feature ensures that you see all records that match your search criteria. To use this feature, follow the steps above but choose the All Records button in the Match area of the dialog box. Figure 13.4 shows an example of the records that were found when searching for the word "Cameron" in a sample database. Notice that the matching characters don't necessarily occur in the same fields; in this case, the match appears in two different fields.

FIG. 13.4
All matching records
are displayed; all others
are hidden.

"Cameron" found
in three records

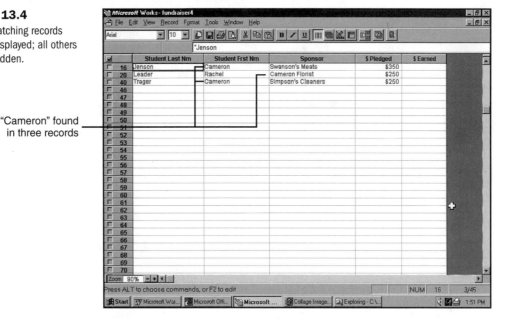

To display all other records; that is, those that didn't match the characters you wanted to find, choose Record, Show, 4 Hidden Records. To redisplay *all* records in the database, choose Record, Show, 1 All Records.

You can also replace entries in the database, just like you do in a word processor document or spreadsheet. Use these steps:

1. To search and replace in selected fields, highlight those fields. To search and replace entries throughout the entire database, place the cursor on any field.

2. Choose Edit, Replace. Works displays the Replace dialog box (see Figure 13.5).

3. In the Find What text box, type the field entry you want to find and replace.

4. In the Replace With text box, type the characters you want to use as replacements.

5. Under the Search options, choose Records if you want Works to search from left to right as it moves through rows. Choose Fields if you want Works to search down each column in turn.

Ch
13

FIG. 13.5
Use the Replace dialog
box to automatically
replace the contents of
a field.

6. To locate the next occurrence, click Find Next. When Works highlights the next occurrence, choose Replace, or Find Next again.

To direct works to replace every occurrence without prompting you, choose Replace All.

To end searching and replacing, choose Cancel.

 TIP With both the Edit, Find and Edit, Replace commands, you can use wild cards to substitute for a character or group of characters. To learn more about using wild cards, refer to "Finding and Replacing Text in a Document," in Chapter 4.

Using Filters

You learned in the previous section how to n use Find to perform simple searches—for example, to find the name of specific company. Sometimes, however, Find isn't specific enough. For instance, you might want to find records where the TotalAmtDue is greater than or equal to $4000.00 *or* the 30DaysPastDue amount is greater than $2000.00 *and* the State equals California (CA).

For searches like these, you use a *filter*, which works like Find but zeros in on records that match a number of criteria. When these records are found, all others are hidden. In Figure 13.6, you see the results that are displayed (only three records) when a filter called "Seattle" was used to find all records whose City is Seattle, whose Last Name is less than or equal to M, and whose Postal Code is greater than or equal to 98124.

Creating a Filter

When you create a filter, you choose the field you want to use, the type of comparison you want to make, and the characters to which you want the field compared.

Table 13.1 lists all the types of comparisons you can use in a filter.

FIG. 13.6

Only three records match the filter criteria.

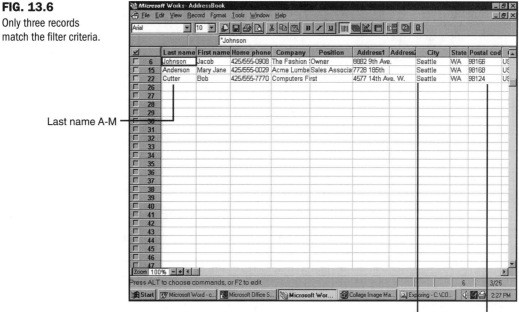

Last name A-M

City is Seattle   ZIP 98124 or greater

Table 13.1   Types of Comparisons Available for Filters

Comparison Type	Meaning
is equal to	Contains exactly the specified characters. For example, the filter *Smith* would not find *Smithsonian* and *100* would not find 1000.
is not equal to	Does not contain the specified characters. (The field might contain the specified characters plus some other text, or it doesn't contain the specified text at all.)
is less than	Is a smaller number than the one specified or begins with an earlier letter of the alphabet than the one specified.
is greater than	Is a larger number than the one specified or begins with a letter of the alphabet than comes after the one specified.
is less than or equal to	Is equal to or a smaller than the number specified, or begins with the same letter or an earlier letter of the alphabet than the one specified.

continues

Ch

13

Table 13.1 Continued

Comparison Type	Meaning
is greater than or equal to	Is equal to or greater than the number specified, or begins with the same letter of the alphabet or a letter that comes after the letter specified.
contains	Contains the specified character, whether as an exact match or as a part of the contents. For example, the filter `Smith` would find `Smithsonian`; `100` would find `1000`.
does not contain	Doesn't contain the specified characters anywhere in the entry.
is blank	The field is completely empty.
is not blank	The field contains some type of entry.
begins with	The first character(s) in the field match the specified characters.
does not begin with	The first character(s) in the field do not match the specified characters.
ends with	The last character(s) in the field entry match the specified characters.

The easiest way to create a filter is by using the Easy Filter option in the Filters dialog box (see Figure 13.8). The Easy Filter option simply compares field entries to the criteria you specify. (You can specify up to five criteria using Easy Filter.) You can also create a filter using a formula, which you'll learn about later in "Creating Advanced Filters."

To create a new filter, use these steps:

1. Choose Tools, Filters, or click the Filters button on the toolbar. Works displays the Filter dialog box; the Filter Name dialog box appears on top of it, as shown in Figure 13.7. (If the First-Time Help dialog box is displayed, you can choose to see a demo on one of the listed topics or click the Don't Display This Message In The Future box and choose OK.)

2. In the Filter Name dialog box, type a descriptive name (up to 15 characters) to replace the suggested name `Filter 1`, then click OK. The Filter Name dialog box closes and the Filter dialog box is still displayed, as shown in Figure 13.8. Note that the Easy Filter option button is already selected.

3. In the first drop-down box, under the Field Name heading, select a field for the first filter criterion.

4. In the first drop-down list under the Comparison heading, select an option for comparing the field content (for example, is equal to, is greater than or equal to, contains, begins with, and so on.)

FIG. 13.7

The Filter Name dialog box appears on top of the Filter dialog box.

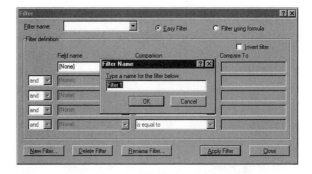

FIG. 13.8

You use the Filter dialog box to choose the filter criteria.

5. In the text box under the Compare To heading, type the value (text or number) to which you want the field's contents compared.

6. To add another criterion, choose *and* or *or* from the drop-down list on the far left side of the second line, then repeat steps 3 through 5 for that line.

 TIP To display only the records for which your filter does *not* apply, click the Invert Filter check box at the upper right of the Filter dialog box.

7. When you are finished entering filter lines, click the Apply Filter button.

To display all records *not* found by the filter, choose Record, Show, 4 Hidden Records. To redisplay all records after applying a filter, choose Record, Show, 1 All Records.

After you apply a filter, the Filter Name dialog box isn't displayed when you choose Tools, Filters. Instead, the Filters dialog box appears with the last filter you used still showing. You can reapply the filter by clicking the Apply Filter button. To create a new filter, click the New Filter button. You can create up to 8 filters for a Works database.

Deleting a Filter

Because you can save only 8 database filters, you might find it necessary to delete a filter at some point to make room for new ones. (If you try to create a ninth filter, you'll be asked to delete an existing one.)

Ch

13

To delete a filter, do this:

1. Choose Tools, Filters. The Filters dialog box shown in Figure 13.8 is displayed.
2. In the Filter Name drop-down list, highlight the filter you want to delete.
3. Click the Delete Filter button. Works displays a warning message asking if you're sure you want to delete the filter and that the operation cannot be undone.
4. Choose Yes.
5. In the Filters dialog box, choose Close.

Creating an Advanced Filter

With the Easy Filter option in the Filters dialog box (refer to Figure 13.8), you can create most of the filters you will ever need. However, if you want to use a mathematical formula in a filter, or if you want to specify more than five criteria, you need to use the Filter Using Formula option in the Filters dialog box.

Figure 13.9 shows how the `Seattle` filter looks when displayed as a formula.

FIG. 13.9
The Filter Using Formula makes a simple formula look like computer code.

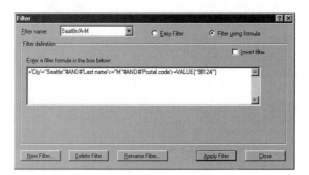

Each filter instruction in the code defines the text or values you want Works to look for. Table 13.2 shows how Works translates each line of the filter into a formula.

Table 13.2 Easy Filter	
View	**Filter Using Formula View**
City equals Seattle	='City'="Seattle"
Last Name is less than or equal to M	"#AND#'Last name'<="M"
Postal Code is greater than or equal to 98124	#AND#'Postal code'>=VALUE("98124")

Keep the following rules in mind when writing a formula:

- Begin each formula with an equal sign
- When including a number to compare to, format it like this: VALUE(*"number"*)
- When including text to compare to, format it like this: *"text"*
- Separate each criterion with *#AND#* or *#OR#* operators, encased in # marks as shown
- Use the operator symbols shown in Table 13.3 to indicate what kind of comparison you want to make

Table 13.3 includes a list of all operators you can use in a filter formula.

Table 13.3   Operator Symbols to Use in Filter Formulas

Description	Operator
is equal to	=
is not equal to	<>
is less than	<
is greater than	>
is less than or equal to	<=
is greater than or equal to	>=
contains	"*text*"
does not contain	<>"*text*"
is blank	""
is not blank	<>""
begins with	"text*"
does not begin with	<> "text*"
ends with	*text"

Note: Asterisks (*) indicate wild card characters.

Just like in a mathematical formula, in filters you group conditions in parentheses. For example, in the following instruction, the OR operator applies to all results of the conditions enclosed in parentheses:

```
=LastName="Johnson"#OR#(Age>30#AND#Sex="M")
```

The filter finds all people who are over 30 *and* are male, *or* whose last name is Johnson.

If you reposition the parentheses, the AND operator applies to all results of the conditions enclosed in parentheses.

```
=LastName=("Johnson"#OR#Age>30)#AND#Sex="M"
```

Ch
13

This filter first finds all people whose name is Johnson *or* who are over 30, *and* then finds all people who are male.

TIP Because the Easy Filter option only lets you specify up to five criteria for a filter, you need to use the Filter Using Formula option to create a filter that specifies additional criteria. You can make the job a little easier by creating the first five criteria using Easy Filter, then switching to Filter Using Formula to add additional criteria.

With the Filter Using Formula option, you can create filters that perform mathematical calculations (such as adding, subtracting, multiplying, dividing, or exponentiating one or more fields). For filters that include math calculations, use the math operators shown in Table 13.4.

Table 13.4   Math Operators for Filters That Include a Formula

Operator	Example	Purpose
+	=(Premium+Principal) >500	Adds two values first, then makes *greater than* comparison
-	=(PastDue-DateDue)>30	Subtracts due date from past due date before making *greater than* comparison
*	=(Cost*Qty)<=100	Multiplies Cost by Quantity before making *less than or equal to* comparison
/	=(Pledge/Miles)>25	Divides Pledge by Miles before making *greater than* comparison
^	=Side^2<200	Raises Side to the power of 2 before making *less than* comparison.

In addition to formulas, you can create filters using a built-in function. Using a function saves you the trouble of typing complex formulas in a filter. Any function that you can use in a database field can be used in a filter. Here is an example:

=PMT(Principal,Rate,Term)*12. The PMT function calculates the periodic (monthly) payment for a loan or investment and the entire formula calculates the amount due yearly.

▶ **See** "Using Functions in Formulas," **p. 148**

You can also use dates in a filter. When you use a date, you must enclose it in single quotation marks, such as '8/19/99'. Here are some examples of filters that use dates:

DateDue-'5/19/97'>90. This filter selects records in which the due date falls more than 90 days after 5/19/97.

Working with Database Reports

Reports let you tell Works to print or display only the fields you want, and you can tell Works to calculate and print report statistics, such as a count of the records, or an average value for a group of records. Figure 13.10 shows an example of a report.

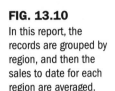

FIG. 13.10
In this report, the records are grouped by region, and then the sales to date for each region are averaged.

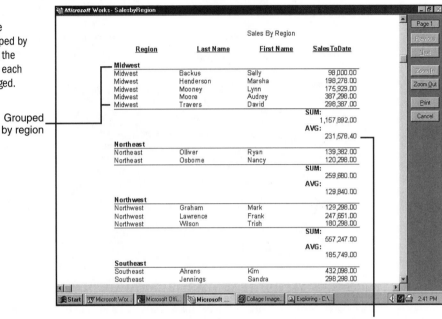

After you create a report that displays information the way you want, you can save the report and use it again later. You can save up to eight reports for each Works database.

In Works, you can create reports in two ways:

- Using the Tools, ReportCreator command, you can create almost any report.
- Using Report view, you can fine-tune a report, and use advanced report features not available in ReportCreator.

ReportCreator walks you through a series of tabs in the ReportCreator dialog box in which you specify your reporting preferences. These preferences include the fields you want in your report, the order in which the fields occur, the title to give your report, how to group records, and the statistics you want to display. After you have created a report, you can enhance it by adding more titles and notes, changing the fonts, changing alignment and number formats, and more.

Ch
13

Creating a Report

Use these steps to create a report with ReportCreator:

1. Display the database (in any view) for which you want to create a report.

2. Choose Tools, ReportCreator. Works displays a Report Name dialog box. (If this is your first time creating a report, you will see the First-Time Help dialog box. Click OK to move past it.)

3. Replace the suggested name (Report 1) with a more descriptive name and click OK.

   The ReportCreator dialog box appears, with the Title tab showing (see Figure 13.11).

FIG. 13.11

The first tab in the ReportCreator dialog box asks for a title for your report.

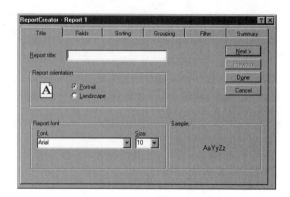

4. Use the suggested title, or replace the text in the report Title field with another title.

   (By default, the report title is the database name, a dash, and the report name you specified in step 3. The default title is a bit awkward, so you probably want to replace it.)

5. Click an orientation button to choose a page layout: Portrait or Landscape.

6. Choose a default font and font size for the report from the Font and Size drop-down lists. Your choices are shown in the Sample area.

   Works uses the font you choose to format *all* text in the report. You can change the font for titles and headings when you customize the report, as explained later in this chapter.

7. Click the Next button to continue. Works displays the Fields tab, as shown in Figure 13.12.

8. In the Fields Available list, highlight the first field you want to include in the report.

   Works prints the first field in the left-most column of the printout, so make sure you select fields in the order that you want them to appear on the report, from left to right.

9. Click the Add button.

   or

   To add all the fields, in the order they are listed in the Fields Available box, click the Add All button.

10. Repeat steps 8 and 9 to add other fields.

FIG. 13.12
Choose the fields you want to include on the Fields tab.

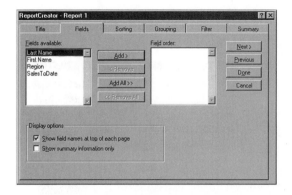

N O T E If you want to remove a field you have added, highlight it in the Field Order list and click the Remove button. To remove all the fields and start over, choose Remove All. (Or, you can double-click a field to add or remove it.) ▮

11. Select or deselect either of the Display Options check boxes:

    Show Field Names at Top of Each Page—when selected, field names are repeated on each page.

    Show Summary Information Only—when selected, your report shows only the summary of the groups you select; individual records are eliminated.

12. Click Next. Works displays the Sorting tab, as shown in Figure 13.13.

FIG. 13.13
Use the Sorting tab to specify in what order the records will appear on the report.

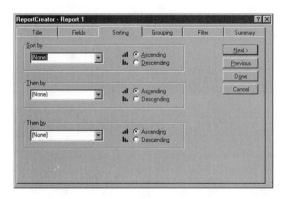

▶ **See** "Sorting Database Records," **p. 232**

13. If you want your records sorted, choose the field to sort by from the Sort By drop-down list, and click the Ascending or Descending button.

14. If you want to sort by additional fields, choose them from one or both of the Then By drop-down lists.

15. Click Next to move on to the next tab. The Grouping tab appears, as shown in Figure 13.14.

Ch
13

N O T E   If you did not choose any fields to sort by, all the options on the Grouping tab will be unavailable, and you can skip to step 17. ■

FIG. 13.14
Use the Grouping tab to choose how to display your sorted records.

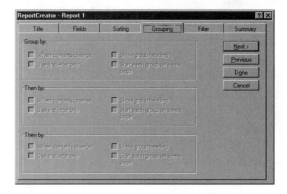

16. For each of the fields you chose to sort by, the following options appear. Select the options you want:

- *When Contents Change*—This option inserts a blank line in a field when the contents of the field change. For instance, if you're sorting by Region, Works displays a blank line after the last record from the Northeast region.

- *Show Group Heading*—When you select this check box, Works prints the field name above each group.

- *Use First Letter Only*—If the field you are sorting by doesn't contain any identical entries, you can group entries by the first letter of the field entry only (such as grouping all the last names that begin with A). Selecting this check box groups by first letter, instead of identical field entries.

- *Start Each Group on a New Page*— Use this option if you want Works to put each group on a separate page.

17. Click Next to move to the Filter tab. The Filter tab appears, as shown in Figure 13.15. (Refer to "Using Filters," earlier in this chapter.)

FIG. 13.15
Use the Filter tab to specify which records to include in the report.

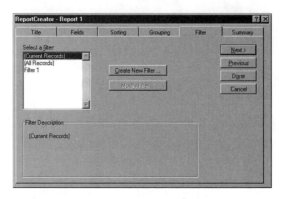

18. The Select a Filter list contains all the filters you have created so far for this database, plus two other entries: (Current Records) and (All Records). Choose one of the following:

- Select Current Records to include all records that were displayed at the time you began the ReportCreator process.

- Select All Records to include every record in the database.

- Select a filter you have already created.

- Click the Create New Filter button to access the Filters dialog box (described in detail earlier in this chapter) and create a new filter.

19. Click Next to continue. The Summary tab appears (see Figure 13.16).

FIG. 13.16

On the Summary tab, you choose what kinds of calculations you want to use to summarize the data.

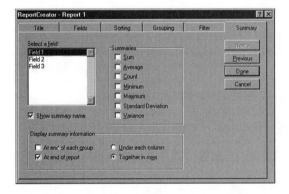

20. Choose the field to summarize from the Select a Field list.

21. Select one or more check boxes from the Summaries section to indicate which calculations to perform.

For example, to total all records in a group, choose Sum. To print the smallest value, choose Minimum, or to print the largest value, choose Maximum.

N O T E Most of the Summaries options apply only to fields that contain numbers. However, the Count option is available for text fields; it counts the number of records in a group. ▪

22. Select any of the following options to further customize the way the summary will appear:

- *Show Summary Name*—This option is selected by default. If you deselect this option, summary type does not appear on the report. For example, if you choose Average, the average is printed but it is not labeled.

- *At End of Each Group*—Selecting this check box summarizes each group individually.

- *At End of Report*—Selecting this check box summarizes the report as a whole.

- *Under Each Column* or *Together in Rows*—Choose one of these options to indicate where you want the summaries to appear.

23. Click the Done button. Works asks if you want to Preview or Modify your definition. Click Preview, and the report appears, as shown in Figure 13.17. (This figure shows the report zoomed in so you can see it more clearly; for this magnification level, click the report twice.) If you choose Modify, the report definition appears on-screen so you can make changes to it.

FIG. 13.17

The fields chosen for the report appear as columns in the report preview.

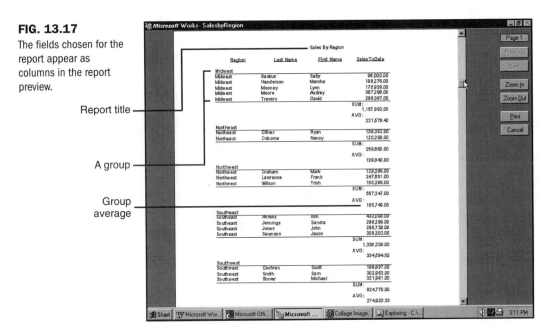

Report title

A group

Group average

You can summarize at the end of each group, at the end of the report, or in both places. For example, you might want to sum at the end of each month to show the monthly sales figures, and then sum at the end of the year for a grand total.

After you create a report, Works saves it automatically with the database when you save your database file. (You won't lose the report if you switch out of Print Preview.)

TIP If you want a printed copy of the report so far, click the Print button before you leave Print Preview. You learn more about printing reports later in this chapter.

To close Print Preview, click the Cancel button. Works takes you to Report view, which no doubt will look a little odd to you at first. You learn about working with Report view in the next section.

▶ **See** "Viewing the Database," **p. 215**

From here, you can move freely between Report, List, Form, and Form Design views by choosing one of these views from the View menu or click the appropriate toolbar button To return to Print Preview, click the Print Preview button on the toolbar or choose File, Print Preview.

When you have created more than one report, you can choose a report to view with the following steps:

1. Choose View, Report.

   The View Report dialog box appears, listing all the reports associated with the database, as shown in Figure 13.18.

FIG. 13.18
Choose the report you want to work with from the View Report dialog box.

2. Select a report from the list.
3. To preview the report, click Preview.

   or

   To change the report specification, click Modify.

Understanding the Report Definition

Once you've created a report, if you switch to Report View, you see a very odd-looking file that looks similar to a database in List view. This is the *report definition*, which defines the layout and format for the report, and how it will look when printed. An example of a report definition is shown in Figure 13.19.

Each row of the report definition contains one of the following labels:

- *Title*   A title row shows the report title that Works prints at the top of the first page.
- *Headings*   A heading row prints a field name or other text at the top of each column.
- *Record*   Record rows indicate which records Works includes in the report.
- *Summ <fieldname>*   This label tells Works to print a statistical summary for each group of records when you sort the report.
- *Summary*   The summary label tells Works to print a statistical summary at the end of the report.

You can see how each of the rows in the report definition in Figure 13.19 translates to the printed report, shown in Figure 13.20.

FIG. 13.19
The report definition determines the layout and format of a report.

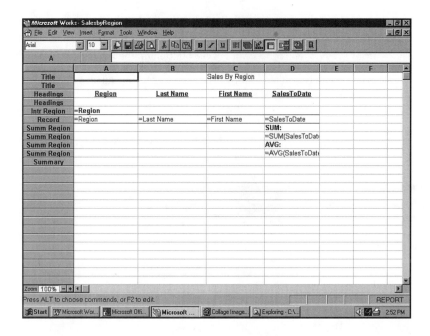

FIG. 13.20
The report definition determines every element of the printed report.

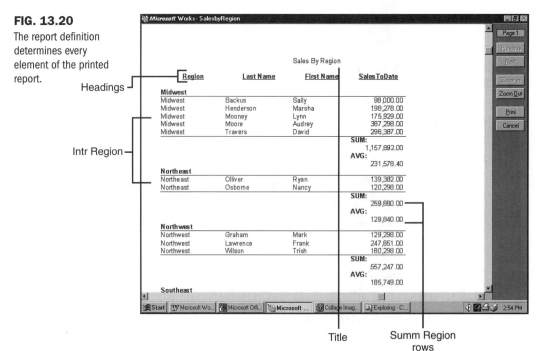

Changing the Report Definition

If you want to make changes to a report definition after a report is created, you can't redisplay the ReportCreator dialog box. Instead, you must use one of the following commands to display the Report Settings dialog box which includes a tab for each command:

Tools, Report Sorting (see Figure 13.21)

Tools, Report Grouping

Tools, Report Filter

FIG. 13.21

The Report Settings dialog box (similar to the ReportCreator dialog box in Figure 13.13) includes Sorting, Grouping, and Filter tabs.

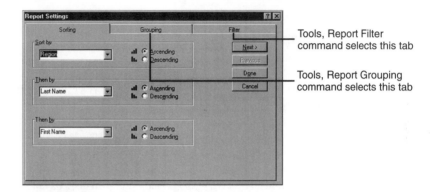

Tools, Report Filter command selects this tab

Tools, Report Grouping command selects this tab

To change the options you originally selected for sorting, grouping, or filter, select the appropriate command and choose new settings in the dialog box. When all settings are correct, click Done. Works returns to Report view, from which you can preview the report or print.

The Title, Fields, and Summary tabs that were included in the Report Settings dialog box (refer to Figure 13.13) are noticeably absent from the ReportCreator dialog box. If you want to make changes to these elements of the report, you must make them directly on the report definition using Report view.

- To change the report title, edit the entry on the Title row of the report definition.
- To change fields that are used in the report, enter new field names (as in =Last Name) in the Record row of the report definition.
- To change summary information, edit the Summ <fieldname> and Summary rows of the report definition.

You can add rows or columns to a report after the report definition has been created. This allows you to add an extra Title row, a blank row, or perhaps another field to the report (to add another field, begin by adding a blank column).

Ch

13

To add rows or columns to a report, use these steps:

1. Select the row or column as your insertion point (a new row is always inserted above the row you select. A new column is always inserted to the left of the column you select).

2. Choose Insert, then choose either Insert Row or Insert Column.

3. If you choose Insert Column, Works inserts the column immediately. If you choose Insert Row, Works displays the Insert Row dialog box shown in Figure 13.22.

FIG. 13.22

Use the Insert Row dialog box to select the type of row to insert.

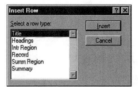

4. Select a row type, then click the Insert button. Works returns to Report view where you can preview or print your report.

T I P You can also delete a row or column from a report definition by choosing Insert, then Delete Row or Delete column.

To add another field to a report, use the previous steps to insert a column, then use these steps:

1. Place the cursor in the Headings row, in the column where you want to add the new field.

2. Insert, Field Name. The Insert Field Name dialog box is displayed.

3. Select a field, then click Insert. Works inserts the field name in the report definition.

4. Place the cursor in the Record row in the column where you just added the new heading.

5. Choose Insert, Field Entry. The Insert Field Entry dialog box is displayed.

6. Select a field name, then click Insert. Works inserts the field entry in the report definition.

When you return to Report view, you can preview or print the report.

Formatting a Report

After you create a report, you can format it to make it more readable and attractive. For example, you can change column widths, row heights, number formats, fonts, and alignment. You can add borders and shading, insert page breaks, and change page and margin settings.

By now you have acquired the skills to make all these changes in a word processor document, spreadsheet, or database file; the techniques are the same for a database report. Display the database in Report view, then choose one of the following commands:

Format, Number

Format, Alignment

Format, Font and Style

Format, Border

Format, Shading

Format, Insert Page Break

File, Page Setup

- ▶ **See** "Printing a Document," **p. 22**
- ▶ **See** "Inserting Page Breaks in a Document," **p. 76**
- ▶ **See** "Applying a Number Format to Selected Cells," **p. 164**
- ▶ **See** "Aligning Entries Within Cells," **p. 166**
- ▶ **See** "Adjusting Row Height," **p. 168**
- ▶ **See** "Choosing a Character Font, Size, Color, and Style," **p. 170**
- ▶ **See** "Adding Borders and Patterns to Cells," **p. 172**

Copying and Deleting Reports

The ability to copy (or *duplicate*) reports is very useful. This feature allows you to create a complex report, then create a slight variation of it by duplicating and editing it rather than starting over from scratch. Follow these steps to duplicate a report:

1. Choose Tools, Duplicate Report.

   Works displays the Duplicate Report dialog box.

2. In the Select a Report list box, highlight the name of the report you want to copy.

3. In the Type a Name Below text box, type a new name of up to 15 characters for the copy.

4. Choose Duplicate.

5. To copy other reports, repeat steps 2 through 4.

6. Choose OK.

The new name is added to the list of reports for the database.

You can and should delete reports that you no longer need. Each database can have no more than eight reports associated with it, so you may need to delete reports before you can create new ones.

Follow these steps to delete a report:

1. Choose Tools, Delete Report.

   Works displays the Delete Report dialog box.

2. In the Select a Report list box, select the report you want to delete.

3. Choose Delete.

4. To delete other reports, repeat steps 2 and 3.

5. Choose OK.

Ch

13

> **CAUTION**
>
> Be careful when deleting reports. You cannot restore a deleted report with the Undo command.

Printing Reports

Printing a Works Database report involves the same steps as printing a database. The only difference between printing reports and databases is that when you choose File, Page Setup from Report view, Works displays a report-specific option in the Other Options tab, as shown in Figure 13.23. This option enables you to print reports without records.

▶ **See** "Printing Database Records," **p. 234**

To print the report without printing any records, just select the Print All but Record Rows check box on the Other Options tab of the Page Setup dialog box. Then you can Print Preview or actually print the report to see how it will look.

When you choose Print All But Record Rows from the Other Options tab, Works prints only the introductory (Intr) and summary (Summ) row types that you specify in the report definition.

 TIP Like charts and spreadsheets, database reports are automatically saved when you save your database file.

FIG. 13.23
In Report view, you use the Other Options tab to specify whether to print the records.

CHAPTER 14

Using the Works Tools Together

The real power of Works is in the integration of its tools. This means that none of the documents you create stand alone. You can add data, drawings, or artwork from other sources to almost any document. You can combine documents, and you can copy, cut, and paste between documents. ■

Four additional Works tools: Draw, WordArt, Clip Art, and Note-it

Use these tools to add interest, draw attention, and create truly professional looking documents.

Sharing information among Works tools

Learn how to cut, copy, and paste between different types of works documents, and how to *link* and *embed* objects in your documents.

Merging database and word processor documents

Use these two types of documents together to create form letters, mail labels, and printed envelopes

Using Draw

You can include simple drawings in a word processor document or a database form (in Design Form view)using the Insert, Drawing command. When you choose this command, a separate Draw window is displayed on top of the word processor or database window you were using. Draw is a separate application program that has its own set of menus and drawing tools. In the document window, Draw inserts a small gray-filled frame that acts as a placeholder for the drawing you create (see Figure 14.1).

FIG. 14.1
The Microsoft Draw window has its own menu and drawing tools.

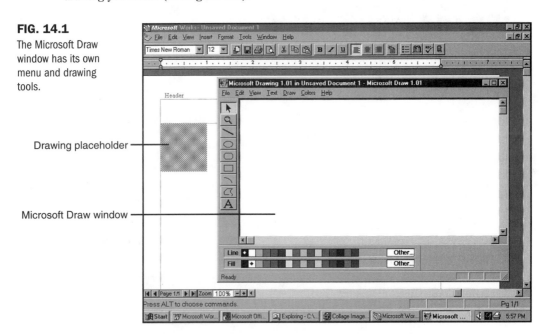

Along the left side of the Microsoft Draw window is a toolbox of drawing tools. You use these tools to select and draw objects. Techniques for using each tool are described in Table 14.1.

Table 14.1 Microsoft Draw Drawing Tools

Tool	Name	Purpose
▶	Pointer tool	Use this tool to select objects.
🔍	Zoom tool	This tool enlarges or reduces your view of an entire drawing.
／	Line tool	Lets you draw straight lines or lines at any of 45° increments (0°, 45°, 90°, 135°, and so on).

Tool	Name	Purpose
⬭	Oval tool	Use this tool to draw a ellipse or a circle.
◯	Rounded rectangle tool	Use to draw a rectangle with rounded corners.
▭	Rectangle tool	Use to draw rectangles and squares.
⌐	Arc tool	Click and drag to draw a pie-wedge shaped object.
⟨	Freeform tool	Click and drag to make a freeform drawing.
A	Text tool	Type up to 255 characters on a single line of text.

Drawing Objects

Using the Draw tools, you can draw many types of objects. The method for drawing a line, circle/ellipse, rectangle/square, rounded rectangle/square, or arc is as follows:

1. Click the drawing tool you want to use.
2. Move the crosshair mouse pointer to the location where you want to draw the object.
3. Press and hold the Shift or Ctrl keys as indicated in Table 14.1 to draw specialized objects (such as a perfect circle or a 45° line). Click and drag the mouse until you're satisfied with the shape of the object.
4. Release the mouse button. Four resize handles appear at the outer corners of the object. (Two resize handles appear in the case of a line.)
5. Click any blank area of the drawing area or click the Pointer tool to deselect the object.

N O T E Many of the drawing tools work in combination with the Shift and Ctrl keys; experiment with them to see how they work. For example, to draw a perfect circle or square (rather than an oval or rectangle), press and hold the Shift key as you use the Oval or Rectangle tool. To draw an object from its center outward, press and hold the Ctrl key as you draw. You can also use Shift and Ctrl at the same time. ■

Selecting Objects

To select a Draw object, click the Pointer tool, then click anywhere on the object. Works displays black squares that form a rectangle surrounding the object (see Figure 14.2). The black squares, called *resize handles,* let you adjust the size of the object. You know an object is selected when the handles are visible.

FIG. 14.2

The visible resize handles indicate the ellipse is selected.

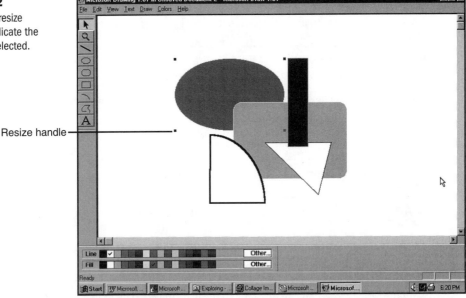

Resize handle——

N O T E When you enter text in a drawing, Works considers text an object. You can select text just like any other type of object. ▇

To select multiple objects at the same time, hold down the Shift key as you click each object individually. When all the objects you want to include are selected, release the Shift key.

 When you want to select all objects in a drawing, choose Edit, Select All, or press Ctrl+A. This command is particularly useful when you want to clear the current drawing and start over.

Another way to select multiple objects is by drawing a selection box around them. Select the Pointer tool, then click and drag the crosshair pointer from the upper-left corner of the first object to the lower-right corner of the last object you want to include in the selection. As you drag the mouse, a selection box in the form of a dashed rectangle defines the area you cover (see Figure 14.3). When you release the mouse button, all objects that you fully enclosed in the selection box are selected. You can add objects to the selection by holding down the Shift key as you click additional objects.

 To group several objects together and treat them as a single object, select the objects and choose Draw, Group or press Ctrl+G. To break up grouped objects, choose Draw, Ungroup or press Ctrl+H.

If you select the wrong object, cancel the selection by clicking any blank part of the drawing area. If you want to remove an object from a selection of multiple objects, hold down the Shift key and click on the object you want to remove.

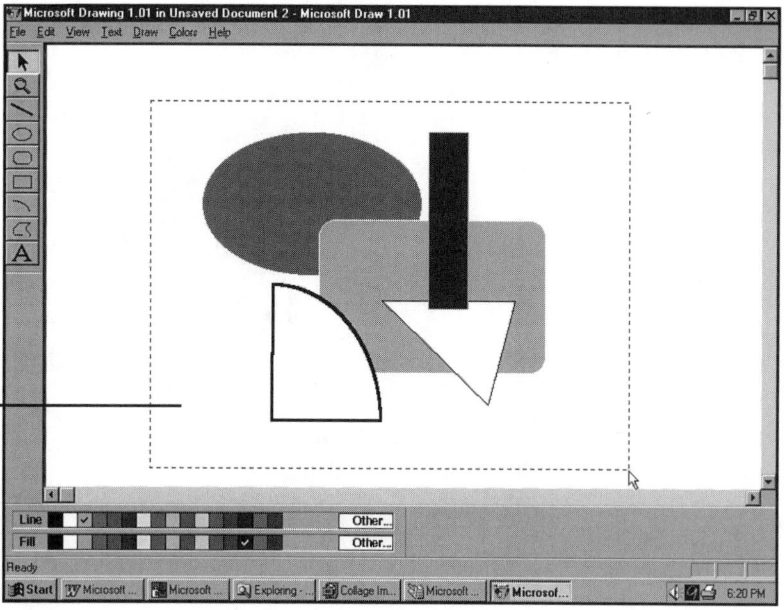

FIG. 14.3
All objects enclosed in the dashed rectangle are being selected.

Selection box ⎯

Enhancing Drawings

You can change the line color or the fill color of the objects you draw. In this context, *line* refers to individual lines, the frame or outline of objects, text, and the foreground of a pattern. *Fill* refers to the interior portion of a closed object or the background of a pattern. Available colors are shown on the color palettes at the bottom of the Draw window (see Figure 14.4). A diamond marker on the palette indicates the default colors Draw uses for line (black) and fill (white) (refer to Figure 14.1). When an object is selected, check marks appear in the Line and Fill palettes indicating the colors used in the current object (refer to Figure 14.4).

To change the line or fill color of an object, select the object, then click a color in the Line or Fill palette. To change the default Line and Fill colors, make sure no objects are selected, then select new Line and Fill colors. The diamond markers move to the new colors you select, indicating these are now the default colors. The new colors remain in effect until you select new default colors.

Another way to enhance an object is to fill it with a two-color pattern. Available patterns are displayed when you choose Draw, Pattern. Pattern examples are shown in Figure 14.5.

Ch
14

FIG. 14.4
Select a line and fill color for all objects and text in a drawing.

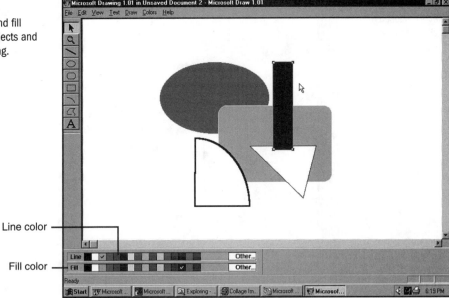

Line color

Fill color

FIG. 14.5
Dress up an object by filling it with a pattern rather than a solid color.

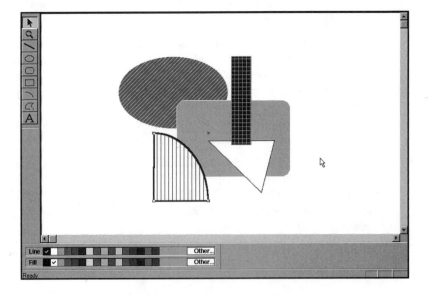

To use a pattern, select an object, then select a pattern style from the Pattern submenu. If you are using the default line and fill colors, Draw makes the pattern background white and the pattern foreground black. To change the colors used in the pattern, select the object, then select line and fill colors from the color palettes at the bottom of the Draw window.

FIG. 14.8
Rotating turns an object 1/4 turn right or left.

Object as originally drawn

Object rotated right

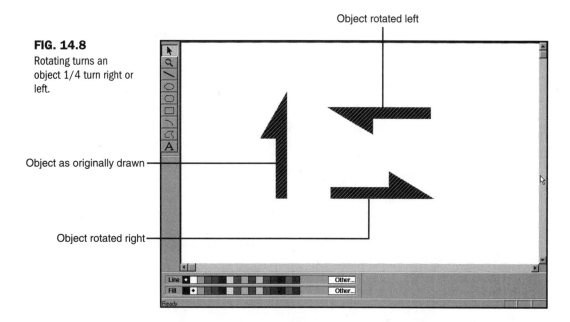

Object rotated left

FIG. 14.9
Flipping makes a vertical or horizontal mirror image of an object.

Object as originally drawn

Object flipped vertically

Object flipped horizontally

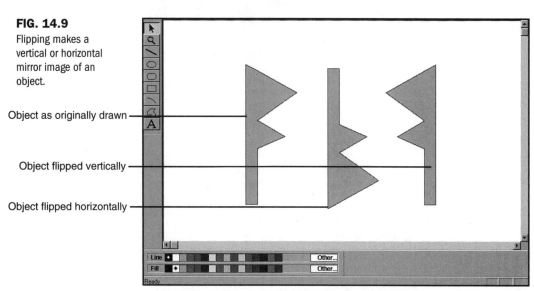

Moving, Copying, and Deleting Objects in a Drawing

When you draw, , moving, copying, and deleting objects are common tasks, and you accomplish them using the same commands and keystrokes you use for text.

■ To move an object, select it and drag it in any direction to a new location. After you have properly positioned the object, release the mouse button.

Ch
14

■ To copy an object, select it, then choose Edit, Copy or press Ctrl+C. This places a copy of the object on the Clipboard. To insert a copy of the object, point to the location you want to copy the object and choose Edit, Paste or press Ctrl+V.

■ To delete an object, select the object, then choose Edit, Clear or press the Delete key. If you think you may want to use the object again later, choose Edit, Cut, which places a copy on the Clipboard.

You can move, copy, and delete more than one object at a time using the same menu commands and keyboard shortcuts; just select all the objects first before choosing a command.

Rearranging the Order of Objects

When you draw several objects one after another and overlap them, each new object you draw appears on top of the previous one, as shown in Figure 14.10.

FIG. 14.10
When objects overlap, the most recent object appears on top.

First object drawn

Last object drawn

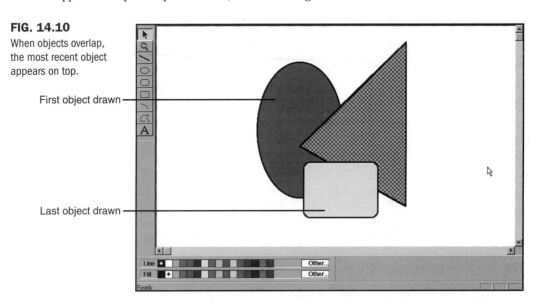

Often, the order in which you draw objects is not the order in which you want them stacked. You can change the order by choosing Edit, Bring To Front (or press Ctrl+=), which brings the selected object to the top of the stack, or Edit, Send To Back (or press Ctrl+-), which sends the selected object to the bottom of the stack. In Figure 14.11, the objects were rearranged using both of these commands.

FIG. 14.11
You can restack objects using the Edit, Bring To Front and Edit, Send To Back commands.

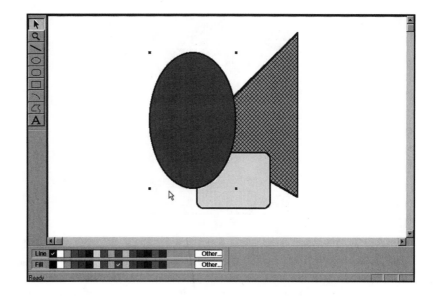

Inserting a Drawing in a Document

You've already seen in Figure 14.1 that Draw inserts a placeholder in your document while you're using Draw. When your drawing is complete, choose File, Exit and Return. Draw displays a dialog box asking if you want to save changes to your drawing. When you choose Yes, the drawing is automatically inserted in your document. From here, you can move or resize the drawing as needed). To reopen a drawing to make changes to it, just double click anywhere in the selected drawing frame. The Draw window is automatically displayed.

▶ **See** "Inserting Objects in a Document," **p. 106**

▶ **See** "Selecting, Sizing, and Moving Objects," **p. 106**

Using Clip Art

If you don't feel confident enough to create your own drawings, you can still insert wonderful illustrations in a document using Clip Art. Even for the adept artist, Clip Art can be useful when you are in a hurry. The Clip Art Gallery is accessible via menu commands from within a database form or word processor document; you don't have to close the word processor or database tool to use Clip Art.

To select a Clip Art picture, move the highlight or cursor in your database form (while in Form Design view) or word processor document to the location where you want to insert a picture. Choose Insert, Clip Art. Works displays the Clip Art Gallery dialog box shown in Figure 14.12.

Ch
14

FIG. 14.12
Use the Clip Art Gallery dialog box to insert a Clip Art picture in your document or database form.

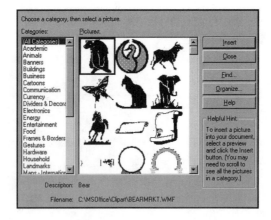

On the left side of the dialog box is a list of categories. The area on the right side displays a sample of all Clip Art pictures in the current category. Figure 14.12 shows a selection of Clip Art pictures in the Landmarks category. Use the scroll bar to see a sample of each picture in a category. If you prefer to scroll through the entire selection, you can select the (All Categories) option in the Categories box.

When you find a Clip Art picture you want to use, click on the picture to select it, then choose Insert. Works closes the Clip Art Gallery dialog box and pastes a copy of the Clip Art picture in your document or database form. Figure 14.13 shows a Clip Art picture used as the logo for Town & Country Interiors' letterhead.

FIG. 14.13
A Clip Art picture is used for a company logo.

Clip Art

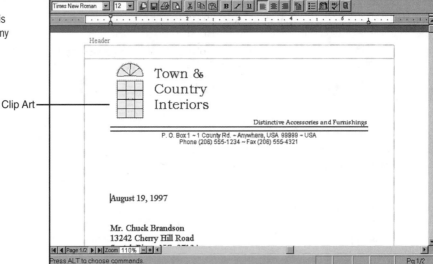

Clip Art pictures usually are quite large—often too large to view at 100% zoom. Switch to a zoom percentage that allows you to see the borders of the picture, then resize as needed using the same methods you learned earlier in this chapter for sizing Draw objects.

To learn how to work with Clip Art in your document, see "Selecting, Sizing, and Moving Objects," in Chapter 6.

To delete a Clip Art picture from a database form or word processor document, first select the picture. Then press the Delete key; or click the Cut button on the toolbar; or choose Edit, Cut. In a word processor document, Works automatically reformats the surrounding text. In a database form, surrounding fields remain unchanged.

Using WordArt

WordArt can turn a dull looking document into a dazzling one. It is a tool that lets you dress up, bend, slant, curve, highlight, shadow, and otherwise enhance text in ways that can't be done with a word processor. In Works, you can insert WordArt in a word processor document or a database form (as long as you're using Form Design view).

From the word processor menu or the database menu, choose Insert, WordArt. Works displays the Enter Your Text Here dialog box shown in Figure 14.14. In the dialog box, the sample text, Your Text Here, is highlighted. When you begin typing your own text, the sample text disappears. At the same time, a grayed frame is automatically inserted in your document; this is the placeholder for the WordArt you create.

FIG. 14.14
WordArt displays a
dialog box and inserts
a placeholder in your
document.

Placeholder

WordArt dialog box

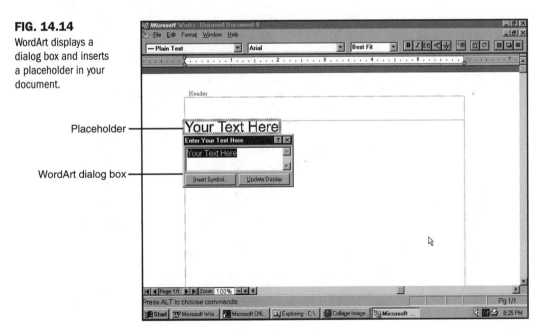

Ch
14

TIP If the Enter Your Text Here dialog box obstructs your view of the WordArt in your document, drag the title bar to move the dialog box out of the way.

Using the WordArt Menus and Toolbar

Like Microsoft Draw, WordArt is a distinct program that has its own menus and toolbars. When you use WordArt, the menus and toolbar in the document window change to reflect WordArt commands. Table 14.2 describes the WordArt toolbar buttons.

Table 14.1   WordArt Toolbar Buttons

Button	Name	Description
— Plain Text	Shape	Click this button to display the Shape drop-down list. After you select a shape, your WordArt text follows the shape. For example, if you select a wave or semicircle, your text bends to form the shape of a wave or semicircle.
Arial	Font	Select a font from the list. The available fonts are the same as those found in the word processor and database components.
Best Fit	Size	Select a point size from the list. Choose the Best Fit option if you want Works to select the best point size to fit the WordArt frame.
B	Bold	Changes the WordArt text to bold. This button toggles the Bold feature on and off.
I	Italic	Changes the WordArt text to italic. This button toggles the Italic feature on and off.
Ee	Even Height	Makes the letters in WordArt—including uppercase and lowercase—all the same height. This button toggles the Even Height feature on and off.
◁	Flip	Click this button to turn each letter on its side. This button toggles the Flip feature on and off.
A	Stretch	Click this button to make your text fill the WordArt frame horizontally and vertically. This button toggles the Stretch feature on and off. When the feature is off, WordArt text aligns in the center.
≣	Align	Select an alignment style to align the text within the WordArt frame. If you don't select a style, WordArt automatically uses the Center alignment style.

Button	Name	Description
![AV icon]	Spacing Between Characters	Displays a dialog box that enables you to control the space between characters in WordArt. You can move characters closer together or farther apart.
![Rotation icon]	Rotation	Displays a dialog box that enables you to rotate text by degrees and adjust the angle or arc of the text.
![Shading icon]	Shading	Displays the Shading dialog box in which you select a two-color shaded pattern and the foreground and background colors to apply to WordArt characters.
![Shadow icon]	Shadow	Displays a drop-down list of shadow styles for individual characters in your WordArt text. To select a color for the shadow, click the More button to display a Shadow dialog box.
![Border icon]	Border	Displays the Border dialog box in which you select a border style and color. Note that in this context, border refers to a character border, not a frame border. When you select a border style or color, Works borders individual characters.

Enhancing WordArt Text

Shaping text is one of the most distinctive features of WordArt. Few word processors, if any, offer this feature. To shape text, type your text in the Enter Your Text Here dialog box, use the Shape drop-down list to select a shape for your WordArt (see Figure 14.15).

FIG. 14.15
Select a shape or an angle from the Shape drop-down list.

 TIP To display the name of a shape, you must select a shape from the Shape drop-down list. The name is then displayed in the Shape button on the toolbar.

In Figure 14.16, you see three examples of WordArt that conform to shapes. The first example uses the Slant Up shape, the second uses the Wave 1 shape, the third uses the Fade Down shape.

Ch
14

FIG. 14.16
These examples show
how you can have fun
with WordArt shapes.

Slant up ——————

Fade down ——————

Wave 1 ——————

T I P The Button Pour and Button Curve shapes require three lines of text in the Enter Your Text Here dialog box. Type the text you want to appear on the top curve, then press Enter and type the text you want to appear on the middle line. Press Enter again then type the text you want to appear on the bottom curve.

You can control the space between characters in WordArt by clicking the Spacing Between Characters button on the toolbar or choosing Format, Spacing Between Characters. Either method opens the Spacing Between Characters dialog box shown in Figure 14.17.

FIG. 14.17
Use the Spacing
Between Characters
dialog box to specify
how tight characters
are.

In the dialog box, *tracking* refers to the space between all characters in the WordArt frame. To move characters closer together, choose Tight or Very Tight, to expand the space between characters, choose Loose or Very Loose. Or, choose Custom option to enter a specific tracking percentage. Figure 14.18 shows examples of text for which the tracking was modified.

FIG. 14.18
Tracking percentages can expand or condense WordArt text.

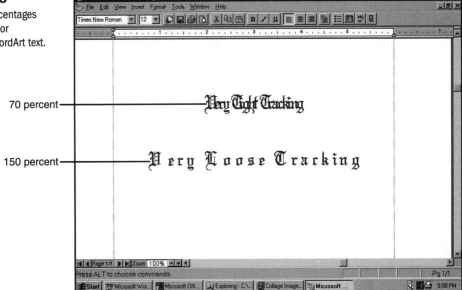

70 percent——

150 percent——

Kerning refers to the space between pairs of characters. Sometimes certain combinations of characters (such as the letters **Ti**) often look like they are spaced too far apart. Kerning moves the two characters closer together. To have WordArt automatically kern pairs of characters for you, choose the Automatically Kern Character Pairs check box.

Changing the Rotation, Arc, and Slant of WordArt Text

After you create WordArt text, you can rotate it, or if you've applied a shape, you can change the depth of its arc or alter its slant. When you rotate WordArt text, you change the way the text revolves (right or left) around its center point. To rotate WordArt text, click the Rotation button on the toolbar or choose Format, Rotation and Effects. Either method opens the Special Effects dialog box shown in Figure 14.19. In the Rotation box, click the up arrow to rotate text to the right; click the down arrow to rotate text to the left. Click OK when you're finished.

FIG. 14.19
Use the up and down arrows in the Rotation box to change the rotation (+ or – up to 360 degrees) of your WordArt text.

Ch
14

When you apply an arc shape (such as Arch Up) to WordArt text, you can control the depth of the arc. Choose Forma$\underline{t}$, $\underline{R}$otation and Effects to display the Special Effects dialog box. In the $\underline{A}$rc Angle box, click the up arrow to make the arc deeper; click the down arrow to make the arc shallower, then click OK.

If you applied any shape other than an arc (such as Slant Up, Slant Down, Fade Up, or Fade Down) to your WordArt text, you can alter the slant of the characters. To do this, choose Forma$\underline{t}$, $\underline{R}$otation and Effects to display the Special Effects dialog box shown in Figure 14.20. This dialog box is similar to the one shown in Figure 14.19, except that the S$\underline{l}$ider box appears in place of the $\underline{A}$rc Angle box. To adjust the slant of characters, click the up or down arrow key in the Slider box, then click OK.

FIG. 14.20

The Slider setting changes the slant of WordArt text.

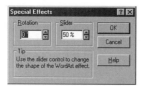

Bordering, Shading, and Shadowing WordArt Text

Bordering is a special effect that makes characters stand out by outlining each character individually. To specify the thickness of the border, choose Format, Border. The Border dialog box appears (see Figure 14.21). The default border color is the background color defined in the Shading dialog box (see Figure 14.23). To change the border color, select a color from the $\underline{C}$olor drop-down list in the Border dialog box. Examples of shadows and borders are shown in Figure 14.24.

FIG. 14.21

Select a border style and color from the Border dialog box.

You might also choose *shading* to enhance WordArt text. When you click the Shading button on the toolbar or choose Forma$\underline{t}$, S$\underline{h}$ading, the Shading dialog box shown in Figure 14.22 opens.

From the $\underline{S}$tyle box, select a shading style. From the Color box, select $\underline{F}$oreground and $\underline{B}$ackground colors. Choose the A$\underline{p}$ply button to apply the selected shading to your WordArt. If you aren't satisfied with the way the shading looks, continue selecting different patterns or colors, then choose A$\underline{p}$ply. When you're happy with the results, choose OK. An example of shaded WordArt is shown in Figure 14.24.

FIG. 14.22
Use the Shading dialog
box to apply a shade
pattern and color to
WordArt.

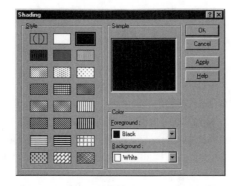

Shadowing is a technique that adds depth to WordArt text by creating the illusion of light cast
on the characters. You can select from several different styles of shadows, and you can specify
the shadow's color rather than simply using gray.

Choose Format, Shadow, to display the Shadow dialog box (see Figure 14.23). You also can
display this dialog box by clicking the Shadow toolbar button, which displays a drop-down list
of shadow styles, then selecting the More option from the drop-down list. To add a shadow to
text, select a shadow style and color, then click OK.

FIG. 14.23
Select a shadow style
and color from the
Shadow dialog box.

FIG. 14.24
Borders make
characters stand out,
shadows add depth,
and shading dresses up
your WordArt text.

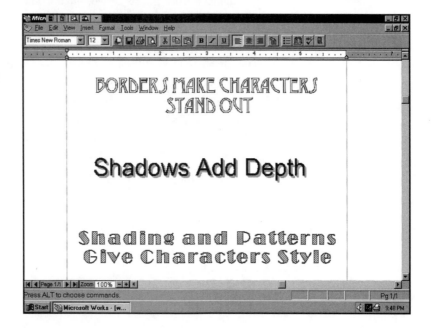

Ch
14

Works immediately applies shadows and borders to your WordArt characters when you choose options in the dialog boxes. To see how your choices look, move the dialog box out of the way if it obstructs your view.

Inserting WordArt in a Document

When your WordArt is complete, double-click anywhere outside of the WordArt dialog box. Your WordArt text appears in your document with the WordArt frame still selected. From here, you can move, copy, or resize the object. To unselect the WordArt, click anywhere in the document. (Refer to Figure 14.16 for an example of WordArt in a word processor document.) To reopen WordArt to make changes to the text or formatting, just double click in the WordArt frame.

▶ **See** "Inserting Objects in a Document," **p. 106**

▶ **See** "Selecting, Sizing, and Moving Objects," **p. 106**

Using Note-It

Ordinarily, when you want to insert a note in a document, you type the text at the appropriate location. To call attention to it, you might format it differently from other text in the document. With Note-It, a tool for inserting notes in a document, you can insert an icon, or picture, instead of the text itself. When you want to read the note, you double-click the icon to pop up the note; otherwise, the text of the note stays hidden.

The Note-It feature is especially useful for including instructions for using a document, inserting a reminder to yourself, or adding a comment for a colleague to read. An example of a note is shown in Figure 14.25. In the figure, one note is closed, and the other note is popped up (open).

To create a Note-It note in a document or a database form, follow these steps:

1. Open the document or database file. In the case of a database, switch to Form Design view. Place the cursor where you want to insert a note.

2. Choose Insert, Note-It to display the Note-It dialog box shown in Figure 14.26.

3. In the Choose a Picture box, select the picture you want to use as your note icon. (Be sure to use the scroll bar to view all the icons—many are available.)

4. To add a note caption, enter the text in the Type Your Caption Here box.

5. Enter the text for your note in the Type Your Note Here box.

6. Choose Big or Small for the font size of the pop-up note.

7. Choose OK to close the dialog box.

Icon for closed note

FIG. 14.25
Note-It notes appear as
icons in a document
until you open the note.

Contents of open note

Icon for open note

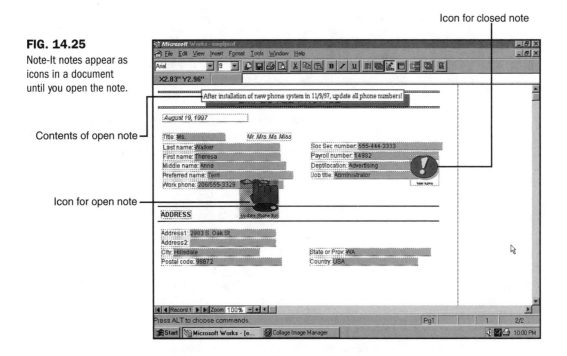

FIG. 14.26
Use the Note-It dialog
box to select a note icon
and enter the note text.

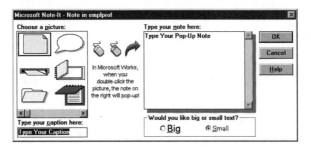

You can edit the text of a note any time by following these steps:

1. Select the Note-It icon.

2. Choose Edit, Microsoft Note-It Object, Edit.

   The Microsoft Note-It dialog box opens. Your note text appears in the Type Your Note
   Here box, and your caption (if you included one) is shown in the Type Your Caption
   Here box. The note icon you are using is selected.

3. To edit your note text or caption, click the appropriate box then use the arrow keys to
   move to the characters you want to change or retype.

Ch
14

4. To change the Note-It icon, select a different picture from the Choose a Picture box.

5. Click OK.

To read a note in a document, just double-click the note icon. The note icon becomes shaded and the note text pops up in a small frame near the top of the document window. After you finish reading the note, click anywhere in the document or press Enter to close the note.

You delete a Note-It note the same way you delete WordArt, Clip Art, or a Microsoft Draw drawing. First, select the Note-It icon. Then choose Edit, Cut, or press the Delete key, or press Ctrl+Z. If you delete a Note-It note by mistake, immediately choose Edit, Undo Editing to restore the note.

Sharing Information Among Works Tools

If you use more than one of the Works tools, there's a good chance that at some time you'll want to share information among different types of documents. For example, you might want to include a spreadsheet chart or a database report in a letter. With Works, you can do this easily. This feature of Works is called *integration* and is perhaps its strongest selling point. And Works provides several methods for sharing information among documents. Each is described in the following sections.

N O T E Because the word processor is the tool most often used for sharing data among Works tools, the examples and figures in this chapter primarily illustrate word processor documents. Be aware that you use exactly the same steps to share information in other types of documents (spreadsheets and databases). ▪

Copying and Moving Information from One Tool to Another

In Chapter 2, you discovered that you can work with more than one document window at a time. And in Chapters 4 and 7, you learned the basic skills for copying and moving text in word processor documents and spreadsheets. These fundamental features of Works are the same features that allow you to copy and move information, not just *within* a document, but also *between* documents.

Suppose, for example, you want to include a spreadsheet in a letter you created using the word processor (see Figure 14.27). Here's the procedure:

1. Open the spreadsheet file (in this case, the *source* document).

2. Open the word processor document (in this case, the *destination* document).

3. Use the Window, Tile command to arrange both windows on the screen at once, or arrange the windows manually by dragging each window's border to resize them.

4. Click in the spreadsheet file and select the cells you want to copy to the word processor document.

5. Click the Copy toolbar button, choose Edit, Copy, or press Ctrl+C.

6. Click in the word processor document and position the cursor where you want to paste the spreadsheet.

7. Click the Paste toolbar button, choose Edit, Paste, or press Ctrl+V. A copy of the spreadsheet is now copied into your word processor document.

Copying from one Works tool to another is as simple as that. The original information in your spreadsheet remains intact, and a copy of it is pasted into your word processor document.

FIG. 14.27

Both source and destination documents are open at once so you can copy from one to the other.

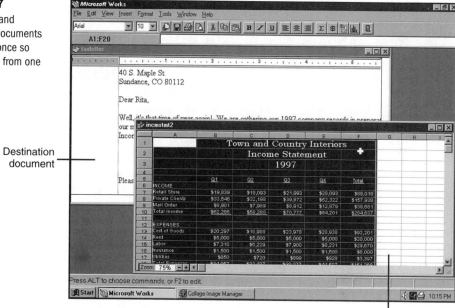

Destination document

Source document

N O T E To move information from the source document rather than copy it, choose the Cut toolbar button, Edit, Cut, or Ctrl+X, then paste it into the destination document. Realize that this permanently removes the selected information from the source document. ■

You can also use the drag-and-drop method, which is even easier than using menu or keyboard commands. Here's how.

1. Open both documents and arrange the windows on the screen so both are visible.

2. In the spreadsheet file, select the cells you want to copy to the word processor document.

3. Point to the border of the selected cells until the mouse's DRAG label appears.

4. Drag the selection into the destination document window. (While still in the source document, the DRAG label changes to MOVE. When you cross over the border of the source window into the destination window, the MOVE label changes to COPY.)

Ch
14

5. Drop the selection (release the mouse button) in the destination document where you want to insert information. When you release the mouse button, Works asks if you want to create a link to the original data. For now, choose No. (You'll learn more about linking later in this chapter.) The information is copied into the destination document.

N O T E   Using the drag-and-drop method, you can *move* rather than *copy* the information from source to destination by holding the Shift key as you drag from one window to another. The mouse label changes to MOVE. ■

Linking Information Between Works Documents

Aside from simply copying information from one document to another, you have two other methods for getting information from here to there. The first is called *linking*, and the information you copy from source to destination is now referred to as an *object*. With linking, Works automatically updates the object in the destination document when the source changes. This means that if you copy a chart into a monthly report, then edit the chart, Works automatically updates the copy of the chart in the monthly report, too.

N O T E   When other Windows-compatible applications say they support DDE (Dynamic Data Exchange), they mean they support linking. This means you can copy information from any application that supports DDE into a Works file. ■

Linking is an extremely powerful feature for two reasons: it ensures consistency between two documents, and it saves you the trouble of updating both documents separately. Use linking when you expect information in the source document to change, or when you need to copy information from one source into several destination documents.

In Figure 14.28, spreadsheet information is copied and linked into a word processor document. In Figure 14.29, the change made in the spreadsheet in cell B7 is automatically changed in the word processor document.

Use the following steps to link spreadsheet data in a word processor document:

1. Open the spreadsheet file.
2. Open the word processor document.
3. Use the Window, Tile command to arrange both windows on the screen at once, or arrange the windows manually by dragging each window's border to resize them.

N O T E   You aren't required to arrange both files on the screen at the same time. If you don't, just switch from one file to the other (in steps 5 and 6) using the Window menu. ■

FIG. 14.28
Spreadsheet informa-
tion is linked to a
document file.

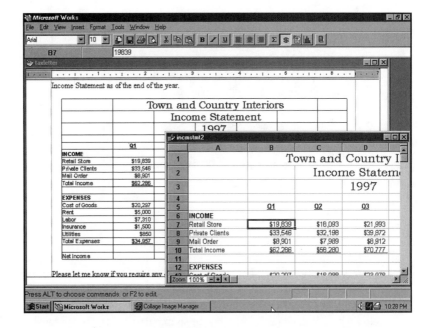

FIG. 14.29
When the spreadsheet
in the source document
is updated, the
destination document
is automatically
updated as well.

Works automatically
changes it here ————

Number was
changed here ————

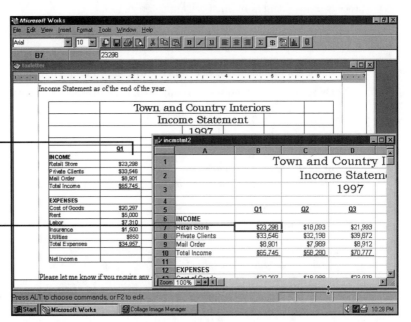

4. In the spreadsheet, select the information you want to link to the destination document.

5. Click the Copy toolbar button, choose Edit, Copy, or press Ctrl+C.

6. Position the cursor in the destination document where you want to paste the information (now called the *object*), then choose Edit, Paste Special. The Paste Special dialog box shown in Figure 14.30 is displayed.

FIG. 14.30

Use the Paste Special dialog box to copy and link an object to a document.

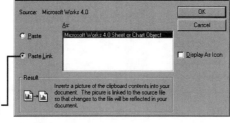

Be sure to click the
Paste Link option

7. Click the Paste Link option.

8. Click OK.

Now when you change information in source document, the spreadsheet copied into the word processor document is automatically updated as well.

Another common task is to copy and link a chart in a word processor document. To do so, use these steps:

1. Open the spreadsheet that contains the chart you want to copy.

2. Display the chart you want to copy, then click the Copy toolbar button.

3. Open the word processor document and place the cursor where you want to insert the chart.

4. Choose Edit, Paste Special.

5. In the Paste Special dialog box, choose the Paste Link option, then click OK. Works inserts a linked copy of the chart in the destination document.

Now if you edit the chart in the source document, the chart in the word processor document is automatically updated as well.

To copy and link a named range of cells from a spreadsheet into a word processor document, you can use the previous steps. In step 2, however, use Edit, Go To to select a named range of cells, then click the Copy toolbar button. Continue with steps 3 through 5 as above. Works copies and links the named range in the word processor document.

You can also link an entire file (rather than just a selection from a file) to another document by following these steps:

1. Open the destination document.

2. Choose Insert Object.

3. In the Insert Object dialog box, choose the Create from File option.

4. In the File text box, type the name of the file to insert, or click the Browse button to find the correct file.

5. Click the Link option.

6. (Optional) To have Works display the inserted object as an icon (rather than the actual contents of the file) click the Display As Icon option.

7. Choose OK.

Works inserts the entire file in your destination document as an icon. Double-click the document icon to view the linked information. (If you didn't choose Display As Icon in step 6, Works automatically opens the source file where you can make changes and save them.)

Embedding an Object in a Document

Another option for sharing information between files is to *embed* an object in a word processor document or database form (in Form Design view). When you embed an object, the information is *not* linked between the files. That is, if you make changes in the source document, the destination document is *not* automatically updated. However, you can easily open the source document without leaving the destination document and make changes to the embedded data. The advantage of embedding an object is that the information becomes part of the destination document and you can make changes to it without opening the original Works tool used to create the object. For instance, if you embed a spreadsheet in a word processor document, you can make changes to the spreadsheet data from within your word processor document just by double-clicking it; you don't have to open the spreadsheet tool, then open the file, then edit it. Table 14.3 lists the types of objects you can insert in word processor files and database forms.

Table 14.3   Insertable Objects in Word Processor and Databases

Type of Object You Can Insert:	In Word Processor document	In Database Form
Table	Yes	No
Chart	Yes	Yes
Spreadsheet	Yes	Yes
Clip Art	Yes	Yes
WordArt	Yes	Yes
Note-It	Yes	Yes
Drawing	Yes	Yes
Object	Yes	Yes

Ch 14

To embed an object in a word processor document or a database form (in Form Design view), position the cursor, then open the Insert menu and choose the type of object to insert. A different dialog box is displayed depending on the type of object you're inserting.

Figure 14.31 shows an example of a new spreadsheet object embedded in a word processor document. Notice that the object has a frame and that, when the object is selected, the word processor toolbar is replaced by the spreadsheet toolbar. As soon as you click anywhere in the document *outside* of the spreadsheet frame, the word processor toolbar returns.

FIG. 14.31

The spreadsheet is an embedded object in a word processor document.

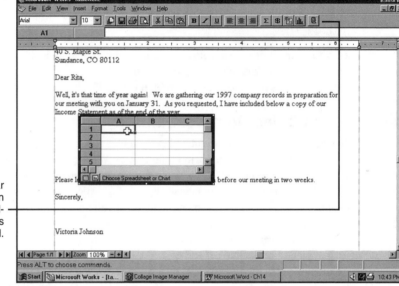

Spreadsheet toolbar appears when embedded spreadsheet object is selected.

Creating Form Letters

Form letters, sometimes called *repetitive* letters, are identical documents you send out to a large number of people. A collection letter for accounts that are overdue is a good example of a form letter. The body of the letter contains essentially the same information, only the specifics (such as amount due, number of days past due, late charges) change based on who the letter is addressed to. If you have a database of clients, employees, students, or suppliers, you can merge the names with any type of form letter, as you learn in the next section. Before you can merge your database file with a form letter, you must first create the form letter.

A form letter is a word processor document that contains inserted codes called *placeholders*. The placeholders tell Works where to print the variable information from your database file. For instance, if you were to print pledge confirmation letters for sponsors of a school fund raiser event, you might include the following as placeholders in your document:

- Sponsor
- Student's name
- amount pledged

To create a form letter, you use the Tools, Form Letters command, which displays a dialog box similar to a TaskWizard. The dialog box contains six tabs and a Next button on each tab, so Works actually leads you through the process of adding fields to the form letter, specifying the database file to be used, choosing printing options, and selecting recipients. To start this process, use the following steps:

1. Create a new word processor document to use as your form letter.

2. Choose Tools, Form Letters. Works displays the Form Letters dialog box shown in Figure 14.32.

FIG. 14.32

The Form Letters dialog box contains several tabs for specifying form letter options.

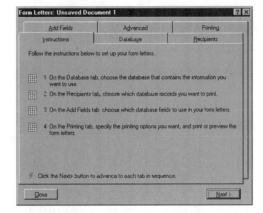

3. The Instructions tab briefly outlines the information you need to provide. Click Next.

4. In the Database tab, select the database file to use, then click Next.

5. In the Recipients tab (see Figure 14.33), choose one of the following options to specify recipients:

> All Records In The Database
>
> Current Records Visible In The Database
>
> Current Records Marked In The Database
>
> Filtered Records In The Database

If you created a filter in your database document, you can select it by clicking the Change Filter button, or click this button to create a new filter.

▶ **See** "Using Filters," **p. 244**

If you want to use Current Records Marked in the Database but no records are marked yet, click the View Database button. Works opens the database where you can mark records by clicking the check box next to the record numbers in the database file. Click the Go Back button to return to the Form Letters dialog box.

Ch
14

FIG. 14.33

The Recipients tab lets you specify which records to include when you print.

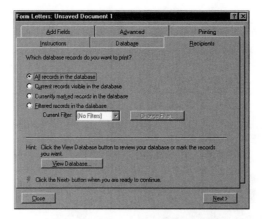

N O T E   The choices you make in the Recipients tab directly determine which records will be printed, so choose all records you want to print at this point. ■

6. In the Add Fields tab, click on each field you want to include in the form letter. (The order in which you select fields is not critical since you'll probably move them in the form letter later.)

7. In the Printing tab, just click Next. (You'll preview and print after you've edited the form letter.)

8. Click the Advanced tab, which gives you the opportunity to Edit your form letter, then click Edit. Works displays the form letter and a dialog box with a Go Back button. The form letter contains all the placeholders you selected and nothing else.

9. Compose your letter, just as you would any word processor document, moving the placeholders where you want them to appear in the document. If you want to use a placeholder twice, copy it. Or, if you decide not to use a placeholder, just delete it. An example of a form letter is shown in Figure 14.34.

    If the Go Back dialog box is in your way for editing, drag it to a different location on the screen.

10. When your form letter is complete, click Go Back.

11. Now choose the Printing tab, then click the Preview button. Click OK when the preview messages dialog box is displayed. Works displays a preview of your form letter, substituting actual data (from your database file) for the placeholders. Check this preview screen carefully, making sure your placeholders are positioned correctly and punctuated the way you want them. Click Cancel to exit Print Preview.

FIG. 14.34

The form letter contains four placeholders where variable information will be inserted.

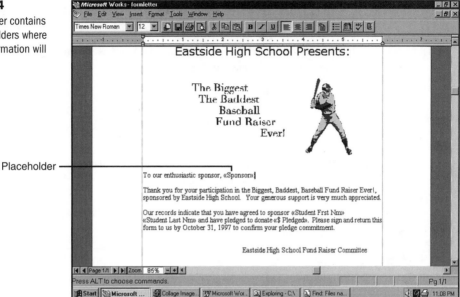

Placeholder

If you need to edit the form letter, choose the Advanced tab and click the Edit button. Works opens your document so you can edit it and places a Go Back dialog box on the screen for you to use to return to the Form Letters dialog box. When you're finished editing, click the Go Back button. You might want to choose the Printing tab again to preview the letter after the changes you made.

12. If you don't want to print the documents at this time, choose Close to exit the Form Letters dialog box. Be sure to save your edited form letter document.

If you want to print, choose the Printing tab, then click Print. A dialog box is displayed asking you want to print the selected records. Choose OK.

Printing Form Letters

You've already seen in the previous section that printing—or, at least, choosing the recipients to receive a printed letter—is part of the form letter creation process. If you chose not to print your letters when you created them, you can print them at any time by opening the form letter document and choosing Tools, Form Letters to display the Form Letters dialog box again. All of the settings you chose previously (the database file; filters, if any, or marked records; etc.) are still in effect. To print a letter for each of the selected records, choose the Printing tab, then click Print.

Ch
14

Creating Mail Labels and Printing Envelopes

The process for creating mail labels is nearly identical to the one you just learned for creating form letters. The primary difference is that you don't create a form document for labels; you just choose fields and specify the layout for the mailing labels.

When you choose the Tools, Labels command in a blank word processor document, then choose Labels again, the Labels dialog box is displayed. It is very similar to the Form Letters dialog box and works in the same TaskWizard-like way: click the Next button to lead you through each of the tabs.

The Database, Recipient, Printing and Advanced tabs are so similar to those used for Form Letters, they require no further explanation. In the Label Size tab, you choose a standard Avery label number, or you can define a custom label size. In the Label Layout tab, you add and arrange fields exactly as you want them to appear on the label. You can also format the labels using the font and size you choose.

N O T E Avery is a brand name for a wide variety of labels (mailing, shipping, file folder, disks, and so on) you can use in your printer. Each type of label is identified by a number; these numbers appear in the list in the dialog box. ■

When you're ready to print, choose the Printing tab. This tab includes a Test button, which prints the first two rows of mailing labels so you can test the label settings.

Printing envelopes is also quite similar to printing mail labels. You specify choices in the Envelopes dialog box, again, very similar to both the Form Letters and Labels tabbed dialog boxes. Choose Tools, Envelopes to display this dialog box. Click the Next button to move through the script-line instructions.

The unique tabs in the Envelopes dialog box are the Main Address, Return Address, and Envelope Size. The Main Address tab is where you insert fields, just like in the Add Fields tab in Figure 14.32. Type the return address, if any, in the Return Address tab. In the Envelope Size tab, you select a standard size or specify a custom size.

Before you print envelopes, be sure to go to the Advanced tab so you can adjust placement of the fields in the envelope document. The Printing tab in the Envelopes dialog box also includes a Test button, which will print one test envelope.

N O T E If you want to print envelopes again at another time, be sure to save your envelope document so don't have to recreate it each time you want to print. ■

CHAPTER 15

Using the Works Communications Tool

With the Works communication tool, a modem on your computer, and standard voice telephone lines, you can connect to a whole world of computer systems and services. ■

A glossary of computer communications terms

If you think a *handshake* is a polite gesture you offer when you meet someone and a *port* is a place where ships dock, this section will bring you up to speed on computer communications terminology.

How to prepare your computer to communicate with another

To communicate with another computer, there is some preparation involved; fortunately when you have everything set, you can save the settings and reuse them.

How to start and end a "session"

Learn how easy it is to connect to and disconnect from another computer.

Learning how to use your computer as a terminal on another computer

In large organizations and corporations, users often access a *mainframe* computer through a *terminal*. With access privileges, you can use your PC as a terminal.

Sending and receiving files

"Communicating" involves sharing information; this section explains how to send files to another computer and receive files in return.

What You Can Do with the Works Communications Tool

In the world of computers, communications is the hottest topic. Access to the so-called "information superhighway," which you learn about in Chapter 16, is spoken of in terms of necessity and inevitability. Before there was an information superhighway, however, computers could communicate with one another for a number of purposes:

- to share files
- to capture text
- to simply "log on" to a mainframe computer from a remote location

In order for computers to "talk" to one to another over a telephone line, there are two requirements. Both systems need to have:

- a device called a *modem* that can interpret the signals a computer sends and receives
- some sort of computer program, however primitive, that gives the user a means to make a request like "I want to send a file" or "I want to receive a file"

You must supply the first requirement; the communications tool in Works satisfies the second requirement. It was specifically designed to accomplish the tasks of sharing files, capturing text, and logging on to a mainframe computer as a terminal.

Understanding Communications Terms

You will feel more comfortable and be better prepared to fully utilize your communications program if you familiarize yourself with typical communications terms; so-called industry *buzz words*. The following list brings you up to speed:

- *ASCII file*, or *text file*   A file that contains only text characters (no formatting) and can be read on almost any computer system by software programs that handle text. ASCII files are often used when you're not sure which text formats the receiving computer can read. (*ASCII* stands for American Standard Code for Information Interchange.)

- *Baud rate*   The rate of speed at which computers send and receive information, such as 2,400, 9,600, or 28,800. The higher the rate, the faster the speed. The two connected computers must set the same baud rate in order to communicate.

- *BBS*, or *Bulletin Board System*   An "electronic" bulletin board, usually set up by a company or organization, that provides information, programs, and files that you can download to your system free of charge.

- *Binary file*   A file that can be read only by a computer because it is coded in only two digits (zeros and ones), hence, the term "binary." Binary files generally include text formatting.

- *Bit*   A contraction of the two words "binary" and "digit," a bit is a single unit of data in binary notation.

■ *Communication session*   The time period during which your computer is connected to another computer via telephone lines.

■ *Data bits*   The number of bits used to define a single character; typical settings are 7 or 8.

■ *Download*   The transfer of a file from another computer system to your own. After the download, the file remains on the originating system and a copy is stored on your computer's hard disk.

■ *Stop bits*   The number used to signal the end of one character; settings are usually 1 or 2.

■ *Handshake*   A required sequence of "pause" and "continue" signals used by two computers to ensure that each one "hears" and continues to receive information from the other and vice versa.

■ *Information service*   An organization that—for a monthly or annual fee—provides dial-up users access to large stores of information on their mainframe computer systems or computer network. Examples include America Online, the Microsoft Network, and CompuServe.

■ *Modem*   A hardware device that attaches to the computer (internally or externally) and interprets the signals a computer sends and receives across standard telephone lines.

■ *Network*   A data communications system that groups two or more computer systems and peripheral devices. Networks generally have far more than two computer systems, and have large data storage devices that allow them to store and make available huge amounts of information to authorized users of the network.

■ *Parity*   A setting used to determine whether information being transmitted contains errors. Settings are *even*, *odd*, or *none*.

■ *Port*   In simple terms, a port is a *connector*. On the back of your computer system, it is where you plug in a cable; inside of your computer system, it is where you plug in a card, such as a video or communications controller.

■ *Transmission protocol*   A formal set of "rules" used to format messages and time their transmission between two computers.

■ *Terminal emulation*   A terminal is a "dumb" device (that is, it has no intelligence of its own) that is attached to a mainframe. Some mainframes only allow certain types of terminals to attach to them, so if you want to use your personal computer as a terminal attached to a mainframe, it must *emulate*, or *imitate*, a particular terminal type.

Using the Communications Toolbar

As with all the other Works tools you've learned about so far, the communications tool in Works has its own toolbar with unique toolbar buttons. The toolbar buttons are described in Table 15.1. Throughout the remainder of this chapter, toolbar buttons are called out in steps.

Table 15.1   Communications Toolbar Buttons

Button	Name	Description
	Works Task Launcher	Displays the Task Launcher dialog box.
	Save	Saves the current file.
	Copy	Copies a selection the Windows Clipboard.
	Paste	Pastes the contents of the Clipboard at the location of the cursor.
	Communications Settings	Displays the Communications tab in the Settings dialog box.
	Terminal Settings	Displays the Terminal tab in the Settings dialog box.
	Phone settings	Displays the Phone tab in the Settings dialog box.
	Transfer Settings	Displays the Transfer tab in the Settings dialog box.
	8-n-1 Settings	Automatically sets three communications settings for you: 8 data bits, no parity, and 1 stop bit.
	7-e-1 Settings	Automatically sets three communications settings for you: 7 data bits, even parity, and 1 stop bit.
	Easy Connect	Displays the Easy Connect dialog box.
	Dial/Hangup	Dials the current phone number or, if already connected, disconnects your phone.
	Pause	Pauses your communications session.
	Capture text	Saves text you receive as a file.
	Sent Text	Sends an ASCII (text) file to the receiving system.
	Send Binary File	Sends a binary file to the receiving system.

Button	Name	Description
	Receive Binary File	Receives a binary file and saves it.
	Address Book	Runs the Address Book TaskWizard.

Ch
15

Setting Up Your Computer for Communications

Before you can communicate with another computer, you must set up your computer to be in "sync" with the other computer. You must know the phone number required to access the other computer, and other information such as the modem settings (baud rate, parity bits, stop bits, data bits), transfer protocol, terminal emulation, and so on.

If you are connecting to an information service such as CompuServe or America Online, or to a corporate computer system, this information is provided for you. If you're communicating with a friend or colleague rather than a corporate system or service, you'll need to know the communications software they are using on their PC; most software packages have a "preferred" set of settings. For each computer or information service you want to connect to, you must set up your computer specifically to connect to that system.

N O T E If you are connecting to a corporate computer or information service, you'll be asked to set a password. Be sure to record the password where you can find it again later, if necessary. ■

Works makes it easy for you to create a new communications file with the Easy Connect dialog box that appears automatically when you use the Communications tool. To create a new communications file, begin with these steps, then follow the steps in the sections that follow to specify particular settings.

1. Click the Works Task Launcher button.
2. Display the Works Tools tab, then choose Communications. The Communications window is displayed and a new blank document called *Unsaved Communication 1* appears in the window. The Easy Connect dialog box shown in Figure 15.1 automatically appears on top of the document window.
3. In the Country Code box, use the United States of America setting if you are calling in the US, otherwise choose a country from the drop-down list.
4. In the Area Code box, type the area code for the system or service you want to dial.
5. In the Phone Number box, type the phone number of the system or service you want to dial. (You can include dashes, spaces, or parentheses; Works ignores them. A comma causes Works to pause before dialing.)
6. In the Name of Service, type a name to identify the connection, such as *CompuServe*, *Library System*, or *Corporate System*.

7. Click OK. The Dial dialog box is displayed. It includes Dial and Cancel buttons.

8. For now, click the Cancel button. The Dial dialog box closes.

Works changes the name of the document from *Unsaved Communication 1* to the name you entered in step 6. The file is automatically saved in the C:\Program Files\MSWorks folder. The next time you open the Easy Connect dialog box, the file name appears in the Services list box.

Now, use the steps in the following sections to specify the correct settings for connecting to this system or service.

FIG. 15.1

Use the Easy Connect dialog box to set up a communications session.

New unsaved communications file

Easy Connect dialog box is automatically displayed

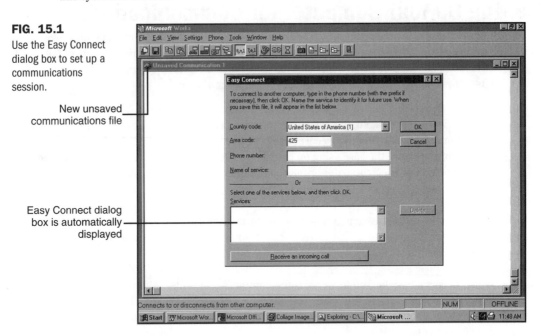

Choosing Phone Settings

Phone settings include the dialing instructions you want Works to follow when dialing another computer or information service. Use these steps to specify phone settings:

1. Choose Settings, Phone, or click the Phone Settings toolbar button. The Settings dialog box shown in Figure 15.2 is displayed with the Phone tab at front.

2. In the Connect Option box, choose only one option: Dial Once (to try dialing once and not try again), Redial (to continue trying if a busy signal is encountered), or Auto Answer (to have Works automatically answer all incoming calls to your modem).

3. In the Redial Attempts box, enter the number of times you want your system to redial after a busy signal is encountered.

4. In the Redial Delay box, specify the number of seconds you want the computer to wait before redialing.

5. Choose OK, or click another tab in the Settings dialog box to set other options.

FIG. 15.2

Use the Phone tab in the Settings dialog box to set up your phone for dialing.

Choosing Communications Settings

In the Settings dialog box, you use the Communications tab to select the communications device you want to use and determine how your computer will communicate with the computer you're dialing.

1. Choose Settings, Communication, or click the Communications Settings toolbar button. The Settings dialog box shown in Figure 15.3 is displayed, this time with the Communication tab at front.

FIG. 15.3

Use the Communication tab in the Settings dialog box to set options for your communications device.

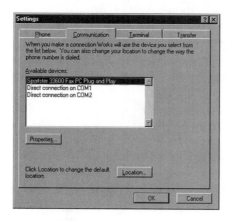

2. The Available Devices box will list your modem; choose it to dial up to another computer. If you are directly cabled to the other computer you want to communicate with, choose COM1 or COM2.

3. Click the Properties button. If you chose COM1 or COM2 in the previous step, the COM1 (or COM2) Properties dialog box shown in Figure 15.4 is displayed.

FIG. 15.4

Choose Port Settings in
the COM1(or COM2)
Properties dialog box.

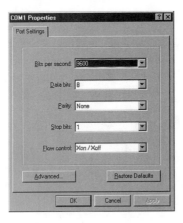

4. Choose the appropriate <u>B</u>its Per Second (baud rate), <u>D</u>ata Bits, <u>P</u>arity, <u>S</u>top Bits, and <u>F</u>low Control settings, then click OK. (You shouldn't need to change <u>A</u>dvanced settings unless you're having trouble receiving data.) The Settings dialog box is displayed with the Communications tab selected.

5. If you selected a modem in step 2, the Properties dialog box shown in Figure 15.5 is displayed when you click the Propertie<u>s</u> button. The General tab is automatically selected.

FIG. 15.5

The Properties box for a
modem device includes
three tabs for various
settings.

6. In the <u>S</u>peaker Volume area, move the slider to Off, High, or a middle position. In the <u>M</u>aximum Speed box, select the highest speed at which your modem can communicate.

7. Click the Connection tab in the Properties dialog box. The Connection tab is shown in Figure 15.6.

8. In the Connection Preferences section, choose the correct <u>D</u>ata Bits, <u>P</u>arity, and <u>S</u>top Bits settings for the computer to which you are connecting. (Remember, if you don't know, the operations staff who manages the computer you're connecting to can provide this information.)

FIG. 15.6

Use the Connection tab to set connection and call preferences.

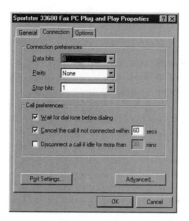

 T I P If you are connecting to a BBS and you don't now the proper settings, choose 8 data bits, no parity, and 1 stop bit, or choose 7 data bits, even parity, and 1 stop bit. These are two commonly used settings—one of them should be compatible with the BBS.

9. In the Call Preferences box, choose any or all three of the dialing options listed.

10. Unless you're having trouble receiving data, you shouldn't need to set Port Settings or Advanced (error control and flow control) options.

11. Click the Options tab in the Properties dialog box to display the dialog box shown in Figure 15.7

FIG. 15.7

Use the Options tab in the Properties dialog box to control connection, dialing, and modem status.

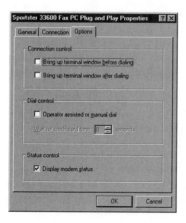

12. Choose whether you want to display a terminal window before or after dialing, and whether or not you need operator-assisted dialing. It is recommended you choose to display the modem status so you can see what your modem is doing as it connects.

13. Click OK to exit the Properties dialog box and return to the Settings dialog box with the Communication tab selected.

14. In the Settings dialog box, click OK to exit the dialog box, or click another tab to choose other settings.

Choosing Terminal Settings

Before you connect to another computer system, you need to determine how your terminal appears to the other computer and how the other computer will display information on your terminal. (Today, we don't refer to the *monitor* on a PC as a *terminal*, but in a sense, it is analogous to a terminal attached to a mainframe computer. In this context, think of your monitor as a terminal.) Some computers will communicate only with specific terminal types. If so, you must choose a terminal type the computer recognizes.

 TIP If you get "garbage" on your screen, this is usually an indication that you need to choose a different terminal type.

1. Choose Settings, Terminal, or click the Terminal Settings toolbar button. The dialog box shown in Figure 15.8 is displayed with the Terminal tab at front.

FIG. 15.8

Use the Terminal tab in the Settings dialog box to choose terminal emulation settings.

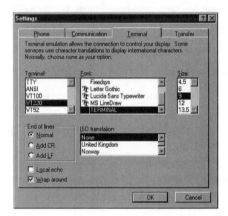

2. In the Terminal list box, choose a terminal type to emulate.

3. From the Font and Size list boxes, choose a display font (or the default TERMINAL font) and a point size.

4. Under the End Of Lines area, use the Normal setting. If lines of text don't begin at the left side of the screen, choose Add CR (add carriage return). If new lines of text overwrite one another on the screen, choose Add LF (add line feed).

5. If you are receiving a file from a foreign country that might include international characters, choose a country in the ISO Translation list box, otherwise, use the None setting.

6. Click Local Echo only if the characters *you type* don't appear on your screen. Click Wrap Around if characters you receive overwrite each other at the right side of your screen on a single line.

7. Choose OK to exit the dialog box or click on another tab to change more settings.

Choosing Transfer Settings

If you're only looking up information on a service or using your PC as a terminal on a main-frame computer, you won't need to choose transfer settings. If you want to send or receive files, however, you must choose transfer settings.

Your computer and remote computer must use the same transfer protocol in order to transfer files. ■

1. Choose <u>S</u>ettings, <u>T</u>ransfer, or click the Transfer Settings button on the toolbar. Works displays the Settings dialog box with the Transfer tab selected (see Figure 15.9).

FIG. 15.9

Choose a transfer protocol in the Transfer tab of the Settings dialog box.

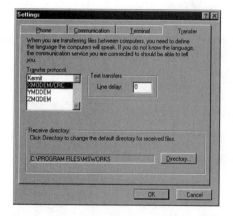

2. The Transfer Protocols list box lists all protocols your computer can use. Choose the one that matches the protocol used on the remote system.

 Xmodem and Kermit are very commonly used file transfer protocols but are not very fast. Ymodem is faster than Xmodem and Kermit, and requires a reliable phone connection. Zmodem is the fastest protocol but is not as commonly used as the others.

3. If the remote computer you are sending to is older and slower than yours and is not receiving files accurately, enter a number (in tenths of a second) in the L<u>i</u>ne Delay text box. Line Delay causes Works to pause briefly after sending each line of text so the receiving computer can keep up with the transfer.

4. Works stores all received files in the C:\Program Files\MSWorks directory. To use a different directory, click the Directory button, choose a directory, then click OK.

5. Click OK to close the Settings dialog box.

Saving Communications Settings

At the beginning of the section "Setting Up Your Computer for Communications," you learned how to use the Easy Connect dialog box to create and save a new communications file. You've just learned how to change some of the settings for that file, so be sure to save the changes you made by choosing File, Save.

Starting and Ending a Communications Session

The easiest way to start a communications session is to use the Easy Connect dialog box. (Refer to "Setting Up Your Computer for Communications" and Figure 15.1, earlier in this chapter.) As you've already seen, when you choose the Communications tool from the Works Task Launcher, the Easy Connect dialog box is displayed automatically. Or, you can choose Phone, Easy Connect (see Figure 15.10). From the Services list box, highlight the name of the system or service you want to connect to, then choose OK. When the Dial dialog box is displayed, click the Dial button to establish the connection.

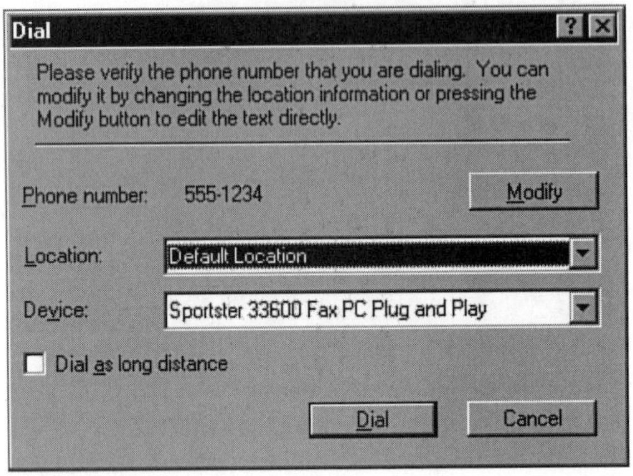

FIG. 15.10
Click the Dial button to dial the phone number shown.

> **N O T E** You can also start a communications session by opening the File menu and clicking the file name at the bottom of the menu. Works automatically opens the file and displays the Dial dialog box shown in Figure 15.10. ■

Once you're connected, you'll begin to see text scroll across your screen. If the system you're connected to requires a user name and password, you will be prompted for them. This is called *logging on*. A counter runs in the lower-right corner of the status bar indicating the amount of time you have been connected.

When you're finished using the system or service to which you're connected, disconnect by following the procedures of the service (*log off* properly if you're logged on), or click the Dial/HangUp button on the toolbar.

Using Your PC as a Terminal

The most common way to communicate with another computer is to use your PC as a terminal on a large mainframe system. For example, many corporations and organizations offer a BBS.

To access a BBS, you must have the dial-in phone number. A user name and password may or may not be required.

In Figure 15.11 you see a screen from a county library system. The primary purpose of this service is to allows authorized users (those who have a valid library card) to search the library system files for books and place books on hold for pick-up. This particular system could also be considered a BBS, because general information about library and other local events appears when you log on to the system.

FIG. 15.11
BBS-type information is displayed by a county library system.

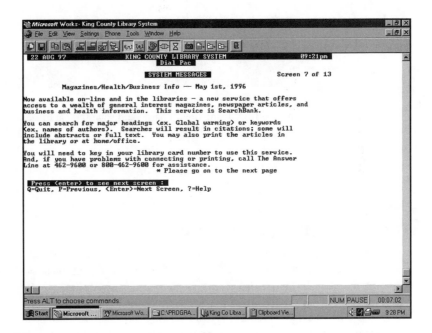

Capturing Text

Most people who use their PC as a terminal will want to perform some of the following tasks: capturing text, sending, or receiving files. These are common tasks. *Capturing* text means that Works saves whatever characters are displayed on your screen from the time you select the capture command until you end it. The text is saved in a document called *capture.txt* or a file name that you specify. Once captured, you can use the information any way you like on your computer (read it, edit it, copy it, cut it, paste it, and so on.) Capturing text is different from receiving a file in that it saves every keystroke you type and every character that the host computer sends and displays on your screen. Essentially, it is a record of your communications session (from the time you start it until you end it).

To capture text, use these steps:

1. Choose Tools, Capture Text, or click the Capture Text toolbar button. The Capture Text dialog box shown in Figure 15.12 is displayed.

FIG. 15.12
Use the Capture Text dialog to name your file.

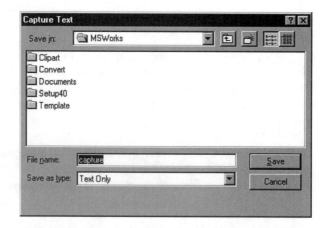

2. Use the Capture Text dialog box to name and save the captured text with a file name just as you name and save other Works files, then click Save. The CAPT indicator appears on the status bar.

3. When you want to stop capturing text, choose Tools, End Capture Text, or click the Capture Text toolbar button again.

Sending and Receiving Files

Sending and receiving files is even more common than capturing text. Using the communications tool, you can send or receive *binary* files or *ASCII* (text) files (see "Understanding Communications Terms," earlier in this chapter).

N O T E   Whether you're sending or receiving files, the remote computer must use the same transfer protocol you're using. To check your protocol setting, choose Settings, Transfer. ▪

To send a binary file, use these steps:

1. With a connection already established, choose Tools, Send File, or click the Send Binary File button on the toolbar. The Send File dialog box shown in Figure 15.13 is displayed.

FIG. 15.13
Choose the file you want to send.

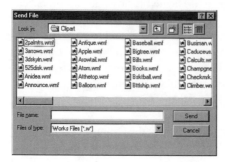

2. Highlight the file you want to send, then click Send. Works begins transmitting the file and displays a transmission status message on your screen.

To send a text file, use these steps:

1. With a connection already established, choose Tools, Send Text, or click the Send Text button on the toolbar. The Send Text dialog box shown in Figure 15.14 is displayed.

FIG. 15.14

Choose the text file you want to send.

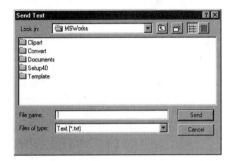

2. Highlight the file you want to send, then click Send. Works begins transmitting the file and displays a transmission status message on your screen.

N O T E If you want to cancel transmission of a binary or a text file, press Esc. You'll be asked to confirm whether you want to cancel the transmission. Choose OK. ▪

You can also send selected text to a remote computer, as opposed to an entire file. For instance, suppose you want to send only two pages of a 50-page document. Sending the entire file would take more time than necessary and require more disk space to store on the remote computer.

To send selected text, use these steps:

1. Open the Works file that contains the text you want to send.

2. Using Easy Connect, connect to the remote computer.

3. Open the Window menu, then switch to the document that contains the text.

4. Select the text, then choose Edit, Copy, or click the Copy toolbar button.

5. Open the Window menu and switch back to your communications document.

6. Choose Edit, Paste Text, or click the Paste toolbar button. Works automatically sends the selected text to the remote computer.

Receiving binary or text files is just as straightforward as sending them. If you're receiving a file from a friend or colleague on an attended remote computer, notify them when you are ready to have them send a file. If the remote computer is unattended (for instance, an information service) use the file transfer procedure for that system to transfer the file to your computer.

To receive a binary or text file, use these steps:

1. Use Easy Connect to connect to the remote computer.

2. Notify the user on the remote computer that you are ready to receive a file, or, if you're connected to an information service, use the file transfer procedure for that system to transfer the file.

3. In Works, choose Tools, Receive File, or click the Receive Binary File toolbar button. Works displays the Receive File dialog box.

4. Type a file name in the File Name text box, or use the suggested file name, then click the Save button.

N O T E   Remember, when receiving files, the remote computer must use the same transfer protocol you're using. To check your protocol setting, choose Settings, Transfer. ■

To end a communications session, refer to "Starting and Ending a Communications Session," earlier in this chapter. ●

CHAPTER 16

Using Internet Explorer

Works 4.5 includes Internet Explorer 3.02, Microsoft's Internet browser. A browser is the software program you use to navigate the Web. ■

Connecting to the Internet

Microsoft makes it easy for you with their Internet Connection Wizard.

Setting communications options

Just like with the Communications tool in Works, with Internet Explorer you'll want to specify communications settings

Using the browser

The primary purpose of the browser is to let you surf the net, whether you go directly to a page, search for a particular topic, or just "jump" from one hyperlink to another.

How to use information from the Internet on your computer

Learn how to save files from the Internet on your PC and use them on your system and in your documents.

Using electronic mail

You learn how to communicate with *anyone* on the World Wide Web via electronic mail

Newsgroups

Learn how to find and subscribe to newsgroups that interest you, and read and reply to newsgroup topics.

Getting Started with the Internet Explorer

When you install Works 4.5, an icon called `SetUp for Microsoft Internet Explorer 3.02` is placed on your desktop. Installing Internet Explorer is as easy as double-clicking the setup icon. When the installation is complete, Works replaces the setup icon on your desktop with `The Internet` icon (a globe with a magnifying glass).

NOTE You might already have a version of Internet Explorer on your computer with Windows 95. If so, you don't need to complete the installation and setup process. ▪

To use the Internet, you must *connect* to it through a service provider (sometimes called an access provider). A provider has a computer that is directly connected the World Wide Web. When you subscribe to a provider's services (for a monthly fee) and dial up to their computer, you're on the net.

Using the Internet Connection Wizard

If you've never used the Internet before and you don't yet have a provider, the quickest and easiest way to connect is by using the Internet Connection Wizard. Using this wizard, Works will configure your system for you, display a list of available providers, and sign you up as a subscriber to the service you choose.

To use the Internet Connection Wizard, follow these steps:

1. From the Window Start menu, choose Programs, then from the submenus, choose Accessories, Internet Tools, Get on the Internet. Works displays the Get Connected! dialog box shown in Figure 16.1.

FIG. 16.1
The first screen of Internet Connection Wizard describes what the Wizard will do for you.

2. Click the Next button. Works displays the Setup Options dialog box shown in Figure 16.2.

FIG. 16.2

Choose the Automatic option to set up your Internet connection quickly and easily.

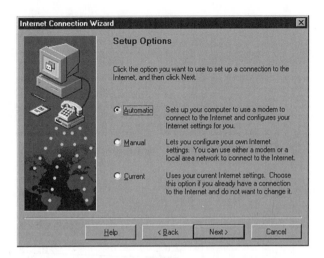

3. Choose the Automatic option to set up your Internet connection quickly and easily, then click the Next button. Works displays the Begin Automatic Setup dialog box that starts the setup process.

4. Click the Next button. Works displays the Location Information dialog box shown in Figure 16.3.

FIG. 16.3

The Wizard narrows its search for providers based on your area code and the first three digits of your phone number.

5. Enter your area code and the first three digits of your phone number in the appropriate boxes, then click Next. Works dials an access number for a list of Internet providers, then displays a list similar to the one shown in Figure 16.4.

Ch

16

FIG. 16.4
The Wizard displays a
list of Internet providers.

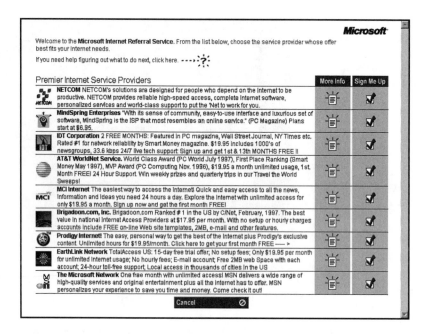

6. If you need help working with this screen, click the Question Mark (?) button. If you want more information about a particular provider, click the More Info button. When you're ready, click the Sign Me Up button for the provider you choose. If you're not ready to choose a provider, click Cancel to exit the Wizard.

If you choose a Sign Me Up button, the Wizard dials the access number for the provider's registration information. You'll need to respond to questions on the screen to complete the process.

Connecting to the Internet

When you double-click the Internet icon on your desktop, you'll see a dialog box for dialing into the network. (Note that you can also start Internet Explorer from your desktop by clicking Start, Programs, Internet Explorer.) Each service provider uses a different dialog box, but they all are designed to dial the access phone number. An example of the Microsoft Network (MSN) Sign In dialog box is shown in Figure 16.5.

The first time you connect, you'll probably be asked to set a password. You'll use this password every time you log on to the access provider's system. Once you are connected to your provider's system, the Internet Explorer screen shown in Figure 16.6 is displayed. (If you are unable to connect, try redialing, or contact your service provider for help or further instructions.) Every browser program defines a different home page as your Start Page. Because Internet Explorer is a Microsoft product, Microsoft's home page is set as your default Start Page. See "Setting Page, Link, and History Options" later in this chapter to learn how to change your start page.

FIG. 16.5

In the MSN Sign In dialog box, you click the Connect button to dial into the network.

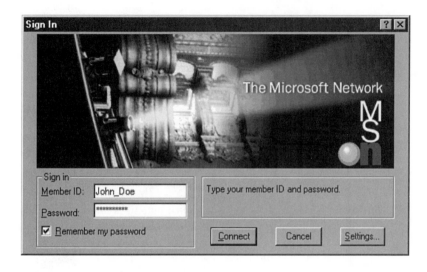

FIG. 16.6

The Internet Explorer screen has its own menus, toolbar, and address line; here the Microsoft home page is displayed.

Home page address

Some of the menus in the Internet Explorer are similar to other applications, such as File, Edit, View, and Help. The Favorites menu lets you save the address of favorite Web sites you want to return to so you don't have to type in the address or search for them again. The Go menu has options that take you to specific sites on the Web.

Ch

16

N O T E If you think of the World Wide Web as a huge library, a *Web site* is analygous to a book in the library. It is a collection of related information, perhaps about the services or products of a company or other type of organization. ▣

An important option on the Go menu is the Open History Folder. Because you are likely to view a large number of pages during any Internet session, Internet Explorer keeps track of every page you've viewed on the Web in the last 20 days (this is the default setting) and saves the list in the file C:\Windows\History. This list makes it easy for you to go back to a particular page you know you've seen rather than having to search for it again. Later in this chapter learn how to set the number of days you want to store in your History as well as other options (see Setting Page, Link, and History Options).

As with all software programs, the toolbar buttons are designed to make selecting common commands quicker and easier. The Internet Explorer toolbar buttons are described in Table 16.1.

Table 16.1 Internet Explorer Toolbar Buttons

Button	Name	Description
	Back	Takes you back to the previous screen you viewed.
	Forward	Takes you forward after you have moved back. (This button is not available if you haven't yet used the Back button.)
	Stop	Stops any activity you've selected, such as going to a site or downloading a file.
	Refresh	Repaints your screen.
	Home	Takes you automatically to your Start page.
	Search	Lets you search the Internet for a particular topic.
	Favorites	Lets you save addresses of your favorite sites so you can return to them quickly and easily.
	Print	Prints the page that is currently displayed on the screen.
	Font	Cycles among different font sizes for display on the screen.
	Mail	Lets you read, send, and receive electronic mail messages.

NOTE The "e" icon at the right end of the menu bar is the Internet Explorer logo. The icon moves when Internet Explorer is accessing or downloading information. To interrupt the current task, click this icon. When not logged on, clicking this icon will display your home page. ■

Below the toolbar is a text box labeled Address. When you want to go to a specific Web site, you enter an address here.

NOTE Every Web site has an *address*, or URL (Universal Resource Locator). You must enter an address to go to a Web site. An example of an address is "http://www.msn.com" ■

At the far right end of the Address bar is a toolbar labeled Links (see Figure 16.6). (A double vertical bar appears to the left of the word *Links*.) If you drag the double vertical bars to the left, you display the Links toolbar next to the Address bar (see Figure 16.7). (Or you can drag it to the left and down to display it below the Address bar.) The Links shown (Best of the Web, Today's Links, Web Gallery, Product News, Microsoft) are hyperlinks Microsoft has defined. Clicking a link takes you directly to the site Microsoft has defined. (See "Setting Page, Link, and History Options" later in this chapter to define your own hyperlinks.)

FIG. 16.7

The Links toolbar is visible next to the address bar.

Links Toolbar —

Configuring Internet Explorer

In Chapter 15, you learned about certain communications settings you must choose before connecting to another computer using the Works Communications tool. Internet Explorer is no different; you must specify some settings in order to connect to the net successfully. (You'll find

Ch
16

that many of the default settings work just fine for you. Change settings only when necessary.) To change various settings, you'll use the View, Options command, which displays the Options dialog box containing six tabs for different types of settings. The following sections describe these most common settings you'll change.

Setting General Viewing Options

Some multimedia objects (such as pictures, sound, and video) are very large files that can take a lot of time to display on a Web page. You can speed up the time it takes to display a Web page by turning off the display of one or more of these options. (The objects still exist; they just aren't displayed.) To turn off multimedia objects, use the General tab in the Options dialog box (see Figure 16.8).

FIG. 16.8

The General tab lets you set personal viewing preferences, some of which improve speed while on the net.

Turn off display of multimedia here

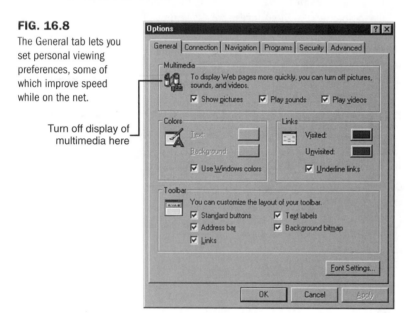

You can also use the General tab to specify text and background colors, colors for links (visited and unvisited), and the toolbar options you want to display. In addition, you can select a display font using the Font Settings button.

Specifying Connection Options

If you used the Internet Connection Wizard to set up Internet Explorer, some of the options in the Connections tab of the Options dialog box are automatically selected for you (see Figure 16.9). To add a service provider, click the Add button; to change settings or the phone number for the provider, click the Properties button. If your provider charges you for connection time, you might want to change the amount of time shown in the Disconnect If Idle box.

FIG. 16.9

Use the Connection tab in the Options dialog box to specify how you want to connect to the Internet.

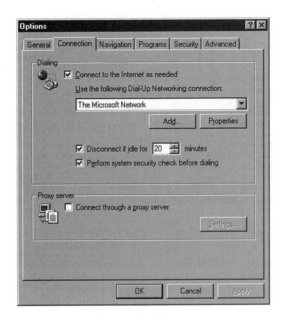

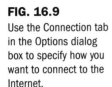

Ch
16

If you connect to the Internet from home, you can ignore the Connect Through a Proxy Server option. This security option is often required by corporations for users who are connecting to the Internet through a LAN. In this case, your corporation's operations staff can give you instructions for using this option.

Setting Page, Link, and History Options

You've already seen in Figure 16.7 an example of Microsoft's home page used as your Start page—that is, the first Web page you see when you connect to the Internet. If you prefer, you can change your Start page using the Navigation tab in the Options dialog box (see Figure 16.10). Here's how:

1. Display the Web page you want to use as a Start page.
2. Choose View, Options, and click the Navigation tab (see Figure 16.10).
3. In the Page box, highlight Start Page.
4. Click the Use Current button, then click OK.

 You don't have to be logged on to set up a start page. Use the preceding steps, but type in the address of the start page in the Address text box in step 3. The next time you log on, the new start page will be displayed.

When you click the Search toolbar button, Internet Explorer automatically displays a default Search page (the page varies depending on your provider). You can specify a different search page using the same steps outlined above, but in step 3, highlight Search Page in the Page drop-down list. Likewise, you can define your own links on the Links toolbar, by following the preceding steps and choosing a quick link from the Page drop-down list mentioned in step 3.

FIG. 16.10

The Navigation tab in the Options dialog box lets you select start page, search page, quick links, and history options.

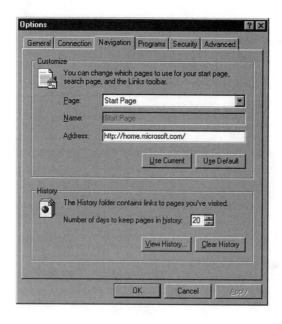

You can set history options, view your history file, and clear your history file using the options in the History section of the Navigation tab (see Figure 16.10). If you want Internet Explorer to keep a history for only 1 day, for example, enter **1** in the Number of Days box. You can view the entire history (stored in the c:\Windows\History file) by clicking the View History button, or empty the History file by choosing the Clear History button.

Specifying Mail and News Services

If you have only one provider, Mail and News services are selected automatically for you. If you have subscribed to more than one provider service, you might have more than one mail or news service option. Use the Programs tab in the Options dialog box to choose from Mail and News services (available services depend on your provider(s). The Programs tab is displayed in Figure 16.11.

Applying a Rating to Web Sites

The Security tab in the Options dialog box covers a variety of security settings. The Content Advisor section allows you to enable a rating system for Web sites so you can deny other users access to certain sites. (Parents, in particular, will appreciate this feature to restrict the sites available to their children.) To use this feature, click the Enable Ratings button on the Security tab shown in Figure 16.12 and follow the directions given. You'll be asked to set a password (as the content advisor supervisor), then set specific ratings options in the Content Advisor dialog box.

FIG. 16.11

Use the Programs tab in the Options dialog box to specify mail service, viewers, and readable file types on the Internet.

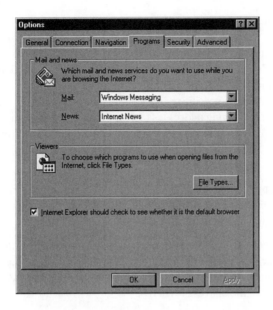

Ch
16

FIG. 16.12

Use the Security tab in the Options dialog box to enable a Web site rating system.

> **N O T E** Some sites have no rating. To allow any user access to these sites, click the Settings button in the Security tab of the Options dialog box, then enter the password. Click the General tab in the Content Advisor dialog box, then click the Users Can See Sites Which Have No Rating option. ■

Using the Browser

The main purpose of an Internet browser is to let you "surf" the Web. *Surfing* is following hyperlinks from one Internet page to another (and many others) to find information you're specifically looking for, or to learn about entirely new topics, ideas, and people from all over the world. This includes going to specific pages, searching for information when you don't have a specific Web site address, saving addresses of your favorite pages so you can revisit them, saving files from the Web on your computer, and printing information from the Web.

Going to a Specific Internet Site

It seems that no matter where you go or what you read today, "www.something" is everywhere. Countless numbers of companies, organizations, associations, societies, clubs, and individuals have Web sites and publish their addresses.

To go to one of the Web sites you've been hearing about, all you need (in addition to a config-ured service provider) is the site's Web address. Type the address in the Address bar of the Internet Explorer and press Enter. If Internet Explorer can't find the page, a message appears telling you to make sure the address is correct.

Searching for Information

Often you don't have an address for a specific Web page, but you have a topic you want to look for, such as "Jurassic-age dinosaurs" or "chocolate amaretto cheesecake" or "Mars landing." When you don't have an exact address, you must search for information by topic using a search engine.

Search engines are computers on the Web that provide search capabilities to the Internet user. Available search engines vary depending on your provider. Examples of common search engines are Excite, Yahoo, InfoSeek, AOL NetFind and Lycos. To display available search engines, click the Search toolbar button. Figure 16.13 shows an example of the Yahoo search engine.

All search engines work in the same way; they all have a box in which you type a topic, a Search or Seek button to begin your search, and they all list suggested categories of informa-tion. In the example shown in Figure 16.13, you use the Search text box to enter the topic you're looking for, then click Search. Assuming "food" is considered a type of entertainment, you might click the Entertainment category before searching for "chocolate amaretto cheese-cake;" this would help narrow down the results quickly.

Most search engines have help for structuring and formatting a search, but few of them make it easy to find. (A Help button doesn't appear on most search engine home pages.) To find help, click the Search or Seek button without entering a topic. This usually leads you to help. Experi-ment with available search engines until you find one you're comfortable with.

Refer to "Setting Page, Link, and History Options" earlier in this chapter for information on setting a Search Page.

Suggested Web sites

FIG. 16.13
A typical search engine
screen.

Other available
search engines

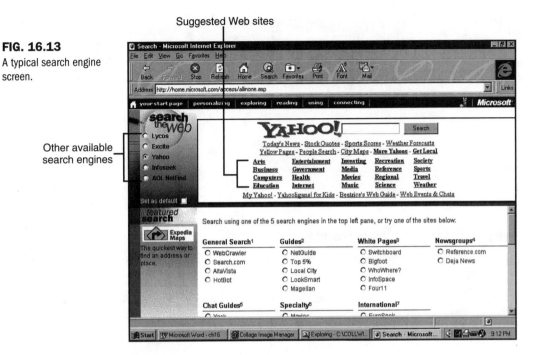

Saving Favorite Sites

As you begin to explore the Web, you'll inevitably find sites you're very interested in and would like to visit again. Because long Web page addresses can be difficult to remember, it's useful to save the addresses of your favorite sites so you can return to them easily.

To add a site to your list of favorites, go to the page you want to add, then choose Favorites, Add to Favorites (or click the Favorites toolbar button, then choose Add to Favorites). In the dialog box that is displayed, use the address that is displayed or type a familiar name for the site and choose OK.

When your list of favorites becomes long, you can organize it by creating folders. For instance, you might want to create Dinosaurs and Cooking as folders, then save your favorite sites in the appropriate category. To do this, choose Favorites, Organize Favorites, which displays the dialog box shown in Figure 16.14.

To create a new folder, click the New Folder button, enter a name, then press Enter.

The easiest way to move a favorite from one folder to another is to drag it. For example, in Figure 16.14, you could click and drag Dinosaurs in Museums and drop it in the Dinosaurs folder. Or, select Dinosaurs in Museums, then click the Move button. In the dialog box that is displayed, select a folder, then click OK. Use the Rename and Delete buttons to rename and delete folders or sites.

FIG. 16.14

Use the Organize Favorites dialog box to add, delete, and rearrange sites.

Saving Files from Web Pages

Sometimes you'll want to save a Web page as a file on your computer. To do this, use these steps:

1. Go to the Web page you want to save, then choose File, Save As File. The Save As dialog box is displayed.

2. Double-click the folder where you want to save the file.

3. In the File Name box, type a name, then click Save.

When you use the previous steps, only the text is saved. If the Web page contains pictures, they are not saved. You can save a picture, audio file, or video file on your computer using these steps:

1. Right click the hyperlink for the object you want to save.

2. From the shortcut menu, choose the Save Target As option. The Save As dialog box is displayed.

3. In the File Name box, type a name for the file, then click the Save button. Internet Explorer saves a copy of the page or picture.

Printing

Using the Print toolbar button or the File, Print command, you can print information directly from a Web page on your printer. When you choose the print command, the Print dialog box shown in Figure 16.15 is displayed. This dialog box should be familiar to you; it is the same one displayed when you choose the print command using other Works tools. Choose the appropriate print settings, then click OK.

▶ **See** "Printing a Document," **p. 22**

Internet Explorer will print only the current page directly to your printer; if you want to print several Web pages, you must select the print command for each page. If you want to print an entire file, its best to save it on you computer, then print it.

FIG. 16.15

The Print dialog box for Internet Explorer looks just like the one displayed by other Works tools.

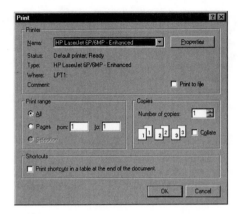

Using Mail

Windows 95 includes a tool that allows you to send and receive electronic mail messages. In order to use it, you must first create a *profile*. The profile includes important information for ensuring the receipt and delivery of messages between your PC and your access provider's system. If you have not yet used e-mail, contact your Internet service provider to help you create your e-mail profile. Once the profile is created, you can access e-mail through Internet Explorer.

Composing and Sending Messages

To compose and send an e-mail message, use these steps:

1. Click the Mail toolbar button, then choose <u>N</u>ew Message. (If the Choose Profile dialog box is displayed, choose a profile, then click OK.) The New Message form shown in Figure 16.16 is displayed.

2. In the T<u>o</u>: text box, type the recipient's Internet mail address, then press Enter. (Internet mail addresses generally consist of the user name, an @ symbol, followed by the provider's system address, then *.com*, such as JDoe@mindwatch.com.)

 You can press Tab after each entry to move consecutively from To:, to CC:, to Subject:, to the message area of the screen.

 To use an address stored in your address book, click the To: box and select a name from the Address Book dialog box that is displayed. If you don't have an address book but want to create one, use the Address Book dialog box that is displayed when you choose <u>T</u>ools, <u>A</u>ddress Book or click the Address Book toolbar button.

FIG. 16.16

Use the New Message form to compose and send an e-mail message.

Send button

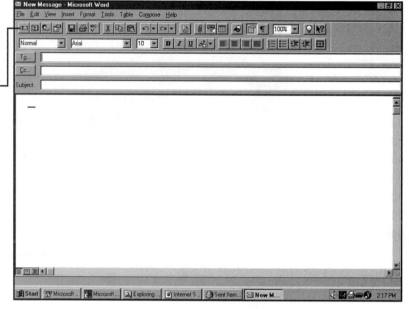

3. If you want to copy anyone on the message, enter their Internet mail address in the CC: text box, then press Enter. (You can also send blind carbon copies by entering an address in the BCC text box.)

4. Type a topic in the Subject: text box. then press Enter.

5. Click in the message area of the screen, then begin typing your message. You can add formatting features to your message using formatting toolbar buttons or commands on the Format menu.

6. When you're ready to send your message, click the Send toolbar button or choose File, Send.

When you choose the Send command, your message is temporarily stored in the Outbox folder. It remains there until the message is delivered from your PC to your access provider's system. At this point, the message is moved from the Outbox folder to the Sent Items folder. The message is then sent from the access provider's system through the network to its final destination.

Reading, Replying to, and Forwarding Mail Messages

To read a mail message, use these steps:

1. Click the Mail toolbar button, then choose Read Mail. The dialog box shown in Figure 16.17 is displayed.

T I P The title in the title bar reflects the last folder you used, so if you last displayed Deleted Items, *Deleted Items-Microsoft Exchange* will appear in the title bar.

FIG. 16.17

New mail messages are listed in your Inbox.

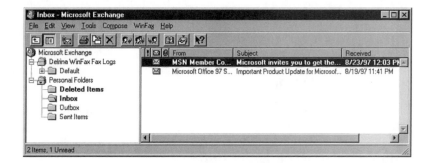

2. If the Inbox isn't selected, click the Inbox folder name on the left side of the dialog box. New unread messages appear in the list on the right side of the dialog box.

3. To read a message, double-click the message. The message is displayed in a screen like the one shown in Figure 16.18.

FIG. 16.18

After reading your message, you can reply to it, or forward it to another user.

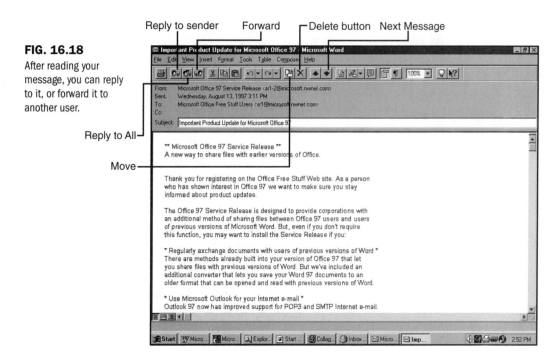

4. After you've read the message you have a number of choices. You can:

- *Reply to the sender* Click the Reply To Sender toolbar button or choose Compose, Reply to Sender.
- *Reply to all* Click the Reply To All toolbar button or choose Compose, Reply to All. (This option sends a reply to the sender and all of the original recipients.)
- *Forward the message* Click the Forward button or choose Compose, Forward. The message is displayed in a screen similar to the one shown in Figure 16.16 but the letters FW for "forward" appear in the title bar. Type entries in the To: and CC: boxes, then click the Send button.

If you do nothing with the message and click the Next button to continue reading other messages, the message stays in the Inbox.

Filing and Deleting Messages

If you save a lot of mail messages on various topics, you might want to create additional mail folders for storing your messages. You already have a mail folder called *Personal Folders;* included in this folder are the *Inbox, Outbox, Deleted Items, and Sent Items* folders. To create additional folders, use these steps:

1. Click the Mail toolbar button, then click Read Mail. The dialog box shown in Figure 16.17 is displayed.
2. Click the folder in which you want to create a new (sub)folder.
3. Choose File, New Folder.
4. In the New Folder dialog box, type a name, then click OK. The folder name is added to the list.

From time to time, you'll want to delete old e-mail messages to keep your folders uncluttered and up to date. To delete a message, use these steps:

1. Click the Mail toolbar button, then click Read Mail. The dialog box shown in Figure 16.17 is displayed.
2. On the left side of the dialog box, select the folder from which you want to delete messages.
3. On the right side of the screen, highlight a message to delete, then click the Delete toolbar button. The message is moved to the Deleted Items folder.
4. Repeat steps 1-3 for all messages you want to delete.

Your deleted messages are kept in the Deleted Items folder (somewhat like the Windows Recycle Bin) so you can retrieve them, if necessary. When you want to permanently delete a message, go to the Deleted Items folder, highlight the message to delete, then click the Delete toolbar button. A warning message appears. Click Yes to delete the message.

Handing Message Attachments

An attachment is a file that is inserted in (sent along with or received along with) the original e-mail message. Often files are sent as attachments if they are large, if they are compressed, or if they don't need to be read immediately (they can just be saved).

To send a message that include an attachment, use these steps:

1. Click the Mail toolbar button, then choose New Message. (If the Choose Profile dialog box is displayed, choose a profile, then click OK.) The New Message screen shown in Figure 16.16 is displayed.

2. Enter recipients addresses in the To: and CC: text boxes, then type a topic in the Subject: text box.

3. In the message area of the screen, begin typing your message. When you're ready to insert a file, choose Insert, File. The Insert File dialog box shown in Figure 16.19 is displayed.

FIG. 16.19

Choose a file to insert in your e-mail message.

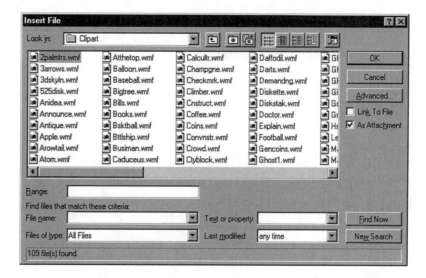

4. Choose a file to insert, then click OK. A file icon is inserted in your e-mail message.

5. When you're ready to send your message, click the Send toolbar button or choose File, Send.

When you receive a message that includes an attached file, you can save the file using these steps:

1. In the message, click the file icon for the inserted file.

2. Choose File, Save As. The Save As dialog box shown in Figure 16.20 is displayed.

Ch
16

FIG. 16.20

Use the Save As dialog box to save an inserted (attached) file.

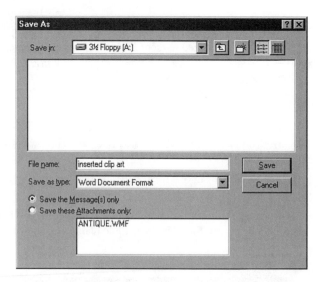

3. In the Save As dialog box, enter a file name, then choose Save the Message(s) Only or Save These Attachments Only.

4. To save the file in a different file type than the one shown, choose a file type in the Save As Type box.

5. To save the file on a different drive or directory, click the Up One Level button or the down arrow in the Save In box to find the right drive or directory.

6. When settings are correct, click the Save button.

Using Newsgroups

Newsgroups are forums in which Internet users from all around the globe can participate in discussions, share information, exchange ideas, and express opinions. Newsgroups exist on an infinite number of topics; from pets to "trekkies," to transcendental meditation, to golf, to Shakespeare. The entire service of newsreading is referred to as Internet News; a newsgroup refers to a forum on a particular topic.

To use newsgroups, you must first add a news server to your Internet Explorer news settings. The news server is the system (operated by your access provider) that stores and handles the exchange of news "messages." Your access provider can supply all the information you need to set up a news server.

Once you have this information, click the Mail toolbar button, then choose Read News. Internet Explorer opens an Internet News window. To set up a server, use the Internet News Configuration Wizard, which is displayed automatically the first time you use Internet News. Or, in the Internet News window that's displayed, choose Options, News, then click the Server tab to set up a news server.

You can add as many news servers as are available to you. If your provider offers more than one news server, or if subscribe to more than one Internet service provider, set up as many news servers as you wish. The more you set up, the wider range of choices you have for newsgroups.

Newsgroups: Subscribing and Unsubscribing

To get started using newsgroups, the first step is to select a newsgroup to which you want to subscribe. Subscribing gives you privileges to read and reply to messages. To subscribe, use these steps:

1. Click the Newsgroups toolbar button. The Newsgroups dialog box shown in Figure 16.21 is displayed. The name of the current news server is highlighted on the left side of the dialog box.

Available news servers   ┌Type a topic here to narrow your search

FIG. 16.21

Use the Newsgroups dialog box to subscribe (or unsubscribe) to a newsgroup.

Current server┘

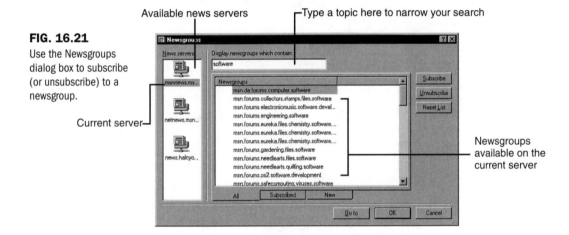

Newsgroups available on the current server

2. Scroll through the Newsgroups list until you find a group you're interested in.

3. Highlight the name, then click Subscribe. An icon is inserted next to the newsgroup name in the list.

4. Repeat steps 2 and 3 to subscribe to more newsgroups.

5. To zero in on a particular subject area, type a topic in the Display Newsgroups Which Contain text box. The newsgroups list now contains only those newsgroups that are related to the subject you specify.

6. To view newsgroups available on another server, click the server name in the left part of the dialog box, then repeat steps 2 and 3 to subscribe.

7. When you're finished subscribing, click OK.

To unsubscribe to a newsgroup, return to the Newsgroups dialog box, highlight the newsgroup name, then click Unsubscribe and click OK.

Viewing Newsgroups

Once you have subscribed to several newsgroups, a group is automatically displayed in your Internet News window. To choose the newsgroup you want to view, click the Newsgroups drop-down list just below the toolbar (see Figure 16.22). In the list, newsgroups are organized by news server. To view a different newsgroup, click it.

Now, scan the list of subjects until you find one you're interested in reading. When you double-click the subject, a separate window opens in which you can read the message (see Figure 16.23). When you're finished reading the message, double-click the Close button in the upper right corner of the window.

FIG. 16.22

The Newsgroups drop-down list shows all newsgroups you have subscribed to, organized by news server.

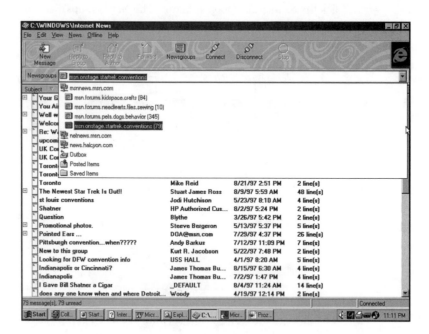

Some messages contain replies to the original message. These messages are marked by an icon with a plus (+) symbol in the left margin. You can display the list of replies by double-clicking the + icon. Read a reply the same way you read any other message.

Replying to or Forwarding a Message

If you find a message you want to respond to, you can create a reply message by using these steps:

1. With the message displayed, click the Reply to Group toolbar button. A window just like the one shown in Figure 16.23 is displayed, except that the name in the title bar begins with *Re:* for reply.

2. If you want to send the reply to additional newsgroups (only on the same server), type the newsgroup name on the Newsgroups: line, separating each name with a semicolon.

3. To send a copy of the reply to the original author, type the author's e-mail address on the CC: line.

4. On the Subject: line, type a new subject for your reply.

5. In the message area, type your message.

6. To send the message, choose File, Post Message, or click the Post Message toolbar button (the first button on the toolbar). Your reply is added underneath the message you're responding to and the plus (+) icon is inserted in the left margin.

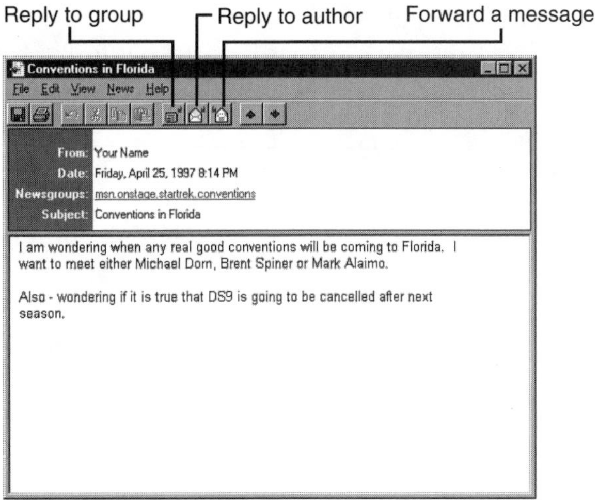

Ch

16

Reply to group   Reply to author   Forward a message

FIG. 16.23

A newsgroup message appears in its own window when you read it.

If you prefer to respond directly to the author of the original message without posting a reply in the newsgroup, use these steps:

1. Display the message you want to respond to.

2. Click the Reply To Author toolbar button. Internet Explorer opens a mail window like the one shown in Figure 16.16 and inserts the text of the newsgroup message and the author's name in the To: box.

3. If you want to send your reply to other users as well, type their names next to the author's name, separating each with a semicolon.

4. In the message area, type your reply.

5. Click the Send toolbar button, or choose File, Send. This message will *not* be added as a reply to the newsgroup.

Creating a New Message

To create a new message in a newsgroup, use these steps:

1. In the Internet New window, click the New Message button. The New Message dialog box is displayed.

2. Use the Newsgroup address shown on the Newsgroup line. If you want to send your message to additional newsgroups (only those on the same server), type a newsgroup name on the Newsgroups: line, separating the entries with a semicolon.

3. To copy someone via e-mail, enter the e-mail address on the CC: line.

4. Type a subject on the Subject line.

5. Type your message in the message area.

6. Choose File, Post Message, or click the Post Message toolbar button.

Exiting Internet Explorer

When you're finished using the Internet, you must log off of your Internet provider's system. This is especially important if your provider charges for usage based on connect time. If you forget to log off, you could end up paying for the time you remained connected to the system, even though you weren't using the Internet.

To log off, choose File, Close. The Internet Explorer screen closes and you'll see a dialog box asking if you want to disconnect from your provider system. (The dialog box will vary slightly depending on your provider.) Choose Yes. The dialog box will display a message telling you when you're disconnected. ●

Index

Complete and Return this Card
for a *FREE* Computer Book Catalog

Thank you for purchasing this book! You have purchased a superior computer book written expressly for your needs. To continue to provide the kind of up-to-date, pertinent coverage you've come to expect from us, we need to hear from you. Please take a minute to complete and return this self-addressed, postage-paid form. In return, we'll send you a free catalog of all our computer books on topics ranging from word processing to programming and the internet.

Mr. ☐   Mrs. ☐   Ms. ☐   Dr. ☐

Name (first) ☐☐☐☐☐☐☐☐☐☐☐☐ (M.I.) ☐ (last) ☐☐☐☐☐☐☐☐☐☐☐☐☐☐☐☐

Address ☐☐☐☐☐☐☐☐☐☐☐☐☐☐☐☐☐☐☐☐☐☐☐☐☐☐☐☐☐☐☐☐☐☐

☐☐☐☐☐☐☐☐☐☐☐☐☐☐☐☐☐☐☐☐☐☐☐☐☐☐☐☐☐☐☐☐☐☐

City ☐☐☐☐☐☐☐☐☐☐☐☐☐☐☐ State ☐☐ Zip ☐☐☐☐☐ ☐☐☐☐

Phone ☐☐☐ ☐☐☐ ☐☐☐☐ Fax ☐☐☐ ☐☐☐ ☐☐☐☐

Company Name ☐☐☐☐☐☐☐☐☐☐☐☐☐☐☐☐☐☐☐☐☐☐☐☐☐☐☐☐☐☐☐

E-mail address ☐☐☐☐☐☐☐☐☐☐☐☐☐☐☐☐☐☐☐☐☐☐☐☐☐☐☐☐☐☐☐

1. Please check at least (3) influencing factors for purchasing this book.

Front or back cover information on book .... ☐
Special approach to the content .... ☐
Completeness of content .... ☐
Author's reputation .... ☐
Publisher's reputation .... ☐
Book cover design or layout .... ☐
Index or table of contents of book .... ☐
Price of book .... ☐
Special effects, graphics, illustrations .... ☐
Other (Please specify): _____ ☐

2. How did you first learn about this book?

Saw in Macmillan Computer Publishing catalog .... ☐
Recommended by store personnel .... ☐
Saw the book on bookshelf at store .... ☐
Recommended by a friend .... ☐
Received advertisement in the mail .... ☐
Saw an advertisement in: _____ ☐
Read book review in: _____ ☐
Other (Please specify): _____ ☐

3. How many computer books have you purchased in the last six months?

This book only .... ☐   3 to 5 books .... ☐
books .... ☐   More than 5 .... ☐

4. Where did you purchase this book?

Bookstore .... ☐
Computer Store .... ☐
Consumer Electronics Store .... ☐
Department Store .... ☐
Office Club .... ☐
Warehouse Club .... ☐
Mail Order .... ☐
Direct from Publisher .... ☐
Internet site .... ☐
Other (Please specify): _____ ☐

5. How long have you been using a computer?

☐ Less than 6 months   ☐ 6 months to a year
☐ 1 to 3 years   ☐ More than 3 years

6. What is your level of experience with personal computers and with the subject of this book?

	With PCs	With subject of book
New	☐	☐
Casual	☐	☐
Accomplished	☐	☐
Expert	☐	☐

Source Code ISBN: 0-7897-1492-2

7. Which of the following best describes your job title?

- Administrative Assistant .... ☐
- Coordinator .... ☐
- Manager/Supervisor .... ☐
- Director .... ☐
- Vice President .... ☐
- President/CEO/COO .... ☐
- Lawyer/Doctor/Medical Professional .... ☐
- Teacher/Educator/Trainer .... ☐
- Engineer/Technician .... ☐
- Consultant .... ☐
- Not employed/Student/Retired .... ☐
- Other (Please specify): _____ ☐

8. Which of the following best describes the area of the company your job title falls under?

- Accounting .... ☐
- Engineering .... ☐
- Manufacturing .... ☐
- Operations .... ☐
- Marketing .... ☐
- Sales .... ☐
- Other (Please specify): _____ ☐

9. What is your age?

- Under 20 .... ☐
- 21-29 .... ☐
- 30-39 .... ☐
- 40-49 .... ☐
- 50-59 .... ☐
- 60-over .... ☐

10. Are you:

- Male .... ☐
- Female .... ☐

11. Which computer publications do you read regularly? (Please list)

_____
_____
_____
_____
_____
_____
_____
_____
_____

Comments: _____
_____
_____

Fold here and scotch-tape to mail.